Prentice Hall

Geometry

Practice and Problem Solving Workbook

PEARSON

Boston, Massachusetts   Chandler, Arizona   Glenview, Illinois   Upper Saddle River, New Jersey

Pearson, Prentice Hall, Pearson Prentice Hall and MathXL are trademarks, in the U.S. and/or other countries, of Pearson Education, Inc., or its affiliates.

PEARSON

ISBN-13: 978-0-13-318596-6
ISBN-10:   0-13-318596-6
6 7 8 9 10   V016   15 14 13

Contents

Chapter 1

Chapter 2

Chapter 7

Chapter 8

Chapter 12

Chapter 13

1-1 Think About a Plan

Nets and Drawings for Visualizing Geometry

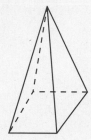

Multiple Representations There are eight different nets for the solid shown at the right. Draw as many of them as you can. (*Hint:* Two nets are the same if you can rotate or flip one to match the other.)

Understanding the Problem

1. What is the net of a solid?

_____

2. What is a result of flipping the net below? Of rotating it?

Planning the Solution

3. Visualize unfolding the solid so that the base shares an edge with all four triangles. Then visualize unfolding the solid so that the base shares an edge with three triangles. Are the nets that result the same? Explain.

_____

4. In Step 3, you saw that a net can have three or four triangles that share an edge with the square base. Are there other possibilities? If so, what are they? Are these the only possibilities?

_____

_____

Finding the Answer

5. Are there other nets that have three or four triangles that share an edge with the square base? Explain.

_____

_____

6. There are four nets that have two triangles that share an edge with the base. For each of these, the triangles may either be on opposite or adjacent sides of the base. Draw each net.

7. How many nets have only one triangle touching the base? Draw as many of them as you can.

1-1 Practice

Form G

Nets and Drawings for Visualizing Geometry

Match each three-dimensional figure with its net.

1.

2.

3.

A.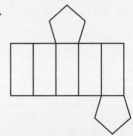

B.

C.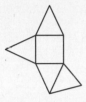

Make an isometric drawing of each cube structure on isometric dot paper.

4.

5.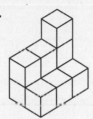

6.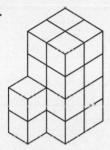

7. **Error Analysis** Two students draw nets for the solid shown below. Who is correct, Student A or Student B? Explain.

Student A:

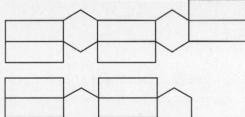

Student B:

8. You want to make a one-piece cardboard cutout for a child to fold and tape together to make a dollhouse. It includes a floor, a complete roof, and four walls. Draw a net for the dollhouse.

1-1 Practice (continued) Form G
Nets and Drawings for Visualizing Geometry

For each isometric drawing, make an orthographic drawing. Assume there are no hidden cubes.

9.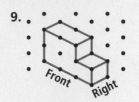

10.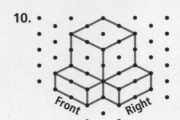

11.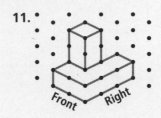

12. **Visualization** Look at the orthographic drawing at the right. Make an isometric drawing of the structure.

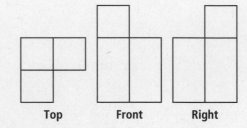

Top   Front   Right

13. Choose the nets that will fold to make a cube.

A.   B.   C.

14. **Writing** To make a net from a container, you start by cutting one of the seams along an edge where two sides meet. If you wanted to make a different net for the container, what would you do differently?

15. **Multiple Representations** Draw two different nets for the solid shown at the right.

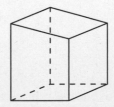

Name _____ Class _____ Date _____

1-1 Standardized Test Prep

Nets and Drawings for Visualizing Geometry

Multiple Choice

For Exercises 1–3, choose the correct letter.

1. Which three-dimensional figure matches the net shown at the right?

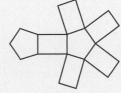

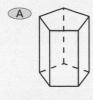 Ⓐ   Ⓑ   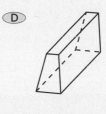 Ⓒ   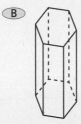 Ⓓ

2. Which cube structure matches the isometric drawing shown at the right?

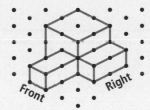

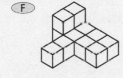 Ⓕ   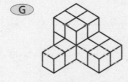 Ⓖ   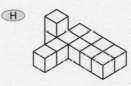 Ⓗ   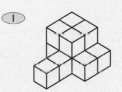 Ⓘ

3. Which top view of an orthographic drawing matches the isometric drawing shown at the right?

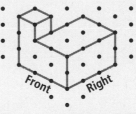

 Ⓐ   Ⓑ   Ⓒ   Ⓓ

Short Response

4. You are building a small shed. You want to describe the area of the ground the shed will cover. Which type of drawing, isometric or orthographic, would best represent the area? Why?

1-2 Think About a Plan

Points, Lines, and Planes

Estimation You can represent the hands on a clock at 6:00 as opposite rays. Estimate the other 11 times on a clock that you can represent as opposite rays.

Know

1. Opposite rays are _____.

2. The hands on the clock represent rays. At 6:00, these rays form opposite rays. This means they form a _____.

Need

3. To solve the problem I need to find the 11 other times that _____

_____.

Plan

4. When the hour hand is between 1 and 2 o'clock, what will the minute hand be between?

   _____

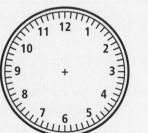 

5. On the two clock faces at the right, draw the hands of a clock at 1:35 and at 1:38.

6. At which time, 1:35 or 1:38, do you think opposite rays form? Explain.

   _____

   _____

   _____

7. Complete the table to show all of the times when the hands on a clock represent opposite rays.

Hour	6	7	8	9	10	11				
Time when opposite rays form	6:00									

1-2 Practice

Points, Lines, and Planes

Form G

Use the figure below for Exercises 1–8. Note that $\overleftrightarrow{RN}$ pierces the plane at N. It is not coplanar with V.

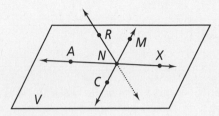

1. Name two segments shown in the figure.

2. What is the intersection of $\overleftrightarrow{CM}$ and $\overleftrightarrow{RN}$?

3. Name three collinear points.

4. What are two other ways to name plane V?

5. Are points R, N, M, and X coplanar?

6. Name two rays shown in the figure.

7. Name the pair of opposite rays with endpoint N.

8. How many lines are shown in the drawing?

For Exercises 9–14, determine whether each statement is *always*, *sometimes*, or *never* true.

9. $\overrightarrow{GH}$ and $\overrightarrow{HG}$ are the same ray.

10. $\overrightarrow{JI}$ and $\overrightarrow{JL}$ are opposite rays.

11. A plane contains only three points.

12. Three noncollinear points are contained in only one plane.

13. If $\overleftrightarrow{EG}$ lies in plane X, point G lies in plane X.

14. If three points are coplanar, they are collinear.

15. **Reasoning** Is it possible for one ray to be shorter in length than another? Explain.

16. **Open-Ended** Draw a figure of two planes that intersect in $\overleftrightarrow{ST}$.

1-2 Practice (continued)
Points, Lines, and Planes

Form G

17. Draw a figure to fit each description.
  a. Through any two points there is exactly one line.

  b. Two distinct lines can intersect in only one point.

18. Reasoning Point *F* lies on $\overrightarrow{EG}$ and point *M* lies on $\overrightarrow{EN}$. If *F*, *E*, and *M* are collinear, what must be true of these rays?

19. Writing What other terms or phrases mean the same as *postulate*?

20. How many segments can be named from the figure at the right?

Use the figure at the right for Exercises 21–29. Name the intersection of each pair of planes or lines.

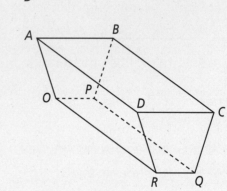

21. planes *ABP* and *BCD*

22. $\overleftrightarrow{RQ}$ and $\overleftrightarrow{RO}$

23. planes *ADR* and *DCQ*

24. planes *BCD* and *BCQ*

25. $\overleftrightarrow{OP}$ and $\overleftrightarrow{QP}$

Name two planes that intersect in the given line.

26. $\overleftrightarrow{RO}$ **27.** $\overleftrightarrow{CQ}$ **28.** $\overleftrightarrow{DA}$ **29.** $\overleftrightarrow{BP}$

Coordinate Geometry Graph the points and state whether they are collinear.

30. $(0, 0), (4, 2), (6, 3)$ **31.** $(0, 0), (6, 0), (9, 0)$

32. $(-1, 1), (2, -2), (4, -3)$ **33.** $(1, 2), (2, 3), (4, 5)$

34. $(-2, 0), (0, 4), (2, 0)$ **35.** $(-4, -1), (-1, -2), (2, -3)$

1-2 Standardized Test Prep

Points, Lines, and Planes

Multiple Choice

For Exercises 1–7, choose the correct letter.

1. Look at the figure at the right. Where do planes *ACE* and *BCD* intersect?

   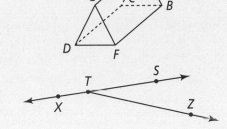

   Ⓐ $\overleftrightarrow{AD}$ Ⓒ $\overleftrightarrow{CB}$

   Ⓑ $\overleftrightarrow{CD}$ Ⓓ $\overleftrightarrow{BF}$

2. Which of the following are opposite rays?

   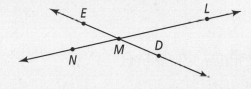

   Ⓕ $\overrightarrow{TS}$ and $\overrightarrow{XS}$ Ⓗ $\overrightarrow{TS}$ and $\overrightarrow{TZ}$

   Ⓖ $\overrightarrow{TX}$ and $\overrightarrow{TZ}$ Ⓘ $\overrightarrow{TS}$ and $\overrightarrow{TX}$

3. What is the smallest number of distinct points that can define a plane?

   Ⓐ 2   Ⓑ 3   Ⓒ 4   Ⓓ infinite

4. At how many points can two distinct lines intersect?

   Ⓕ 1   Ⓖ 2   Ⓗ 3   Ⓘ 4

5. In the figure at the right, which line is the same as $\overleftrightarrow{ED}$?

   Ⓐ $\overleftrightarrow{ML}$ Ⓒ $\overleftrightarrow{NL}$

   Ⓑ $\overleftrightarrow{DM}$ Ⓓ $\overleftrightarrow{MN}$

6. If two lines are coplanar, which of the following must be true?

   Ⓕ The lines intersect.

   Ⓖ The lines never intersect.

   Ⓗ All points on the lines are coplanar.

   Ⓘ The lines share at least one point.

7. What is the intersection of two distinct, non-parallel planes?

   Ⓐ a point   Ⓑ a line   Ⓒ a line segment   Ⓓ a ray

Short Response

8. Point *C* does not lie on $\overleftrightarrow{XY}$. Can point *C* lie in the same plane as $\overleftrightarrow{XY}$? Explain.

1-3

Think About a Plan

Measuring Segments

If $AD = 12$ and $AC = 4y - 36$, find the value of y.
Then find AC and DC.

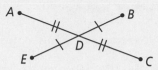

Understanding the Problem

1. What are the two congruence relationships that the diagram shows?

2. What is the value of DC? ⬜

3. Write an equation that describes the relationship between AC, DC, and AD.

Planning the Solution

4. How can you use the equation in Exercise 3 above to find the value of y?

_____

_____

Getting an Answer

5. Write an equation for y using the method described in Exercise 4 above.

6. Solve for y.

7. $AC = 4y - 36$. Substitute the value of y to find AC.

8. Check your answer. Does it make the equation that you wrote in Step 5 true? _____

1-3 Practice   Form G
Measuring Segments

In Exercises 1–6, use the figure below. Find the length of each segment.

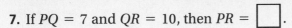

1. $\overline{AB}$ **2.** $\overline{BC}$ **3.** $\overline{AC}$

4. $\overline{AD}$ **5.** $\overline{BD}$ **6.** $\overline{CD}$

For Exercises 7–11, use the figure at the right.

7. If $PQ = 7$ and $QR = 10$, then $PR = \boxed{}$.

8. If $PQ = 20$ and $QR = 22$, then $PR = \boxed{}$.

9. If $PR = 25$ and $PQ = 12$, then $QR = \boxed{}$.

10. If $PR = 19$ and $QR = 12$, then $PQ = \boxed{}$.

11. If $PR = 10$ and $PQ = 4$, then $QR = \boxed{}$.

Use the number line below for Exercises 12–16. Tell whether the segments are congruent.

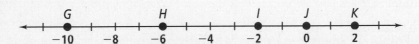

12. $\overline{GH}$ and $\overline{HI}$ **13.** $\overline{GH}$ and $\overline{IK}$ **14.** $\overline{HJ}$ and $\overline{IK}$

15. $\overline{IJ}$ and $\overline{JK}$ **16.** $\overline{HJ}$ and $\overline{GI}$ **17.** $\overline{HK}$ and $\overline{GI}$

18. Reasoning Points A, Q, and O are collinear. $AO = 10$, $AQ = 15$, and $OQ = 5$. What must be true about their positions on the line?

Algebra Use the figure at the right for Exercises 19 and 20.

19. Given: $ST = 3x + 3$ and $TU = 2x + 9$.
   a. What is the value of ST?
   b. What is the value of TU?

20. Given: $ST = x + 3$ and $TU = 4x - 6$.
   a. What is the value of ST?   **b.** What is the value of SU?

21. Algebra On a number line, suppose point E has a coordinate of 3, $EG = 6$, and $EX = 12$. Is point G the midpoint of $\overline{EX}$? What are possible coordinates for G and X?

1-3 Practice (continued) Form G
Measuring Segments

On a number line, the coordinates of P, Q, R, and S are -12, -5, 0, and 7, respectively.

22. Draw a sketch of this number line. Use this sketch to answer Exercises 23–26.

23. Which line segment is the shortest?

24. Which line segment is the longest?

25. Which line segments are congruent?

26. What is the coordinate of the midpoint of $\overline{PR}$?

27. You plan to drive north from city A to town B and then continue north to city C. The distance between city A and town B is 39 mi, and the distance between town B and city C is 99 mi.
  a. Assuming you follow a straight driving path, after how many miles of driving will you reach the midpoint between city A and city C?
  b. If you drive an average of 46 mi/h, how long will it take you to drive from city A to city C?

28. Algebra Point O lies between points M and P on a line. $OM = 34z$ and $OP = 36z - 7$. If point N is the midpoint of $\overline{MP}$, what algebraic equation can you use to find MN?

Algebra Use the diagram at the right for Exercises 29–32.

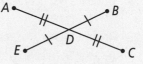

29. If $AD = 20$ and $AC = 3x + 4$, find the value of x. Then find AC and DC.

30. If $ED = 5y + 6$ and $DB = y + 30$, find the value of y. Then find ED, DB, and EB.

31. If $DC = 6x$ and $DA = 4x + 18$, find the value of x. Then find AD, DC, and AC.

32. If $EB = 4y - 12$ and $ED = y + 17$, find the value of y. Then find ED, DB, and EB.

33. Writing Is it possible that $PQ + QR < PR$? Explain.

1-3 Standardized Test Prep

Measuring Segments

Gridded Response

Solve each exercise and enter your answer on the grid provided.

1. What is the length of $\overline{BD}$?

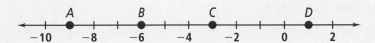

2. Points G, H, and I are collinear and H is between G and I. If $GH = 12$ and $GI = 23$, what is HI?

3. Look at the diagram below. If $XY = 7$ and $XZ = 30$, what is the value of t?

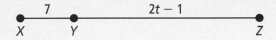

For Exercises 4 and 5, use the figure at the right.

4. M is the midpoint of $\overline{LN}$. What is LM?

5. What is LN?

Answers

1.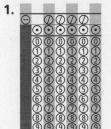
2.
3.
4.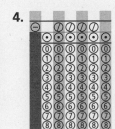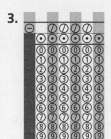
5.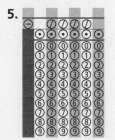

1-4 Think About a Plan

Measuring Angles

Use the diagram at the right. Solve for *x*. Find the angle
measures to check your work.

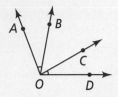

$m\angle AOB = 4x - 2$, $m\angle BOC = 5x + 10$, $m\angle COD = 2x + 14$

Understanding the Problem

1. The diagram shows that $\angle AOB$ and _____ are congruent.

2. So, $m\angle AOB =$ _____.

Planning the Solution

3. How can you use the information in Step 2 to write an equation for *x*?

_____

_____

4. Write an equation for *x*.

_____

Getting an Answer

5. Solve for *x*.

6. Find the measures of the angles by substituting for *x*.

   $m\angle AOB = \boxed{}$

   $m\angle BOC = \boxed{}$

   $m\angle COD = \boxed{}$

7. Measure the angles using a protractor to check your answers. Are
   they reasonable?

_____

1-4 Practice
Measuring Angles

Form G

Use the diagram below for Exercises 1–11. Find the measure of each angle.

1. ∠MLN

2. ∠NLP

3. ∠NLQ

4. ∠OLP

5. ∠MLQ

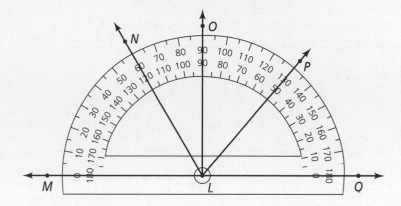

Classify each angle as *acute*, *right*, *obtuse*, or *straight*.

6. ∠MLN	7. ∠NLO	8. ∠MLP
9. ∠OLP	10. ∠OLQ	11. ∠MLQ

Use the figure at the right for Exercises 12 and 13.

12. What is another name for ∠XYW?

13. What is another name for ∠WYZ?

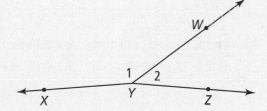

Use a protractor. Measure and classify each angle.

14.

15.

16.

17.

18.

1-4 **Practice** (continued)   Form G

Measuring Angles

19. $\angle JKL$ and $\angle CDE$ are congruent. If $m\angle JKL = 137$, what is $m\angle CDE$?

Use the figure at the right for Exercises 20–23.
$m\angle FXH = 130$ and $m\angle FXG = 49$.

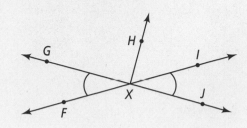

20. $\angle FXG \cong$ ☐

21. $m\angle GXH =$ ☐

22. Name a straight angle in the figure.

23. $\angle IXJ \cong$ ☐

24. Algebra If $m\angle RZT = 110$, $m\angle RZS = 3s$, and $m\angle TZS = 8s$, what are $m\angle RZS$ and $m\angle TZS$?

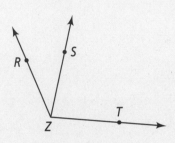

25. Algebra $m\angle OZP = 4r + 2$, $m\angle PZQ = 5r - 12$, and $m\angle OZQ = 125$. What are $m\angle OZP$ and $m\angle PZQ$?

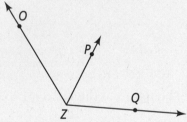

26. Reasoning Elsa draws an angle that measures 56. Tristan draws a congruent angle. Tristan says his angle is obtuse. Is he correct? Why or why not?

27. Lisa makes a cherry pie and an apple pie. She cuts the cherry pie into six equal wedges and she cuts the apple pie into eight equal wedges. How many degrees greater is the measure of a cherry pie wedge than the measure of an apple pie wedge?

28. Reasoning $\angle JNR$ and $\angle RNX$ are congruent. If the sum of the measures of the two angles is 180, what type of angle are they?

29. A new pizza place in town cuts their circular pizzas into 12 equal slices. What is the measure of the angle of each slice?

1-4 Standardized Test Prep

Measuring Angles

Multiple Choice

For Exercises 1–5, choose the correct letter.

1. What is $m\angle BAC$?

   Ⓐ 25

   Ⓑ 50

   Ⓒ 130

   Ⓓ 155

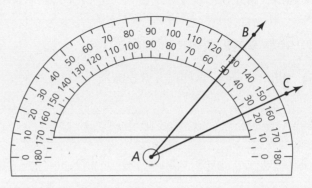

2. What is another name for $\angle 4$?

   Ⓕ $\angle VWS$ Ⓗ $\angle SVW$

   Ⓖ $\angle SWV$ Ⓘ $\angle WVT$

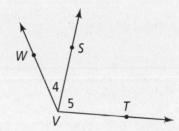

3. $m\angle KLM = 129$ and $m\angle MNO = 129$. What is true about these two angles?

   Ⓐ They are both acute angles.   Ⓒ They are both right angles.

   Ⓑ They are congruent.   Ⓓ They are both straight angles.

4. $m\angle MRT = 133$. What is $m\angle MRN$?

   Ⓕ 24   Ⓗ 46

   Ⓖ 48   Ⓘ 87

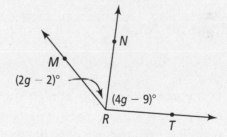

5. $\angle LJB$ and $\angle IJM$ are congruent. If the sum of the measures of the angles is 90, what type of angle are they?

   Ⓐ acute   Ⓑ obtuse   Ⓒ right   Ⓓ straight

Short Response

6. $m\angle RNY + m\angle GNC = 128$ and $\angle RNY \cong \angle GNC$. What is true about these two angles?

1-5 Think About a Plan

Exploring Angle Pairs

Reasoning When $\overrightarrow{BX}$ bisects $\angle ABC$, $\angle ABX \cong \angle CBX$. One student claims there is always a related equation $m\angle ABX = \frac{1}{2}m\angle ABC$. Another student claims the related equation is $2m\angle ABX = m\angle ABC$. Who is correct? Explain.

Understanding the Problem

1. What does it mean for $\overrightarrow{BX}$ to bisect $\angle ABC$?

   _____

   _____

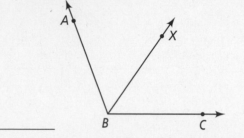

2. How is $m\angle ABC$ related to $m\angle ABX$ and $m\angle CBX$?

   _____

3. How are $m\angle ABX$ and $m\angle CBX$ related?

   _____

Planning the Solution

4. Based on your answers, write an equation relating $m\angle ABC$ and $m\angle ABX$.

5. Based on your answers, write an equation relating $m\angle ABC$ and $m\angle CBX$.

6. Based on your answers, write an equation relating $m\angle ABX$ and $m\angle CBX$.

Getting an Answer

7. Do any of your equations match an equation given in the exercise?

   _____

8. Can you show using algebra that one of your equations is equivalent to another equation in the exercise? Explain.

   _____

   _____

9. Which student is correct? Explain.

   _____

1-5 Practice

Form G

Exploring Angle Pairs

Use the diagram at the right. Is each statement true? Explain.

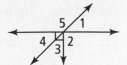

1. $\angle 2$ and $\angle 5$ are adjacent angles.

2. $\angle 1$ and $\angle 4$ are vertical angles.

3. $\angle 4$ and $\angle 5$ are complementary.

Name an angle or angles in the diagram described by each of the following.

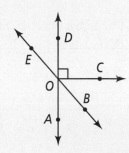

4. complementary to $\angle BOC$

5. supplementary to $\angle DOB$

6. adjacent and supplementary to $\angle AOC$

Use the diagram below for Exercises 7 and 8. Solve for x.
Find the angle measures.

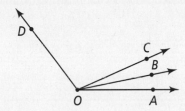

7. $m\angle AOB = 4x - 1$; $m\angle BOC = 2x + 15$; $m\angle AOC = 8x + 8$

8. $m\angle COD = 8x + 13$; $m\angle BOC = 3x - 10$; $m\angle BOD = 12x - 6$

9. $\angle ABC$ and $\angle EBF$ are a pair of vertical angles; $m\angle ABC = 3x + 8$ and $m\angle EBF = 2x + 48$. What are $m\angle ABC$ and $m\angle EBF$?

10. $\angle JKL$ and $\angle MNP$ are complementary; $m\angle JKL = 2x - 3$ and $m\angle MNP = 5x + 2$. What are $m\angle JKL$ and $m\angle MNP$?

For Exercises 11–14, can you make each conclusion from the information in the diagram? Explain.

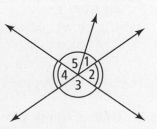

11. $\angle 3 \cong \angle 4$

12. $\angle 2 \cong \angle 4$

13. $m\angle 1 + m\angle 5 = m\angle 3$

14. $m\angle 3 = 90$

15. $\overrightarrow{KM}$ bisects $\angle JKL$. If $m\angle JKM = 86$, what is $m\angle JKL$?

16. $\overrightarrow{SV}$ bisects $\angle RST$. If $m\angle RST = 62$, what is $m\angle RSV$?

1-5

Practice (continued)   Form G

Exploring Angle Pairs

$\overrightarrow{QS}$ bisects $\angle PQR$. Solve for x and find $m\angle PQR$.

17. $m\angle PQS = 3x;\ m\angle SQR = 5x - 20$

18. $m\angle PQS = 2x + 1;\ m\angle RQS = 4x - 15$

19. $m\angle PQR = 3x - 12;\ m\angle PQS = 30$

20. $m\angle PQS = 2x + 10;\ m\angle SQR = 5x - 17$

For Exercises 21–24, can you make each conclusion from the information in the diagram below? Explain.

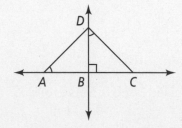

21. $\angle DAB$ and $\angle CDB$ are congruent.

22. $\angle ADB$ and $\angle CDB$ are complementary.

23. $\angle ADB$ and $\angle CDB$ are congruent.

24. $\angle ADB$ and $\angle BCD$ are congruent.

25. Algebra $\angle MLN$ and $\angle JLK$ are complementary, $m\angle MLN = 7x - 1$, and $m\angle JLK = 4x + 3$.
   a. Solve for x.
   b. Find $m\angle MLN$ and $m\angle JKL$.
   c. Show how you can check your answer.

26. Reasoning Describe all the situations in which the following statements are true.
   a. Two vertical angles are also complementary.
   b. A linear pair is also supplementary.
   c. Two supplementary angles are also a linear pair.
   d. Two vertical angles are also a linear pair.

27. Open-Ended Write and solve an equation using an angle bisector to find the measure of an angle.

1-5 Standardized Test Prep

Exploring Angle Pairs

Multiple Choice

For Exercises 1–6, choose the correct letter.

1. $\angle CDE$ and $\angle FDE$ are supplementary, $m\angle CDE = 3x + 10$, and $m\angle FDE = 6x + 8$. What is $m\angle FDE$?

   Ⓐ 18   Ⓑ 64   Ⓒ 108   Ⓓ 116

2. $\overrightarrow{SV}$ bisects $\angle RST$. If $m\angle RSV = 64$, what is $m\angle RST$?

   Ⓕ 32   Ⓖ 64   Ⓗ 116   Ⓘ 128

Use the diagram at the right for Exercises 3 and 4.

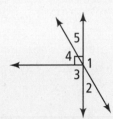

3. Which of the following pairs are vertical angles?

   Ⓐ $\angle 1$ and $\angle 2$ Ⓒ $\angle 2$ and $\angle 5$

   Ⓑ $\angle 2$ and $\angle 3$ Ⓓ $\angle 4$ and $\angle 5$

4. Which of the following pairs are supplementary?

   Ⓕ $\angle 1$ and $\angle 2$ Ⓗ $\angle 2$ and $\angle 3$

   Ⓖ $\angle 2$ and $\angle 5$ Ⓘ $\angle 4$ and $\angle 5$

Use the diagram at the right for Exercises 5 and 6.

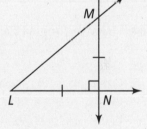

5. Which of the following conclusions can you make from the information in the diagram?

   Ⓐ $\angle MNL \cong \angle LMN$ Ⓒ $\overline{LM} \cong \overline{MN}$

   Ⓑ $m\angle MNL = 2m\angle LMN$ Ⓓ $LM = 2MN$

6. Which of the following conclusions cannot be made from the information in the diagram?

   Ⓕ $\overline{MN} \cong \overline{LN}$ Ⓗ $\angle NLM$ is supplementary to $\angle NML$.

   Ⓖ $\angle NLM \cong \angle NML$ Ⓘ $\angle NLM$ is complementary to $\angle NML$.

Short Response

7. $\angle ABC$ and $\angle DBE$ are vertical angles, $m\angle ABC = 3x + 20$, and $m\angle DBE = 4x - 10$. Write and solve an equation to find $m\angle ABC$ and $m\angle DBE$.

1-6 Think About a Plan

Basic Constructions

a. Draw a large triangle with three acute angles. Construct the bisector of the three angles. What appears to be true about the three angle bisectors?

b. Repeat the constructions with a triangle that has one obtuse angle.

c. **Make a Conjecture** What appears to be true about the three angle bisectors of any triangle?

1. In this problem, you will draw three rays for each triangle. Each ray starts at a vertex and passes through the interior of the triangle.

   a. What is the maximum number of points of intersection between the rays? ☐

   b. What is the minimum number? ☐

2. On a separate piece of paper, draw △ABC such that all three angles are acute angles and the triangle takes up most of the paper.

3. In your own words, what are the steps for drawing the angle bisector of ∠A?

   _____

   _____

   _____

4. Draw the angle bisector of ∠A. Then draw the angle bisectors for ∠B and ∠C.

5. On a separate piece of paper, draw △DEF such that one of the three angles is an obtuse angle and the triangle takes up most of the paper. Construct the angle bisectors for ∠D, ∠E, and ∠F.

6. How many points of intersection are there for the three angle bisectors of △ABC? ☐

7. How many points of intersection are there for the three angle bisectors of △DEF? ☐

8. Suppose a friend draws △DHI. Without looking at the triangle, what do you think will be true of the three angle bisectors of its angles?

   _____

1-6 Practice

Form G

Basic Constructions

For Exercises 1–13, do the construction using the figures below. Check your work with a ruler or a protractor.

1. Construct $\overline{AB}$ congruent to $\overline{XY}$.

2. Construct the perpendicular bisector of $\overline{XY}$.

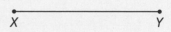

X _____ Y

3. Construct a triangle whose sides are all the same length as $\overline{XY}$.

4. Construct $\overline{AB}$ so that $AB = MN + OP$.

5. Construct $\overline{KL}$ so that $KL = OP - MN$.

6. Construct the perpendicular bisector of $\overline{MN}$.

M — N

7. Construct the perpendicular bisector of $\overline{OP}$.

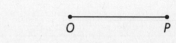

O _____ P

8. Construct $\angle A$ so that $m\angle A = m\angle 1 + m\angle 2$.

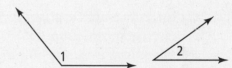

9. Construct $\angle B$ so that $m\angle B = m\angle 1 - m\angle 2$.

10. Construct $\angle C$ so that $m\angle C = 2m\angle 2$.

11. Construct $\angle D$ so that $m\angle D = 2m\angle 1$.

12. Construct $\angle Y$ so that $m\angle Y = \frac{1}{2}m\angle 2$.

13. Construct $\angle Z$ so that $m\angle Z = \frac{1}{2}m\angle X$.

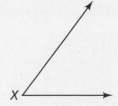

1-6 Practice (continued) Form G
Basic Constructions

14. Draw a segment $\overline{AB}$. Construct a segment whose length is $\frac{1}{4}AB$.
   a. How is the line segment you need to construct related to the perpendicular bisector of $\overline{AB}$?

   b. How can you use the previous constructions to help you?

15. Answer the questions about an angle in a plane. Explain each answer.
   a. How many angle bisectors does an angle have in the plane?
   b. How many rays in the plane bisect the angle?
   c. How many rays in space bisect the angle?

16. **Writing** Explain how to do each construction with a compass and straightedge.
   a. Draw an $\angle A$. Construct the angle bisector of $\angle A$.

   b. Divide $\angle A$ into four congruent angles.

17. Draw a segment $\overline{ST}$.
   a. Construct a right triangle with two sides that have the measure $\frac{1}{2}ST$.
   b. **Reasoning** Describe how to construct a 45° angle. Then describe how to construct an isosceles right triangle.

18. Draw a segment $\overline{VW}$.
   a. Construct a square $ABCD$ whose sides have length VW.
   b. Describe how to construct the perpendicular bisectors of sides $\overline{AB}$ and $\overline{BC}$.

1-6 Standardized Test Prep

Basic Constructions

Multiple Choice

For Exercises 1–4, choose the correct letter.

1. You are asked to construct a segment congruent to $\overline{AB}$. As a first step, you draw a ray. Which of the following, if true of the ray, would be most helpful?

   A The ray is drawn on the paper shorter than $\overline{AB}$.

   B The ray is drawn on the paper longer than $\overline{AB}$.

   C The ray is drawn parallel to $\overline{AB}$.

   D The ray is drawn perpendicular to $\overline{AB}$.

2. Which of the following must be true about a perpendicular bisector and the segment it bisects?

   F The perpendicular bisector and the segment bisect each other.

   G The angle of intersection depends on the length of the line segment.

   H The perpendicular bisector intersects the segment at a 45° angle.

   I The perpendicular bisector intersects the segment at a 90° angle.

3. Which of the following is true about the bisectors of a segment in a plane?

   A Every segment has exactly one bisector.

   B Every segment has exactly two bisectors.

   C Every segment has infinitely many bisectors.

   D Every segment has infinitely many perpendicular bisectors.

4. Which of the following materials is not used when making basic constructions?

   F a ruler   G a compass   H a straightedge   I a pencil

Extended Response

5. How do you construct a perpendicular bisector of $\overline{AB}$? Use three steps.

1-7 Think About a Plan

Midpoint and Distance in the Coordinate Plane

Do you use the Midpoint Formula or the Distance Formula to find the following?

a. Given points K and P, find the distance from K to the midpoint of $\overline{KP}$.

b. Given point K and the midpoint of $\overline{KP}$, find KP.

Understanding the Problem

1. What does the Midpoint Formula help you find?

_____

2. What does the Distance Formula help you find?

_____

Planning the Solution

3. What does part (a) of the problem ask you to find?

_____

4. What does part (b) of the problem ask you to find?

_____

Getting the Answer

5. What formula would you use for part (a)?

_____

6. What formula would you use for part (b)?

_____

7. In Steps 5 and 6, how could you explain why you need to use one formula instead of the other?

_____

_____

1-7 Practice   Form G

Midpoint and Distance in the Coordinate Plane

Find the coordinate of the midpoint of the segment with the given endpoints.

1. 3 and 5   **2.** −7 and 4   **3.** 5 and −9   **4.** −6 and −10

Find the coordinates of the midpoint of $\overline{AB}$.

5. $A(6, 7)$, $B(4, 3)$ **6.** $A(-1, 5)$, $B(2, -3)$

7. $A(14, -2)$, $B(7, -8)$ **8.** $A(0, 0)$, $B(-5, 12)$

9. $A(2.8, 1.1)$, $B(-3.4, 5.7)$ **10.** $A(2\frac{1}{2}, -\frac{1}{4})$, $B(3\frac{1}{4}, -1)$

The coordinates of point Y are given. The midpoint of $\overline{XY}$ is $(3, -5)$. Find the coordinates of point X.

11. $Y(0, 2)$ **12.** $Y(-10, 5)$ **13.** $Y(7, 1)$

14. $Y(4, -8)$ **15.** $Y(-1, -9)$ **16.** $Y(2.5, -6.5)$

Find the distance between each pair of points. If necessary, round to the nearest tenth.

17. $A(6, 7)$, $B(-1, 7)$ **18.** $C(5, -5)$, $D(5, 3)$

19. $E(-1, 0)$, $F(12, 0)$ **20.** $Q(2, -6)$, $T(10, 0)$

21. $H(20, -4)$, $I(-4, 3)$ **22.** $J(-5, 5)$, $K(-3, -2)$

The room shown below right is 14 ft by 10 ft. Find the dimensions of each piece of furniture to the nearest tenth.

23. length and width of the dresser

24. length and width of the table

25. length and width of the bed

26. Reasoning The midpoint of $\overline{AB}$ is on the
y-axis, and $\overline{AB}$ is parallel to the x-axis. Point A
is located in Quadrant III. Which quadrant
contains point B? Explain.

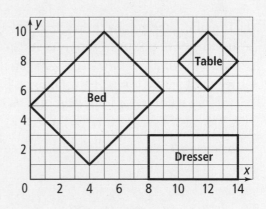

1-7 Practice (continued)   Form G

Midpoint and Distance in the Coordinate Plane

For each graph, find (a) XY to the nearest tenth and (b) the coordinates of the midpoint of $\overline{XY}$.

27.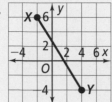

28.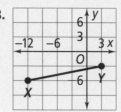

29. **Coordinate Geometry** Graph the points $A(0, 0)$, $B(3, 3)$, $C(9, 3)$, and $D(12, 0)$. Draw trapezoid $ABCD$ and diagonals $\overline{AC}$ and $\overline{BD}$. Add point $E(6, 2)$ at the intersection of diagonals $\overline{AC}$ and $\overline{BD}$.
    a. Find BE and CE. What do you notice?
    b. Find AE and DE. What do you notice?
    c. **Make a Conjecture** What appears to be true about the diagonals of a trapezoid?

30. **Open-Ended** Point $B(-3, -3)$ is the endpoint of many segments.
    a. Find the coordinates of the midpoint and the other endpoint of four noncollinear segments that have point B as their endpoint.

    b. You know that a segment with endpoint B lies entirely in Quadrant III. What does that tell you about the other endpoint?

    c. How many possible segments parallel to either the y-axis or the x-axis match this description? Explain.

31. The plan at the right shows three storage closets in an apartment building. Find the center of each closet and the length of the closet's diagonal to the nearest tenth of a foot. (*Hint:* The diagonals bisect each other, so the center is the midpoint of each diagonal.)
    a. closet 1
    b. closet 2
    c. closet 3

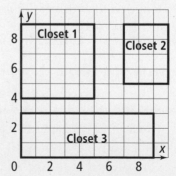

32. **Writing** In your own words, describe how to find the distance between two points on a coordinate plane.

1-7 Standardized Test Prep

Midpoint and Distance in the Coordinate Plane

Multiple Choice

For Exercises 1–7, choose the correct letter.

1. What is the other endpoint of the segment with midpoint −3 and endpoint −7?

   (A) −11   (B) −5   (C) 1   (D) 4

2. The endpoints of $\overline{ST}$ are $S(2, -2)$ and $T(4, 2)$. What are the coordinates of the midpoint of $\overline{ST}$?

   (F) (3, 0)   (G) (0, 3)   (H) (3, −2)   (I) (3, 2)

3. What is the distance between $A(-8, 4)$ and $B(4, -1)$?

   (A) 7   (B) 10   (C) 13   (D) 17

4. The midpoint of $\overline{XZ}$ is Y. Which of the following is true?

   (F) $XZ = XY$ (G) $XZ = \frac{1}{2}XY$ (H) $YZ = \frac{1}{2}XY$ (I) $YZ = \frac{1}{2}XZ$

Use the graph at the right for Exercises 5 and 6.

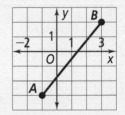

5. According to the graph, what is the midpoint of $\overline{AB}$?

   (A) (1, 0)   (C) (1, 0.5)

   (B) (1, −0.5)   (D) (1.5, −0.5)

6. According to the graph, what is AB to the nearest tenth?

   (F) 2.2   (G) 3   (H) 5   (I) 6.4

7. The midpoint of $\overline{CD}$ is $M(-3, -7)$. If the coordinates of C are $(-2, -10)$, what are the coordinates of D?

   (A) (−4, −4)   (B) (−1, −13)   (C) (−2.5, −8.5)   (D) (−5, −17)

Short Response

8. The midpoint of $\overline{AB}$ is in Quadrant IV, and $\overline{AB}$ is parallel to the y-axis.
   a. What quadrant or quadrants cannot contain either point A or B? Explain.

   b. What else can you determine about points A and B?

1-8 Think About a Plan

Perimeter, Circumference, and Area

Pet Care You want to adopt a puppy from your local animal shelter. First, you plan to build an outdoor playpen along the side of your house, as shown on the right. You want to lay down special dog grass for the pen's floor. If dog grass costs $1.70 per square foot, how much will you spend?

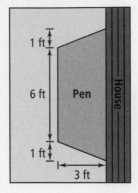

Understanding the Problem

1. What are you trying to find?

_____

Planning the Solution

2. What additional information do you need to know to answer the question?

_____

3. How will you use that additional information to answer the question?

_____

Getting the Answer

4. How can you find the area of the playpen?

_____

_____

_____

5. How do you find the total cost of the grass?

_____

6. What is the total cost of the grass? Show your work.

1-8

Practice

Form G

Perimeter, Circumference, and Area

Find the perimeter of each figure.

1.

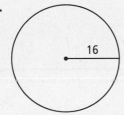

5 cm

9 cm

2.

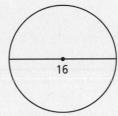

7 cm

3. An 8-ft-by-10-ft rug leaves 1 ft of the bedroom floor exposed on all four sides. Find the perimeter of the bedroom floor.

Find the circumference of each circle in terms of π.

4.

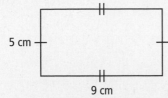

16

5.

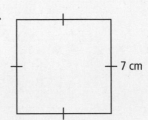

16

6.

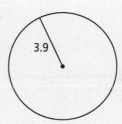

3.9

Graph each figure in the coordinate plane. Find the perimeter.

7. $X(-4, 2)$, $Y(2, 10)$, $Z(2, 2)$

8. $R(1, 2)$, $S(1, -2)$, $T(4, -2)$

9. $A(0, 0)$, $B(0, 5)$, $C(6, 5)$, $D(6, 0)$

10. $L(-3, 2)$, $M(2, 14)$, $N(2, 20)$, $P(-3, 20)$

Find the area of the rectangle with the given base and height.

11. 4 ft, 15 in.

12. 90 in., 3 yd

13. 3 m, 130 cm

Find the area of each circle in terms of π.

14.

12.5

15.

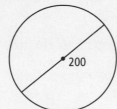

200

16.

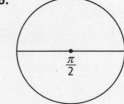

$\frac{\pi}{2}$

1-8 Practice (continued) Form G

Perimeter, Circumference, and Area

Find the area of each shaded region. All angles are right angles.

17.

18.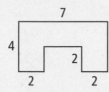

19.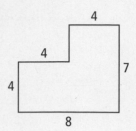

Find the circumference and area of each circle, using $\pi = 3.14$. If necessary, round to the nearest tenth.

20. $r = 5$ m

21. $d = 2.1$ in.

22. $d = 2$ m

23. $r = 4.7$ ft

24. The area of a circle is 25π in.^{2}. What is its radius?

25. A rectangle has twice the area of a square. The rectangle is 18 in. by 4 in. What is the perimeter of the square?

26. Reasoning If two circles have the same circumference, what do you know about their areas? Explain.

27. Coordinate Geometry The center of a circle is $A(-3, 3)$, and $B(1, 6)$ is on the circle. Find the area of the circle in terms of π.

28. Algebra Use the formula for the circumference of a circle to write a formula for the area of a circle in terms of its circumference.

29. Coordinate Geometry On graph paper, draw polygon $ABCDEF$ with vertices $A(0, 0)$, $B(0, 10)$, $C(5, 10)$, $D(5, 7)$, $E(9, 7)$, and $F(9, 0)$. Find the perimeter and the area of the polygon.

30. The units of the floor plan at the right are in feet. Find the perimeter and area of each room.
   a. the kitchen
   b. the bedroom
   c. the bathroom
   d. the closet
   e. What is the area of the main hallway? Explain how you could find this area using the area of each room.

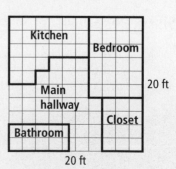

1-8   Standardized Test Prep

Perimeter, Circumference, and Area

Multiple Choice

For Exercises 1–6, choose the correct letter.

1. A 12-ft-by-15-ft swimming pool has a 3-ft-wide no-slip surface around it. What is the outer perimeter of the no-slip surface?

   Ⓐ 78 ft   Ⓑ 78 ft^2 Ⓒ 198 ft   Ⓓ 198 ft^2

2. What is the circumference of the circle at the right in terms of π?

   Ⓕ 1.1π Ⓗ 2.2π

   Ⓖ 1.21π Ⓘ 4.4π

3. What is the perimeter of $\triangle PQR$ with vertices $P(-2, 9)$, $Q(7, -3)$, and $R(-2, -3)$ in the coordinate plane?

   Ⓐ 21 units   Ⓑ 25 units   Ⓒ 34 units   Ⓓ 36 units

4. You are tiling a kitchen floor that is 10 ft wide by 4 yd long. How many square yards of tile do you need?

   Ⓕ $13\frac{1}{3}$ yd^2 Ⓖ $13\frac{1}{2}$ yd^2 Ⓗ 20 yd^2 Ⓘ 40 yd^2

5. The diameter of $\odot Z$ is 5 in. What is its area in terms of π?

   Ⓐ 2.5π in.^{2} Ⓑ 5π in.^{2} Ⓒ 6.25π in.^{2} Ⓓ 25π in.^{2}

6. All angles in the figure at the right are right angles. What is the area of the figure?

   Ⓕ 14   Ⓗ 28

   Ⓖ 18   Ⓘ 36

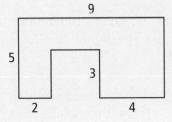

Short Response

7. **a.** If two squares have the same area, what do you know about the measures of their sides? Explain.

   b. If two rectangles have the same area, what do you know about the measures of their sides? Explain.

2-1 Think About a Plan

Patterns and Inductive Reasoning

Bird Migration During bird migration, volunteers get up early on Bird Day to record the number of bird species they observe in their community during a 24-h period. Results are posted online to help scientists and students track the migration.

a. Make a graph of the data.

b. Use the graph and inductive reasoning to make a conjecture about the number of bird species the volunteers in this community will observe in 2015.

Bird Count

Year	Number of Species
2004	70
2005	83
2006	80
2007	85
2008	90

Understanding the Problem

1. What does the problem ask you to predict?

_____

2. What approach to organizing the data is suggested in the problem?

_____

Planning the Solution

3. On your graph, what data should be represented by the horizontal axis?

_____

4. On your graph, what data should be represented by the vertical axis?

_____

5. Graph the data on the grid at the right. Don't forget to label the axes.

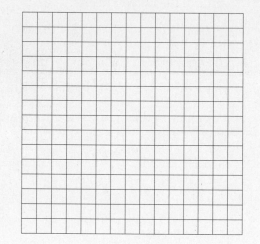

Getting an Answer

6. Look at the data points. Is there an upward or downward trend? What is the approximate increase or decrease in the number of bird species observed per year?

_____

7. Based on the pattern in the graph of the data, how many bird species do you think will be observed in 2015?

2-1 Practice   Form G

Patterns and Inductive Reasoning

Find a pattern for each sequence. Use the pattern to show the next two terms.

1. 5, 11, 18, 26, . . .   **2.** A, B, D, E, G, H, . . .

3. −3, 6, −12, 24, −48, . . .   **4.** 1, 5, 30, 210, 1680, . . .

5.

Use the sequence and inductive reasoning to make a conjecture.

Sequence A:

6. How many sides does the fifth figure of Sequence A have?

7. How many sides does the tenth figure of Sequence A have?

8. How many sides does the fourteenth figure of Sequence A have?

Sequence B: −5, 4, −2, −5, 4, −2, −5, 4, −2, . . .

9. What is the tenth term of Sequence B?

10. What is the fifteenth term of Sequence B?

Make a conjecture for each scenario. Show your work.

11. the square of an odd number   **12.** the cube of a negative number

13. the product of two even   **14.** the product of a multiple of 5
numbers and an odd number   and a multiple of 2

**Find a pattern for each sequence. Use inductive reasoning to show the
next two terms.**

15. 3, 5, 9, 17, . . .   **16.** 1, 4, 6, 24, 26, . . .

17. 5, 3, 9, 7, 21, . . .   **18.** 1, −2, 2, −4, 0, . . .

19. 0.3, −0.09, 0.0027, . . .   **20.** $\frac{2}{3}, \frac{4}{9}, \frac{8}{27}, \ldots$

21. 2, 3, 5, 8, 13, 21, . . .   **22.** 4, 7, 12, 19, 28, . . .

2-1 Practice (continued)   Form G

Patterns and Inductive Reasoning

Use inductive reasoning to make a prediction for each scenario.

23. A farmer keeps track of the water his livestock uses each month.
    a. Predict the amount of water used in August.
    b. Is it reasonable to use the graph to predict water consumption for October? Explain.

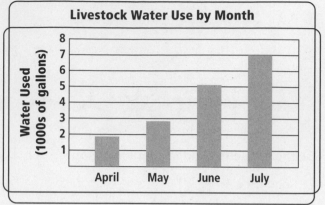

Livestock Water Use by Month

24. Hannah sells snow cones during soccer tournaments. She records data for snow cone sales and temperature.
    a. Predict the amount of snow cone sales when the temperature is 100°F.
    b. Is it reasonable to use the graph to predict sales for when the temperature is 15°F? Explain.

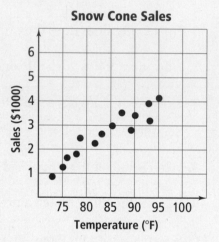

Snow Cone Sales

Find one counterexample to show that each conjecture is false.

25. The sum of two integers is always positive.

26. The product of two mixed numbers is never a whole number.

27. All four-sided figures are rectangles.

28. **Patterns** Draw the next two figures in the sequence shown below.

29. **Open-Ended** Use letters of the alphabet and create two different sequences that begin with the same two letters.

30. **Writing** Think about all of the things you did this morning. Choose one activity and explain how you used inductive reasoning to complete it.

2-1 Standardized Test Prep

Patterns and Inductive Reasoning

Gridded Response

Solve each exercise and enter your answer on the grid provided.

1. What is the next term of this sequence?

   1, 3, 5, 8, 11, 15, 19, 24, . . .

2. What is the next term of this sequence?

   $\frac{1}{2}, \frac{2}{6}, \frac{3}{18}, \frac{4}{54}, \ldots$

3. What is the next term of this sequence?

   $-5, 5, -6, 6, -7, 7, -8, \ldots$

4. What is the missing term in this sequence?

   0.95, 0.85, 0.90, 0.80, __?__, 0.75, 0.80, . . .

5. Jim makes the following conjecture.

   Other than 1, there are no numbers less than 100 that are both perfect squares and perfect cubes.

   What is a counterexample that proves his conjecture false?

Answers

1.

2.
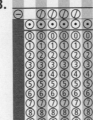

3.
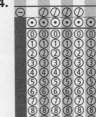

4.
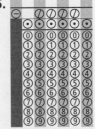

5.

Name _____ Class _____ Date _____

2-2 Think About a Plan
Conditional Statements

Error Analysis Natalie claims that a given conditional and its contrapositive are both true. Sean claims that the given conditional is true but its contrapositive is false. Who is correct and how do you know?

Understanding the Problem

1. What is the main point of disagreement between Natalie and Sean?

   _____

   _____

2. Do you think it is possible to write a conditional statement that is true, but has a false contrapositive? Explain.

   _____

3. How could you use examples of true and false conditionals to decide who is correct?

   _____

   _____

   _____

Planning the Solution

4. Use a table to test some conditional statements. Write several conditional statements and their contrapositives. Use the table to show their truth values. One example has been completed for you. Use additional paper if necessary.

Conditional	True or false?	Contrapositive	True or false?
If a dog has spots, then the dog can fly.	false	If a dog cannot fly, then the dog does not have spots.	false

Getting an Answer

5. What does the pattern in your table tell you about whether Natalie or Sean is probably correct?

   _____

   _____

2-2

Practice

Form G

Conditional Statements

Identify the hypothesis and conclusion of each conditional.

1. If a number is divisible by 2, then the number is even.

2. If the sidewalks are wet, then it has been raining.

3. The dog will bark if a stranger walks by the house.

4. If a triangle has three congruent angles, then the triangle is equilateral.

Write each sentence as a conditional.

5. A regular pentagon has exactly five congruent sides.

6. All uranium is radioactive.

7. Two complementary angles form a right angle.

8. A catfish is a fish that has no scales.

Write a conditional statement that each Venn diagram illustrates.

9.

10.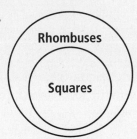

Determine if the conditional is *true* or *false*. If it is false, find a counterexample.

11. If the figure has four congruent angles, then the figure is a square.

12. If an animal barks, then it is a seal.

2-2

Practice (continued)   Form G
Conditional Statements

Write the converse, inverse, and contrapositive of the given conditional statement. Determine the truth value of all three statements. If a statement is false, give a counterexample.

13. If two angles are complementary, then their measures sum to 90.

14. If the temperature outside is below freezing, then ice can form on the sidewalks.

15. If a figure is a rectangle, then it has exactly four sides.

Draw a Venn diagram to illustrate each statement.

16. If a figure is a square, then it is a rectangle.

17. If the game is rugby, then the game is a team sport.

18. Open-Ended Write a conditional statement that is false and has a true converse. Then write the converse, inverse, and contrapositive. Determine the truth values for each statement.

19. Multiple Representations Use the definitions of *p, q,* and *r* to write each conditional statement below in symbolic form.
p: The weather is rainy.   *q:* The sky is cloudy.   *r:* The ground is wet.
  a. If the weather is not rainy, then the sky is not cloudy.
  b. If the ground is wet, then the weather is rainy.
  c. If the sky is not cloudy, then the ground is wet.

2-2 Standardized Test Prep

Conditional Statements

Multiple Choice

For Exercises 1–4, choose the correct letter.

1. What is the hypothesis of the given statement?

   If pigs had wings, you could fly.

   Ⓐ Pigs have wings.   Ⓒ Pigs do not have wings.

   Ⓑ You can fly.   Ⓓ You cannot fly.

2. Which statement is the converse of the given statement?

   If you make an insurance claim, then your rates will go up.

   Ⓕ If your insurance rates do not go up, then you have not made a claim.

   Ⓖ If you do not make an insurance claim, then your rates will not go up.

   Ⓗ If your insurance rates go up, then you have made an insurance claim.

   Ⓘ If you make an insurance claim, then your rates will not go up.

3. Which statement is the contrapositive of the given statement?

   If a person is a banjo player, then the person is a musician.

   Ⓐ If a person is not a musician, then the person is not a banjo player.

   Ⓑ If a person is not a banjo player, then the person is a musician.

   Ⓒ If a person is not a banjo player, then the person is not a musician.

   Ⓓ If a person is a musician, then the person is a banjo player.

4. How are the two statements given below related to each other?

   X: If you run for 10 minutes, then you will raise your heart rate.

   Z: If you do not run for 10 minutes, then you will not raise your heart rate.

   Ⓕ *Z* is the contrapositive of *X*.   Ⓗ *Z* is the inverse of *X*.

   Ⓖ *Z* is the converse of *X*.   Ⓘ *Z* is the retrograde of *X*.

Short Response

5. What are the inverse and the contrapositive of the following conditional?

   If a movie is a comedy, then it is funny.

2-3   Think About a Plan

Biconditionals and Definitions

Error Analysis Your friend defines a right angle as an angle that is greater than an acute angle. Use a biconditional to show that this is not a good definition.

1. What is your friend's statement?

    _____

    _____

2. The exercise tells you to use a biconditional. What would be a good first step before you write a biconditional?

    _____

3. Rewrite your friend's statement as a biconditional.

    _____

    _____

4. Now write the two conditionals that make up the biconditional. Fill in the blanks to complete the two conditional statements.

    a. If an angle is a(n) _____ angle, then the measure of the angle is _____ than the measure of a(n) _____ angle.

    b. If the measure of an angle is _____ than the measure of a(n) _____, then the angle is a(n) _____ .

5. Look at the two conditionals. Are both conditionals true? Explain.

    _____

    _____

6. What would be the best way to explain that your friend's definition is not a good definition?

    _____

    _____

2-3 Practice

Form G

Biconditionals and Definitions

Each conditional statement below is true. Write its converse. If the converse is also true, combine the statements as a biconditional.

1. If a number is divisible by 2, then the number is even.

2. If two angles have the same measure, then the angles are congruent.

3. If $x > 5$, then $|x| > 5$.

4. If a closed figure is a pentagon, then it has exactly five sides.

5. If two numbers are both even, then the sum of the two numbers is even.

Write the two statements that form each biconditional.

6. Two lines are perpendicular if and only if they intersect to form four right angles.

7. A whole number is divisible by 3 if and only if the sum of the digits of the whole number is divisible by 3.

8. A whole number is an odd number if and only if it is not divisible by 2.

9. A person lives in Alaska if and only if the person lives in the northernmost state in the United States.

2-3

Practice (continued)   Form G
Biconditionals and Definitions

Test each statement below to see if it is reversible. If so, write it as a true biconditional. If not, write *not reversible*.

10. If a quadrilateral is a square, then the quadrilateral has four congruent angles.

11. An isosceles triangle is a triangle with two congruent angles.

12. A circle is a figure with no sides.

13. If a quadrilateral is a trapezoid, it has exactly two sides that are parallel.

14. A person who lives in Miami is a person who lives in Florida.

Is each statement below a good definition? If not, explain.

15. Two rays intersect if and only if they lie in the same plane.

16. A redwood tree is an evergreen tree that grows very tall.

17. A rectangle is a quadrilateral with four congruent angles.

18. A hexagon is a polygon with exactly six sides.

Write each statement as a biconditional.

19. A square is a rectangle with four congruent sides.

20. An equilateral triangle is a triangle with three congruent angles.

21. A factor of a whole number is a whole number that divides evenly into the given number.

22. **Open-Ended** Write a definition of your choice. Then write the definition as a biconditional.

2-3 Standardized Test Prep

Biconditionals and Definitions

Multiple Choice

For Exercises 1–3, choose the correct letter.

1. Which statement is a good definition of a rectangle?

    Ⓐ A rectangle is a shape with four sides.

    Ⓑ A rectangle is a shape with two pairs of parallel sides.

    Ⓒ A rectangle is a quadrilateral with four congruent angles.

    Ⓓ A rectangle is a parallelogram with four congruent sides.

2. Conditional: If a triangle is scalene, then the triangle has no congruent sides.

    Which statement shows the conditional written as a true biconditional?

    Ⓕ A triangle is scalene if and only if it has no congruent sides.

    Ⓖ If a triangle has no congruent sides, then the triangle is scalene.

    Ⓗ If a triangle has some congruent sides, then the triangle is not scalene.

    Ⓘ A triangle is equilateral if and only if it is not scalene.

3. Biconditional: A triangle is equilateral if and only if the triangle has three congruent angles.

    Which choice shows the two conditionals that make up the biconditional?

    Ⓐ If a triangle has three sides, then it is equilateral. If the triangle is equilateral, then it has three sides.

    Ⓑ If a triangle is equilateral, then it has three congruent angles. If a triangle has three congruent angles, then it is equilateral.

    Ⓒ If a triangle is scalene, then the triangle is not equilateral. If a triangle is equilateral, then the triangle is not scalene.

    Ⓓ An equilateral triangle has symmetry. If a triangle has symmetry, it is equilateral.

Short Response

4. Write this definition as a true biconditional two different ways.

    Definition: A rhombus is a parallelogram with four congruent sides.

2-4 | Think About a Plan

Deductive Reasoning

Writing Give an example of a rule used in your school that could be written as a conditional. Explain how the Law of Detachment is used in applying that rule.

Understanding the Problem

1. What is the problem asking you to do?

   _____

   _____

Planning the Solution

2. List a school rule that could be written as a conditional.

   Example: Do not park your car in spaces marked "reserved" or your car
   will be towed.

   _____

   _____

Getting an Answer

3. Rewrite the school rule as a conditional.

   Example: If you park your car in a space marked "reserved," then your car
   will be towed.

   _____

   _____

4. Identify the hypothesis and the conclusion of the conditional you wrote for
   the school rule.

   Example: Hypothesis: You park your car in a space marked "reserved."

              Conclusion: Your car will be towed.

   _____

   _____

5. The Law of Detachment states that if the hypothesis of a true conditional is
   true, then the conclusion is true. Explain how the Law of Detachment is
   used when applying your school rule.

   _____

   _____

2-4 Practice   *Form G*
Deductive Reasoning

If possible, use the Law of Detachment to make a conclusion. If it is not possible to make a conclusion, tell why.

1. If a triangle is a right triangle, then the triangle has one 90° angle.
   $\triangle ABC$ is a right triangle.

2. If a parallelogram has four congruent sides, then the parallelogram is a rhombus.
   The parallelogram has four congruent sides.

3. If $x > 7$, then $|x| > 7$.
   $x < 7$

4. If cats prowl, mice will scatter.
   Mice are scattering.

5. If the light is flashing yellow, then you may drive with caution through the intersection.
   The light is flashing yellow.

6. If a triangle has two congruent sides, then the triangle is isosceles.
   In $\triangle DEF$, $\overline{DE} \cong \overline{EF}$.

If possible, use the Law of Syllogism to make a conclusion. If it is not possible to make a conclusion, tell why.

7. To take Calculus, you must first take Algebra 2.
   To take Algebra 2, you must first take Algebra 1.

8. If a tree has ragged bark, then the tree is unhealthy.
   If a tree has ragged bark, then the tree might be a birch tree.

9. A quadrilateral has four congruent sides if and only if it is a rhombus.
   A square is a rhombus.

2-4 **Practice** (continued)   *Form G*

Deductive Reasoning

If possible, use the Law of Syllogism to make a conclusion. If it is not possible to make a conclusion, tell why.

10. If you like to snow ski, then you will like Colorado.

If you like to wakeboard, then you will like Florida.

11. If it is Tuesday, then the cafeteria is serving meat loaf.

When the cafeteria serves meat loaf, Harlan brings a sack lunch.

12. If a polygon is a square, then it has exactly four congruent angles.

If a polygon has exactly four congruent angles, then it is a rectangle.

Use the Law of Detachment and the Law of Syllogism to make conclusions from the following statements. If it is not possible to make a conclusion, tell why.

13. If you live in Fairbanks, then you live in Alaska. If you live in Alaska, then you live in the largest state in the United States. Alan lives in Fairbanks.

14. A rectangle is a quadrilateral with four congruent angles. A rectangle is a parallelogram with four congruent angles. A square is a rectangle.

15. If it is summer, the days will be warm. If people are swimming, the days are warm. If the air conditioning is turned on inside, then it is warm outside.

16. If it is raining, the temperature is greater than 32°F. If the temperature is greater than 32°F, then it is not freezing outside. It is raining.

17. During the school week, if it does not rain, the soccer team will have practice. If the soccer team has practice, the team members will warm up by jogging two miles. It does not rain on Wednesday.

18. Open-Ended Write a set of statements that uses the Law of Syllogism to make a conclusion.

19. Writing Give an example of how a police officer uses the Law of Detachment.

2-4 Standardized Test Prep

Deductive Reasoning

Multiple Choice

For Exercises 1–3, choose the correct letter.

1. Which statement is a valid conclusion based on the argument?

If a polygon is a regular pentagon, then the polygon has exactly five congruent angles.

The polygon is a regular pentagon.

Ⓐ Therefore, the polygon is a rectangle.

Ⓑ Therefore, the polygon is a regular quadrilateral.

Ⓒ Therefore, the polygon has exactly five congruent angles.

Ⓓ Therefore, the polygon has congruent sides.

2. Using the Law of Syllogism, which of the following completes the statement to form a valid conclusion?

If it is snowing heavily, then school will be canceled.

If school is canceled, the big test will not be given today.

It is snowing heavily, therefore

Ⓕ look out for the snowplows while driving to school.

Ⓖ the big test will not be given today.

Ⓗ the roads will be hard to drive on.

Ⓘ you should call the school to see if school is canceled.

3. Using the Law of Detachment, which statement is a valid conclusion?

If Jordin has a temperature of 100° or more, then Jordin should stay home from school.

Jordin has a temperature of 101°.

Ⓐ Jordin should see the school nurse.

Ⓑ Jordin should stay home from school.

Ⓒ Jordin should take his temperature again.

Ⓓ Jordin has a temperature of 100° or more.

Short Response

4. Use the Law of Syllogism to make a valid conclusion.

If a blub is screaming, then a frot is swimming.

If a frot is swimming, then a greep is flinging.

2-5

Think About a Plan

Reasoning in Algebra and Geometry

Write a two-column proof.

Given: $KM = 35$

$$\overset{\textstyle 2x-5 \quad\quad 2x}{\underset{\textstyle K \quad\ L \quad\quad M}{\bullet\!\!-\!\!\bullet\!\!-\!\!-\!\!\bullet}}$$

Prove: $KL = 15$

Know

1. What information are you given? Where does this information belong in the proof?

   _____

2. Use the figure. What information do you know from the figure?

   _____

Need

3. To solve the problem, what will you need to prove? Where does this statement belong in the proof?

   _____

Plan

4. You can determine information using the figure. Analyze the figure. What equation can you write?

5. How can you use the equation and the information you know to find the value of x?

   _____

6. How can you use the value of x to show that $KL = 15$?

   _____

7. Use the space below to write the proof.

Statements	Reasons
1) $KM = 35$	1) Given

Name _____ Class _____ Date _____

2-5   Practice   Form G
Reasoning in Algebra and Geometry

Fill in the reason that justifies each step.

1. $0.25x + 2x + 12 = 39$ Given

       $2.25x + 12 = 39$ **a.** _?_

          $2.25x = 27$ **b.** _?_

        $225x = 2700$ **c.** _?_

              $x = 12$ **d.** _?_

2. Given: $m\angle ABC = 80$

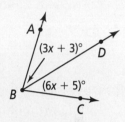

   $m\angle ABD + m\angle DBC = m\angle ABC$ Angle Addition Postulate

   $(3x + 3) + (6x + 5) = 80$ Substitution Property

            $9x + 8 = 80$ **a.** _?_

                $9x = 72$ **b.** _?_

                  $x = 0$ **c.** _?_

3. Given: $KL = 3(PM)$

     $5x = 3(2x - 4)$ Substitution Property

     $5x = 6x - 12$ **a.** _?_

       $-x = -12$ **b.** _?_

          $x = 12$ **c.** _?_

4. Given: $XY = YZ$

   $8m + 5 = 6m + 17$ Substitution Property

   $2m + 5 = 17$ **a.** _?_

     $2m = 12$ **b.** _?_

       $m = 6$ **c.** _?_

Name the property of equality or congruence that justifies going from the first statement to the second statement.

5. $\overline{XY} \cong \overline{TZ}$

    $\overline{TZ} \cong \overline{XY}$

6. $3(x + 2) = 15$

    $3x + 6 = 15$

7. $4n + 6 - 2n = 9$

    $2n + 6 = 9$

8. $\angle A \cong \angle B$ and $\angle B \cong \angle C$

    $\angle A \cong \angle C$

2-5

Practice (continued)

Form G

Reasoning in Algebra and Geometry

9. Write a two-column proof.

Given: $\angle QWT$ and $\angle TWX$ are complementary.

Prove: $x = 28$

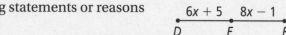

Statements	Reasons
1) $\angle QWT$ and $\angle TWX$ are complementary	1) ?
2) $m\angle QWT + m\angle TWX = 90$	2) ?
3) $2x + x + 6 = 90$	3) ?
4) $3x + 6 = 90$	4) ?
5) $3x = 84$	5) ?
6) $x = 28$	6) ?

10. Developing Proof Fill in the missing statements or reasons for the two-column proof.

Given: E is the midpoint of $\overline{DF}$.

Prove: $DE = 23$

Statements	Reasons
1) E is the midpoint of $\overline{DF}$.	1) ?
2) ?	2) Definition of midpoint
3) $6x + 5 = 8x - 1$	3) ?
4) $5 = 2x - 1$	4) ?
5) ?	5) Addition Property of Equality
6) ?	6) Division Property of Equality
7) $DE = 6x + 5$	7) Given
8) $DE = 6(3) + 5$	8) ?
9) $DE = 23$	9) ?

11. Write a two-column proof.

Given: $m\angle PMN = m\angle RBC$

Prove: $m\angle ABR + m\angle PMN = m\angle ABC$

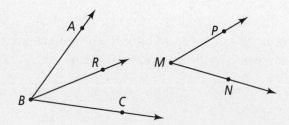

2-5 Standardized Test Prep

Reasoning in Algebra and Geometry

Multiple Choice

For Exercises 1–6, choose the correct letter.

1. According to the Transitive Property of Equality, if $TX = XY$, and $XY = YZ$, then $TX = \boxed{}$.

   Ⓐ TX Ⓑ XY Ⓒ YZ Ⓓ TZ

2. What property is illustrated by the statement, if $KL = LM$, then $LM = KL$?

   Ⓕ Reflexive Property of Equality   Ⓗ Transitive Property of Equality

   Ⓖ Symmetric Property of Equality   Ⓘ Division Property of Equality

Use the list of reasons below for Exercises 3–6. Choose the correct reason for each algebraic statement.

   Ⓐ Subtraction Property of Equality   Ⓒ Distributive Property

   Ⓑ Combine like terms.   Ⓓ Division Property of Equality

Statements	Reasons
$3(x + 2) + 1 = 8$	Given
$6x + 6 + 1 = 8$	3) _?_
$6x + 7 = 8$	4) _?_
$6x = 1$	5) _?_
$x = \frac{1}{6}$	6) _?_

Extended Response

7. Write a two-column proof.

   Given: A is the midpoint of $\overline{ZP}$.

        $XY = ZA$

   Prove: $XY = AP$

2-6

Think About a Plan

Proving Angles Congruent

Reasoning Explain why this statement is true:
If $m\angle ABC + m\angle XYZ = 180$ and $\angle ABC \cong \angle XYZ$, then $\angle ABC$ and $\angle XYZ$ are right angles.

Understanding the Problem

1. The statement is a conditional. Break the conditional down into its parts. What is the hypothesis?

   _____

2. What is the conclusion of the conditional?

   _____

3. What makes an angle a right angle? _____

4. What does the symbol $\cong$ mean about the angles? _____

Planning the Solution

5. For the statement to be true, the sum of the measures of the two angles must equal _____ and the angles must have the same measure.

6. Write an equation to represent the hypothesis. Because $\angle ABC \cong \angle XYZ$, they have the same measure, so use the same variable m to represent the measure of each angle.

7. Simplify the equation.

Getting an Answer

8. What is the value of m?

9. Does this value of m mean that $\angle ABC$ and $\angle XYZ$ are right angles?

   _____

10. How can you explain why the statement is true?

   _____

   _____

   _____

2-6 Practice   Form G

Proving Angles Congruent

Find the value of x.

1.

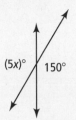
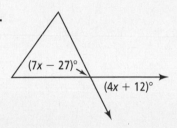
(5x)°   150°

2.

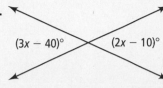
(3x − 40)°   (2x − 10)°

3.

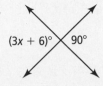
(3x + 6)°   90°

4.

(7x − 27)°
(4x + 12)°

5.

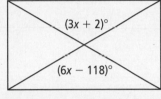
(3x + 2)°
(6x − 118)°

6.

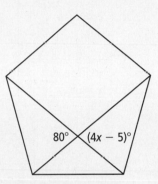
80° (4x − 5)°

Find m∠1 using the given information.

7. $m\angle 1 = 5x$, $m\angle 4 = 2x + 90$

8. $m\angle 1 = 8x - 120$, $m\angle 4 = 4x + 16$

9. $m\angle 2 = 180 - 3x$, $m\angle 3 = 2x$

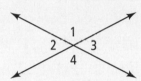
1
2 3
4

Complete the proofs by filling in the blanks.

10. **Given:** $\angle A \cong \angle BDA$

    Prove: $x = 5$

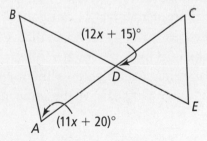
B   C
(12x + 15)°
D
E
A (11x + 20)°

Statements	Reasons
1) __?__	1) Given
2) __?__	2) Vertical Angles are ≅.
3) $\angle A \cong \angle CDE$	3) __?__
4) __?__	4) Definition of Congruence
5) $11x + 20 = 12x + 15$	5) __?__
6) __?__	6) Subtraction Property of Equality
7) __?__	7) __?__

2-6 **Practice** (continued)   Form G
Proving Angles Congruent

11. Given: ∠5 ≅ ∠2

Prove: ∠8 ≅ ∠4

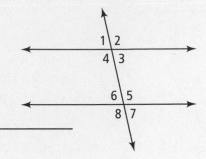

Statements	Reasons
1) _?_	1) Given
2) ∠2 ≅ ∠4	2) _?_
3) _?_	3) Transitive Property of Congruence
4) _?_	4) Vertical Angles are ≅.
5) ∠8 ≅ ∠4	5) _?_

12. Complete the paragraph proof below.

Given: ∠1 and ∠2 are complementary
∠2 and ∠3 are complementary
$\overline{BD}$ bisects ∠ABC

Prove: m∠1 = 45

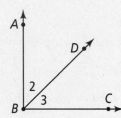

We know that _____ and _____ are complementary and ∠2 and ∠3 are complementary because these facts are given. By the _____, m∠2 + m∠3 = 90. Given that $\overline{BD}$ bisects ∠ABC, it follows that _____. Using substitution, _____, or 2(m∠3) = 90. Using the _____, m∠3 = 45. By the Congruent Complements Theorem, _____. It follows that _____, because congruent angles have the same measure and _____ by substitution.

13. Writing Look back at the proof in Exercise 11. Rewrite the proof as a paragraph proof.

Name _____ Class _____ Date _____

2-6 Standardized Test Prep
Proving Angles Congruent

Multiple Choice

For Exercises 1–5, choose the correct letter.

1. $\angle A$ and $\angle B$ are supplementary, and $\angle A$ and $\angle C$ are supplementary. Which conclusion is valid?

   (A) $\angle B$ and $\angle C$ are supplementary.

   (B) $\angle B$ and $\angle C$ are complementary.

   (C) $\angle B$ and $\angle C$ are acute.

   (D) $\angle B$ and $\angle C$ are congruent.

2. The measure of $\angle B$ is one-half the measure of its complement. What is the measure of $\angle B$?

   (F) 30 (G) 45 (H) 60 (I) 90

3. $\angle T$ and $\angle R$ are vertical angles. $m\angle T = 3x + 36$ and $m\angle R = 6x - 9$. What is the measure of $\angle T$?

   (A) 15 (B) 81 (C) 87 (D) 99

Use the figure at the right for Exercises 4 and 5.

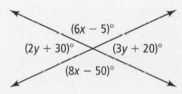

4. What is the value of x?

   (F) 8.9 (H) 16.8

   (G) 22.5 (I) 27.5

5. What is the value of y?

   (A) −10 (C) 2

   (B) −2 (D) 10

6. $\angle A$ and $\angle B$ are complementary angles. If $m\angle A = 5x - 2$, and $m\angle B = 3x + 4$, what is the value of x?

   (F) 3 (G) 6 (H) 11 (I) 22.25

Short Response

7. In the figure at the right, if $m\angle 1 = 37$, and $\angle 1 \cong \angle 3$, what is $m\angle 4$? Explain.

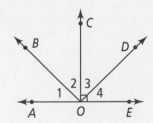

3-1

Think About a Plan

Lines and Angles

Recreation You and a friend are driving go-karts on two different tracks. As you drive on a straight section heading east, your friend passes above you on a straight section heading south. Are these sections of the two tracks *parallel, skew,* or *neither?* Explain.

Understanding the Problem

1. How are parallel lines and skew lines alike?

   _____

2. How are parallel lines and skew lines different?

   _____

Planning the Solution

3. What geometric concepts do you need to find out about the tracks?

   _____

Getting an Answer

4. Make a sketch of the situation in the problem.

5. Would the track sections you drew intersect? _____

6. Are the track sections you drew coplanar? _____

7. Use what you know about the properties of parallel and skew lines to explain whether the track sections are *parallel, skew,* or *neither.*

   _____

   _____

3-1 Practice

Form G

Lines and Angles

Use the diagram to name each of the following.

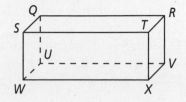

1. a pair of parallel planes

2. all lines that are parallel to $\overleftrightarrow{RV}$

3. four lines that are skew to $\overleftrightarrow{WX}$

4. all lines that are parallel to plane $QUVR$

5. a plane parallel to plane $QUWS$

In Exercises 6–11, describe the statement as *true* or *false*. If false, explain.

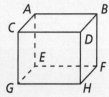

6. $\overleftrightarrow{AE}$ and $\overleftrightarrow{EF}$ are skew lines.

7. plane $DBF \parallel$ plane ABD

8. $\overleftrightarrow{GH} \parallel \overleftrightarrow{EF}$

9. $\overleftrightarrow{DB} \parallel \overleftrightarrow{AE}$

10. plane $EFH \parallel$ plane ABD

11. $\overleftrightarrow{FH}$ and $\overleftrightarrow{CD}$ are skew lines.

12. You are driving over a bridge that runs east to west. Below the bridge, a highway runs north to south. Are the bridge and the highway *parallel, skew,* or *neither?* Explain.

13. **Open-Ended** List parts of your classroom that fit each description below.
    a. parallel to the top of a window

    b. skew with one side of the door

    c. parallel to the plane of the floor

14. **Reasoning** Your friend says that the sides of a ladder and the rungs of a ladder are skew. Is this true? Explain.

15. **Visualization** If two planes are parallel, must all lines within those planes be parallel? Explain.

3-1

Practice (continued)   Form G

Lines and Angles

Identify all pairs of each type of angle in the diagram below right.

16. corresponding angles

17. same-side interior angles

18. alternate interior angles

19. alternate exterior angles

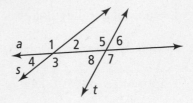

**Decide whether the angles are *alternate interior angles*,
same-side interior angles, *corresponding angles*, or
alternate exterior angles.**

20. $\angle 2$ and $\angle 7$ **21.** $\angle 5$ and $\angle 4$

22. $\angle 8$ and $\angle 3$ **23.** $\angle 6$ and $\angle 4$

24. $\angle 1$ and $\angle 5$

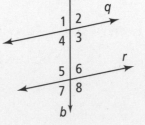

25. Draw a Diagram Line *e* intersects trapezoid *ABCD*. Sketch a diagram that
meets the following conditions.

   a. $\overleftrightarrow{AB}$ and $\overleftrightarrow{DC}$ are parallel.

   b. $\angle 1$ and $\angle 6$ are alternate exterior angles.

   c. $\angle 2$ and $\angle 3$ are same-side interior angles.

   d. $\angle 4$ and $\angle 5$ are each supplementary to $\angle 3$.

26. Writing Describe three real-world objects that represent two lines
intersected by a transversal.

27. The map at the right shows the intersection
of Maple Street and Oak Street by Main
Street. Name the angle pairs represented
by the locations listed below.

   a. town hall and gas station

   b. school and library

   c. library and post office

   d. school and gas station

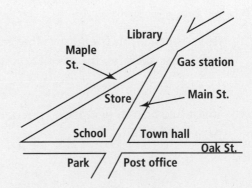

3-1 Standardized Test Prep
Lines and Angles

Multiple Choice

For Exercises 1–7, choose the correct letter.

For Exercises 1–3, use the figure at the right.

1. Which line segment is parallel to $\overline{GE}$?
   - Ⓐ $\overline{DH}$
   - Ⓒ $\overline{FG}$
   - Ⓑ $\overline{KI}$
   - Ⓓ $\overline{HI}$

2. Which two line segments are skew?
   - Ⓕ $\overline{DE}$ and $\overline{GE}$
   - Ⓗ $\overline{EI}$ and $\overline{GK}$
   - Ⓖ $\overline{GK}$ and $\overline{DH}$
   - Ⓘ $\overline{HI}$ and $\overline{DF}$

3. Which line segment is parallel to plane $FGKJ$?
   - Ⓐ $\overline{FD}$
   - Ⓑ $\overline{HI}$
   - Ⓒ $\overline{GE}$
   - Ⓓ $\overline{KI}$

For Exercises 4–7, use the figure at the right.

4. Which is a pair of alternate interior angles?
   - Ⓕ $\angle 3$ and $\angle 6$
   - Ⓗ $\angle 6$ and $\angle 5$
   - Ⓖ $\angle 2$ and $\angle 7$
   - Ⓘ $\angle 4$ and $\angle 6$

5. Which angle corresponds to $\angle 7$?
   - Ⓐ $\angle 1$
   - Ⓑ $\angle 3$
   - Ⓒ $\angle 4$
   - Ⓓ $\angle 6$

6. Which pair of angles are alternate exterior angles?
   - Ⓕ $\angle 1$ and $\angle 5$
   - Ⓖ $\angle 3$ and $\angle 6$
   - Ⓗ $\angle 5$ and $\angle 8$
   - Ⓘ $\angle 1$ and $\angle 8$

7. Which pair of angles are same-side interior angles?
   - Ⓐ $\angle 1$ and $\angle 5$
   - Ⓑ $\angle 3$ and $\angle 6$
   - Ⓒ $\angle 4$ and $\angle 8$
   - Ⓓ $\angle 3$ and $\angle 5$

Short Response

8. Describe the parallel planes, parallel lines, and skew lines in a cube.
   Draw a sketch to illustrate your answer.

3-2

Think About a Plan

Properties of Parallel Lines

Outdoor Recreation Campers often use a "bear bag" at night to avoid attracting animals to their food supply. In the bear bag system at the right, a camper pulls one end of the rope to raise and lower the food bag.

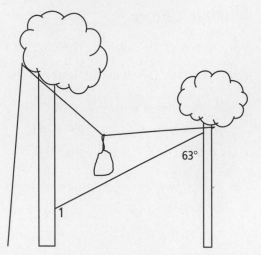

a. Suppose a camper pulls the rope taut between the two parallel trees, as shown. What is $m\angle 1$?

b. Are $\angle 1$ and the given angle *alternate interior angles, same-side interior angles,* or *corresponding angles?*

Understanding the Problem

1. Look at the diagram. How could you describe the diagonal taut rope and the trees in terms of lines and transversals?

   _____

2. What do you know about the special angle pairs formed when parallel lines are intersected by a transversal?

   _____

3. What strategy can you use to solve the problem?

   _____

   _____

Planning the Solution

4. What special angle pair do $\angle 1$ and the given angle make up? How do you know?

   _____

   _____

5. What do you know about the relationship between these types of angles?

   _____

Getting an Answer

6. What is an equation you can use to find $m\angle 1$?

7. What is the solution to the equation?

3-2

Practice

Form G

Properties of Parallel Lines

Identify all the numbered angles that are congruent to the given angle. Justify your answers.

1.

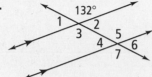

2.

3.

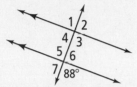

4.

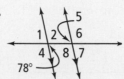

Find $m\angle 1$ and $m\angle 2$. Justify each answer.

5.

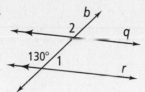

6.

7.

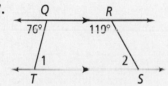

8.

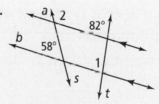

Algebra Find the value of x and y. Then find the measure of each labeled angle.

9.

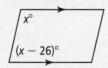

10.

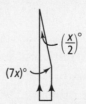

11.

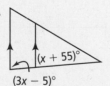

12.

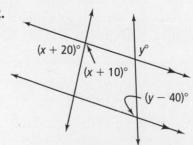

Prentice Hall Gold Geometry • Practice and Problem Solving Workbook

3-2

Practice (continued)

Form G

Properties of Parallel Lines

13. Write a two-column proof.

Given: $a \parallel b$, $x \parallel y$

Prove: $\angle 4$ is supplementary to $\angle 15$.

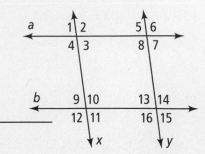

Statements	Reasons

14. Visualization One pair of parallel lines intersect a second pair of parallel lines. One of the angles of intersection has a measure of 60. How can you determine the measure of the four interior angles? Draw a sketch to support your answer.

15. Error Analysis Which solution for the figure at the right is incorrect? Explain.

$$2x - 40 = x + 10 \qquad\qquad 2x - 40 + (x + 10) = 180$$
$$x - 40 = 10 \qquad\qquad\qquad 3x - 30 = 180$$
$$x = 50 \qquad\qquad\qquad\qquad 3x = 210$$
$$\qquad\qquad\qquad\qquad\qquad x = 70$$

16. A zip line consists of a pulley attached to a cable that is strung at an angle between two objects. In the zip line at the right, one end of the cable is attached to a tree. The other end is attached to a post parallel to the tree. What is the measure of $\angle 1$? What type of angle pair do $\angle 1$ and the given angle represent?

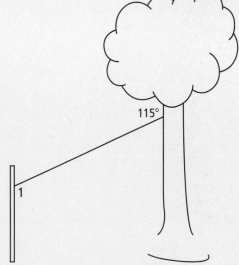

3-2   Standardized Test Prep

Properties of Parallel Lines

Multiple Choice

For Exercises 1–6, choose the correct letter.

For Exercises 1–4, use the figure at the right.

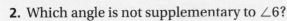

1. Which angle is congruent to ∠1?

   Ⓐ ∠2   Ⓒ ∠6

   Ⓑ ∠5   Ⓓ ∠7

2. Which angle is not supplementary to ∠6?

   Ⓕ ∠2   Ⓖ ∠4   Ⓗ ∠5   Ⓘ ∠8

3. Which can be used to prove directly that ∠1 ≅ ∠8?

   Ⓐ Alternate Interior Angles Theorem

   Ⓑ Corresponding Angles Theorem

   Ⓒ Same-Side Interior Angles Postulate

   Ⓓ Alternate Exterior Angles Theorem

4. If $m\angle 5 = 42$, what is $m\angle 4$?

   Ⓕ 42   Ⓖ 48   Ⓗ 128   Ⓘ 138

For Exercises 5 and 6, use the figure at the right.

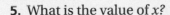

5. What is the value of x?

   Ⓐ 10   Ⓒ 30

   Ⓑ 25   Ⓓ 120

6. What is the measure of ∠1?

   Ⓕ 45   Ⓖ 60   Ⓗ 120   Ⓘ 125

Short Response

7. Write a two-column proof of the Alternate Exterior Angles Theorem (Theorem 3-3).

   Given: $r \parallel s$

   Prove: $\angle 1 \cong \angle 8$

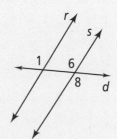

3-3 Think About a Plan

Proving Lines Parallel

Algebra Determine the value of x for which $r \parallel s$.
Then find $m\angle 1$ and $m\angle 2$.

Given: $m\angle 1 = 20 - 8x$, $m\angle 2 = 30 - 16x$

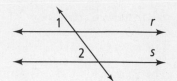

1. Is $\angle 1$ an interior angle or an exterior angle? Is $\angle 2$ an interior angle or an exterior angle?

   _____

2. Do $\angle 1$ and $\angle 2$ lie on the same side of the transversal or on opposite sides of the transversal?

   _____

3. What type of angle pair are $\angle 1$ and $\angle 2$?

   _____

4. If $r \parallel s$, and $\angle 1$ and $\angle 2$ are the type of angle pair you named above, how are the angles related?

   _____

5. What equation can you write using the given information?

6. What is the value of x?

7. Substitute the value of x into each expression. What are the measures of each angle?

   $m\angle 1 = 20 - 8x = $ ☐

   $m\angle 2 = 30 - 16x = $ ☐

8. Would this value of x prove that $r \parallel s$? Explain.

   _____

   _____

3-3 Practice Form G
Proving Lines Parallel

Which lines or segments are parallel? Justify your answer.

1.
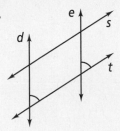

2.
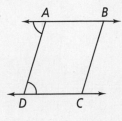

3.
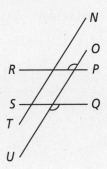

4.
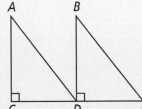

5.
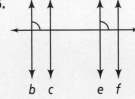

6.
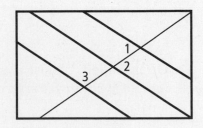

7. Developing Proof Complete the flow proof below.

Given: $\angle 1$ and $\angle 2$ are supplementary; $x \parallel y$

Prove: $q \parallel r$

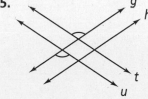

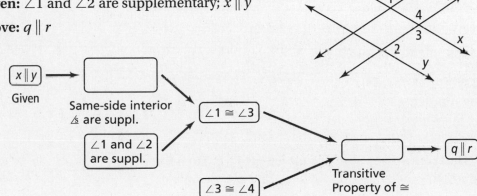

8. The art club is designing a new flag for the marching band. In the diagram, $m\angle 1 = 45$, $m\angle 2 = 45$, and $m\angle 3 = 145$. Does the flag contain three parallel lines? Explain.

3-3 Practice (continued)   Form G
Proving Lines Parallel

Algebra Determine the value of x for which $r \parallel s$. Then find the measure of each labeled angle.

9.

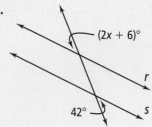

10.

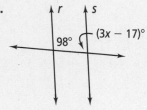

11.

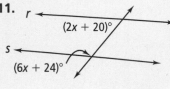

12.

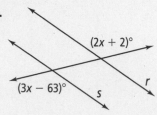

13.

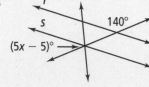

14.

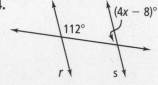

Developing Proof Use the given information to determine which lines, if any, are parallel. Justify each conclusion with a theorem or postulate.

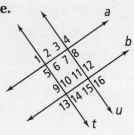

15. $\angle 11$ is supplementary to $\angle 10$.

16. $\angle 6 \cong \angle 9$

17. $\angle 13$ is supplementary to $\angle 14$.

18. $\angle 13 \cong \angle 15$

19. $\angle 12$ is supplementary to $\angle 3$.

20. $\angle 2 \cong \angle 13$

Algebra Determine the value of x for which $j \parallel k$. Then find $m\angle 1$ and $m\angle 2$.

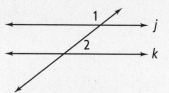

21. $m\angle 1 = 7x + 14$, $m\angle 2 = 2x + 4$

22. $m\angle 1 = 4x - 5$, $m\angle 2 = x + 20$

23. Open-Ended Choose a value for x and write an expression for one of the angles in terms of x that will prove that g and h are parallel.

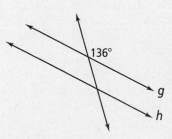

3-3

Standardized Test Prep

Proving Lines Parallel

Multiple Choice

For Exercises 1–6, choose the correct letter.

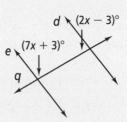

1. For what value of x is $d \parallel e$?

   Ⓐ 20   Ⓑ 25   Ⓒ 35   Ⓓ 37

For Exercises 2 and 3, use the figure below right.

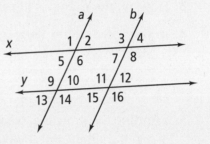

2. Which statement proves that $a \parallel b$?

   Ⓕ $\angle 8$ is supplementary to $\angle 12$.   Ⓗ $\angle 1 \cong \angle 6$

   Ⓖ $\angle 10$ is supplementary to $\angle 11$.   Ⓘ $\angle 5 \cong \angle 13$

3. Which statement proves that $x \parallel y$?

   Ⓐ $\angle 2$ is supplementary to $\angle 3$.   Ⓒ $\angle 6 \cong \angle 9$

   Ⓑ $\angle 14$ is supplementary to $\angle 15$.   Ⓓ $\angle 12 \cong \angle 13$

For Exercises 4–6, use the figure at the right.

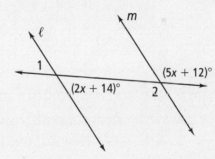

4. If $\ell \parallel m$, what is $m\angle 1$?

   Ⓕ 22   Ⓖ 58   Ⓗ 122   Ⓘ 130

5. For what value of x is $\ell \parallel m$?

   Ⓐ 22   Ⓑ 54   Ⓒ 58   Ⓓ 122

6. If $\ell \parallel m$, what is $m\angle 2$?

   Ⓕ 22   Ⓖ 58   Ⓗ 122   Ⓘ 130

Short Response

7. Write a flow proof.

   Given: $\angle 2$ and $\angle 3$ are supplementary.

   Prove: $c \parallel d$

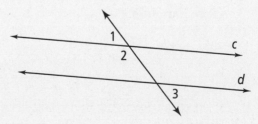

3-4 Think About a Plan

Parallel and Perpendicular Lines

Quilting You plan to sew two triangles of fabric together to make a square for a quilting project. The triangles are both right triangles and have the same side and angle measures. What must also be true about the triangles in order to guarantee that the opposite sides of the fabric square are parallel? Explain.

1. What do you know about the triangles? _____

2. What figures can you make by sewing different sides together? _____

3. How are the triangles the same? _____

4. In your own words, what question are you trying to answer?

_____

_____

5. Examine the drawings below. △ABC and △DCB are congruent and sides $\overline{BC}$ on each triangle are sewn together.

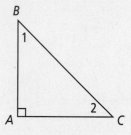 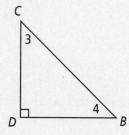 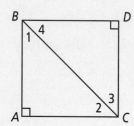

   a. Which angles are congruent to each other?
   b. Is $\overline{AC} \parallel \overline{BD}$? How do you know?

_____

   c. Is $\overline{AB} \parallel \overline{CD}$? How do you know?

_____

6. What fact about the triangles makes the opposite sides of the fabric piece parallel?

_____

_____

_____

7. How would you explain this relationship?

_____

_____

3-4

Practice   Form G

Parallel and Perpendicular Lines

1. Suppose you are laying tiles. You place several different rectangles together to form a larger rectangle.
   a. $\overline{BC}$ is parallel to $\overline{DF}$, $\overline{DF}$ is parallel to $\overline{GH}$. What is the relationship between $\overline{BC}$ and $\overline{GH}$? Explain.

   b. $\overline{BK}$ is parallel to $\overline{EL}$. $\overline{GH}$ is perpendicular to $\overline{BK}$. What is the relationship between $\overline{GH}$ and $\overline{EL}$?

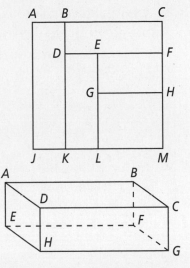

2. **Error Analysis** A student says that according to Theorem 3-9, $\overleftrightarrow{AB}$ and $\overleftrightarrow{BC}$ must be parallel because they are both perpendicular to $\overleftrightarrow{BF}$. Explain the student's error.

3. **Developing Proof** Copy and complete this paragraph proof.

   Given: $q \parallel r$, $r \parallel s$, $b \perp q$, and $a \perp s$

   Prove: $a \parallel b$

   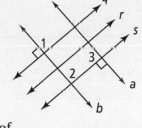

   Proof: Because it is given that $q \parallel r$ and $r \parallel s$, then $q \parallel s$ by the _____. This means that $\angle 1 \cong \angle$ _____ because they are _____. Because $b \perp q$, $m\angle 1 = 90$. So, $m\angle 2 =$ _____. This means $s \perp b$, by definition of perpendicular lines. It is given that $a \perp s$, so $a \parallel b$ by Theorem _____.

4. **Open-Ended** Draw a diagram that meets the criteria listed below. Then describe how all the lines are related to each other.
   a. $q \parallel r$ b. $r \perp s$
   c. $t \parallel q$ d. $u \perp t$

5. A puppeteer cuts the pieces shown at the right to frame the stage of a puppet theater. Will the sides of the pieces on the left and right be parallel?

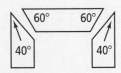

In Exercises 6 and 7, a, b, c, and d are distinct lines in the same plane. For each combination of relationships, tell how a and c relate. Justify your answer.

6. $a \perp b$; $b \perp c$ 7. $a \perp b$; $b \parallel c$

3-4 Practice (continued) Form G
Parallel and Perpendicular Lines

8. Write a paragraph proof.
   Given: $\overleftrightarrow{NP} \perp \overleftrightarrow{NO}$; $\overleftrightarrow{NP} \perp \overleftrightarrow{PQ}$
           $\angle PQS$ and $\angle QSR$ are supplementary.
   Prove: $\overleftrightarrow{NO} \parallel \overleftrightarrow{RS}$

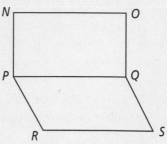

9. The recreation department is setting up the football field. They check to make sure that the 50-yd line and the end zone lines are perpendicular to the right sideline. Does this mean both sidelines are parallel? Explain.

10. **Draw a Diagram** Apple Road is perpendicular to Blueberry Lane. Blueberry Lane is parallel to Cornflower Drive. Cornflower Drive is perpendicular to Daffodil Lane. Daffodil Lane is parallel to Evergreen Drive. Draw a diagram to explain how each street is related to every other street. What can you conclude about Apple Road and Evergreen Drive? Explain.

11. **Compare and Contrast** How is the Transitive Property of Parallel Lines similar to the Transitive Property of Congruence? How are they different?

12. **Writing** How is Theorem 3-9 related to the postulates and theorems you learned in Lesson 3-3?

The following statements describe a set of railroad tracks. Based only on the statement, make a conclusion about the rails or the railroad ties. Explain.

13. The railroad ties are each perpendicular to one rail.

14. The rails are parallel. One railroad tie is perpendicular to one rail.

3-4   Standardized Test Prep

Parallel and Perpendicular Lines

Multiple Choice

For Exercises 1–5, choose the correct letter.

1. Which can be used to prove $d \perp t$?

   Ⓐ Transitive Property of Parallel Lines

   Ⓑ Transitive Property of Congruence

   Ⓒ Perpendicular Transversal Theorem

   Ⓓ Converse of the Corresponding Angles Theorem

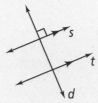

2. A carpenter is building a frame. Which values of a and b will ensure that the sides of the finished frame are parallel?

   Ⓕ $a = 40$ and $b = 60$ Ⓗ $a = 30$ and $b = 60$

   Ⓖ $a = 45$ and $b = 50$ Ⓘ $a = 40$ and $b = 40$

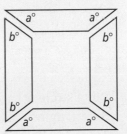

For Exercises 3 and 4, use the map at the right.

3. If Adam Ct. is perpendicular to Bertha Dr. and Charles St., what must be true?

   Ⓐ Adam Ct. $\perp$ Edward Rd.   Ⓒ Adam Ct. $\parallel$ Dana La.

   Ⓑ Bertha Dr. $\parallel$ Charles St.   Ⓓ Dana La. $\perp$ Charles St.

4. Adam Ct. is perpendicular to Charles St. and Charles St. is parallel to Edward Rd. What must be true?

   Ⓕ Adam Ct. $\perp$ Edward Rd.   Ⓗ Bertha Dr. $\parallel$ Charles St.

   Ⓖ Adam Ct. $\parallel$ Dana La.   Ⓘ Dana La. $\perp$ Charles St.

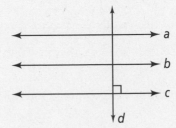

5. If $a \perp b$, $b \perp c$, $c \parallel d$, and $d \perp e$, which is not true?

   Ⓐ $a \perp e$ Ⓒ $a \parallel d$

   Ⓑ $a \parallel c$ Ⓓ $b \parallel d$

Short Response

6. Write a paragraph proof.

   Given: $a \parallel b$, $b \parallel c$, and $d \perp c$

   Prove: $a \perp d$

3-5
Think About a Plan
Parallel Lines and Triangles

Algebra A right triangle has exterior angles at each of its acute angles with measures in the ratio 13 : 14. Find the measures of the two acute angles of the right triangle.

Know

1. What is the sum of all the interior angles in a right triangle?

2. One angle in a right triangle measures 90. What is the sum of the other two angles?

3. What is the sum of an interior angle and its adjacent exterior angle?

Need

4. What strategy can you use to keep track of the interior and exterior angles of the triangle?

_____

_____

5. Draw a diagram, labeling the interior acute angles $\angle 1$ and $\angle 2$ and their corresponding exterior angles $\angle 3$ and $\angle 4$.

Plan

6. Use what you know to find the following sums:
   a. $m\angle 1 + m\angle 2 + m\angle 3 + m\angle 4$
   b. $m\angle 3 + m\angle 4$

7. The ratio of $m\angle 3$ to $m\angle 4$ is 13 : 14. Use this to find the measures of $\angle 3$ and $\angle 4$. Explain your work.

_____

_____

8. How can you use $m\angle 3$ and $m\angle 4$ to find the measures of the interior angles? What are the interior angle measures?

_____

Name _____ Class _____ Date _____

3-5 Practice   Form G
Parallel Lines and Triangles

Find $m\angle 1$.

1.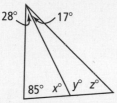

2.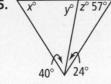

3.
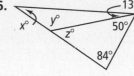

Algebra Find the value of each variable.

4.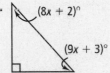

5.

6.
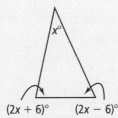

7. Use the diagram at the right to answer the questions.
   a. Which angle is an exterior angle?

   b. What are its remote interior angles?

   c. Find $m\angle 1$ and $m\angle 2$.

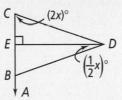

Find the value of the variables and the measures of the angles.

8.
$(8x + 2)°$
$(9x + 3)°$

9.
$x°$
$(2x + 6)°$ $(2x - 6)°$

10. In the figure at the right, $\overline{ED} \perp \overline{CB}$ and $\overline{ED}$ bisects $\angle CDB$. Find $m\angle DBA$.

C $(2x)°$
E
B $\left(\frac{1}{2}x\right)°$ D
A

11. **Reasoning** What is the measure of each angle in an isosceles right triangle? Explain.

12. The ratio of the angle measures of the acute angles in a right triangle is $2 : 3$. Find the measures of the acute angles.

3-5 **Practice** (continued)   Form G

Parallel Lines and Triangles

13. **Paragraph Proof** Prove that the sum of the exterior angles of a triangle is always 360°.

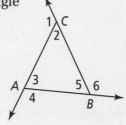

Given: $\triangle ABC$

Prove: $m\angle 1 + m\angle 4 + m\angle 6 = 360$

14. A ramp built for wheelchairs is shown below.

a. Find the measures of the remote interior angles for $\angle R$.

b. Find $m\angle R$.

15. **Error Analysis** A student draws a diagram of $\triangle ABC$ with angle bisector $\overrightarrow{AD}$ as shown, and says that the measure of $\angle CAD$ must be 30°.
   a. What is the student's error in reasoning?

   b. Draw a diagram that would show an alternate answer.

Find each missing angle measure.

16. 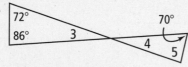   17.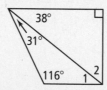

18. **Reasoning** Two angles of a triangle measure 53 and 39. What is the measure of the largest exterior angle of the triangle? Explain.

3-5 Standardized Test Prep

Parallel Lines and Triangles

Gridded Response

1. What is the value of *w*?

2. What is the value of *z*?

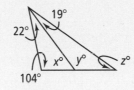

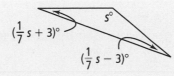

3. What is the value of *s*?

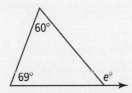

4. What is the value of *e*?

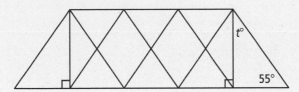

5. What is the value of *t* on the truss of the bridge?

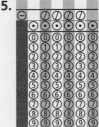

Answers

1. 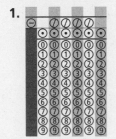 2. 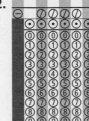 3.  4.  5.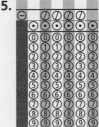

3-6 | Think About a Plan

Constructing Parallel and Perpendicular Lines

Construct a right triangle with legs of lengths *a* and *b*.

1. Use the space at the bottom of the page to make your construction.

   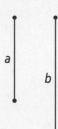

   a. What type of angle will the two legs make? _____

   b. What will be the length of the shorter leg? ___

   c. What will be the length of the longer leg? ___

2. How can you construct a leg with length *b*?

   _____

   _____

3. How can you construct a perpendicular at one end of leg *b*? Construct leg *b* and its perpendicular according to your plan.

   _____

   _____

   _____

   _____

4. What steps do you still need to complete to finish constructing the triangle?

   _____

   _____

5. Complete the construction. Check your triangle to make sure it is drawn correctly.

   a. Is it a right triangle? _____

   b. What is the shorter leg length? ___

   c. What is the longer leg length? ___

3-6 Practice   Form G

Constructing Parallel and Perpendicular Lines

1. Draw a figure like the given one. Then construct the line through point Y that is parallel to $\overleftrightarrow{AB}$.

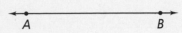

Draw two segments. Label their lengths a and b. Construct a quadrilateral with one pair of parallel sides as described.

2. The sides have lengths a and $2b$.   3. The sides have lengths $\frac{1}{2}a$ and b.

4. Draw a figure like the given one. Then construct the line perpendicular to ℓ at point P.

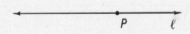

5. Draw a figure like the given one. Then construct the line through point P and perpendicular to $\overleftrightarrow{AB}$.

• P

6. Construct an equilateral triangle.

3-6

Practice (continued)   Form G

Constructing Parallel and Perpendicular Lines

For Exercises 7–11, use the segments at the right.

7. Draw a line ℓ. Construct a segment of length c that is perpendicular to line ℓ.

8. Construct a rectangle with base b and height a.

9. Construct a square with sides of length c.

10. Construct a right triangle with legs of lengths a and c.

11. Draw a line segment m with length c. Construct two line segments perpendicular to line segment m with lengths a and b, respectively.

12. Construct a quadrilateral with exactly one pair of parallel sides, beginning with line n and a point P not on line n.

3-6 Standardized Test Prep

Constructing Parallel and Perpendicular Lines

Multiple Choice

For Exercises 1–3, choose the correct letter.

1. Which diagram below shows the first step in parallel line construction on a point outside a line?

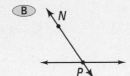

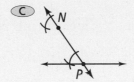

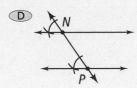

2. What kind of line is being constructed in this series of diagrams?

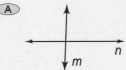 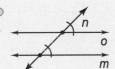 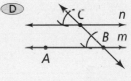

(F) parallel   (G) perpendicular   (H) congruent   (I) similar

3. Which diagram below shows line *m* parallel to line *n*?

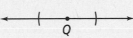 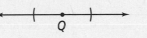 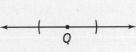

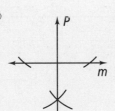

Short Response

4. **Error Analysis** Explain the error in the construction at the right. The student is attempting to draw a perpendicular line through a point not on the line.

3-7 Think About a Plan

Equations of Lines in the Coordinate Plane

Accessibility By law, the maximum slope of an access ramp in new construction is $\frac{1}{12}$. The plan for the new library shows a 3-ft height from the ground to the main entrance. The distance from the sidewalk to the building is 10 ft. If you assume the ramp does not have any turns, can you design a ramp that complies with the law? Explain.

1. What does the word *slope* mean in this context?

_____

2. What does the law require for the access ramp slope?

_____

3. What are the height and maximum length for the access ramp?

_____

4. What is the slope for that ramp?

5. How does the slope compare with the required slope?

_____

_____

6. Can you design a ramp that complies with the law? Explain.

_____

_____

3-7 Practice

Form G

Equations of Lines in the Coordinate Plane

Find the slope of the line passing through the given points.

1.
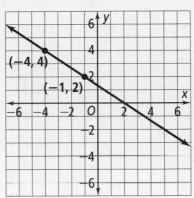

2.
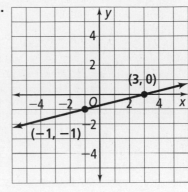

3. $(2, 3), (-1, -6)$

4. $(-6, -2), (-3, -6)$

5. $(2, 9), (4, -7)$

Graph each line.

6. $y = 3x - 4$

7. $y - 2 = (x + 3)$

8. $y + 2 = -4(x + 3)$

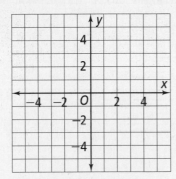
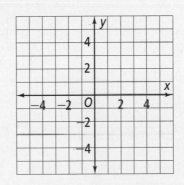
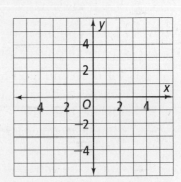

Use the given information to write an equation for each line.

9. slope 6, y-intercept 4

10. slope $-\frac{1}{3}$, y-intercept -2

11.
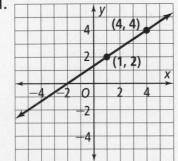

12.
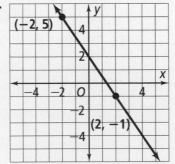

13. through $(-2, 0)$ and $(3, 10)$

14. through $(10, 2)$ and $(2, -2)$

3-7   **Practice** (continued)   *Form G*

Equations of Lines in the Coordinate Plane

Graph each line.

15. $y = -4$ **16.** $x = 3$ **17.** $y = 5$

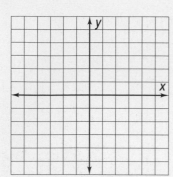   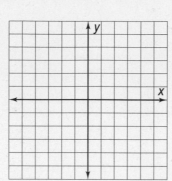   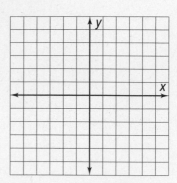

18. Open-Ended Write equations for three lines that contain the point (0, 2).

Write each equation in slope-intercept form.

19. $y - 3 = 4(x + 2)$ **20.** $y - 2 = -2(x - 5)$ **21.** $y + 1 = -\frac{1}{2}(x + 4)$

22. A wireless phone company charges $20 for a basic plan each month plus $0.25/min for each call.

   a. Write an equation to show how much the company charges, where x is the number of minutes used and y is the total cost.

   b. Find the total cost for 300 minutes, 350 minutes, and 400 minutes.

   c. Graph the equation using the values for 300 and 400 minutes.

Graph each pair of lines. Then find their point of intersection.

23. $y = -5, x = -2$ **24.** $y = 6, x = -1$

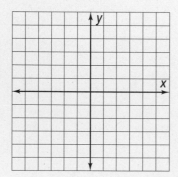   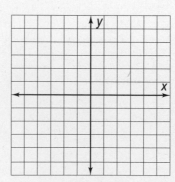

3-7 Standardized Test Prep

Equations of Lines in the Coordinate Plane

Multiple Choice

For Exercises 1–4, choose the correct letter.

1. What is the slope of the line passing through the points $(2, 7)$ and $(-1, 3)$?

   Ⓐ $\frac{2}{7}$　　　　Ⓑ $\frac{3}{4}$　　　　Ⓒ $\frac{4}{3}$　　　　Ⓓ $\frac{1}{3}$

2. What is the correct equation of the line shown at the right?

   Ⓕ $y = \frac{3}{2}x + 3$　　　　Ⓗ $y = \frac{2}{3}x + 3$

   Ⓖ $y = -\frac{3}{2}x - 3$　　　　Ⓘ $y = -\frac{2}{3}x - 3$

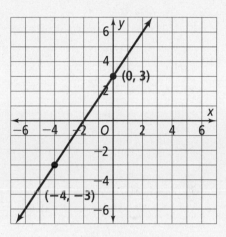

3. The x-intercept of a line is -5 and the y-intercept of the line is -2. What is the equation of the line?

   Ⓐ $y = -\frac{5}{2}x - 5$　　　　Ⓒ $y = -\frac{5}{2}x - 2$

   Ⓑ $y = \frac{2}{5}x + 2$　　　　Ⓓ $y = -\frac{2}{5}x - 2$

4. What is the slope-intercept form of the equation $y - 7 = -\frac{5}{2}(x + 4)$?

   Ⓕ $y - 2 = -\frac{5}{2}(x + 2)$　　Ⓗ $y = -\frac{4}{7}x + 2$

   Ⓖ $y + 7 = -x + \frac{5}{2}$　　　Ⓘ $y = -\frac{5}{2}x - 3$

Short Response

5. **Error Analysis** A student has attempted to graph an equation that contains the point $(1, -4)$ and has a slope of $\frac{1}{3}$.
   a. What is the correct equation in slope-intercept form?
   b. What is the student's error on the graph?

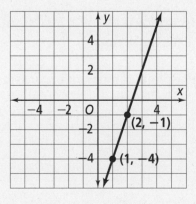

3-8 Think About a Plan

Slopes of Parallel and Perpendicular Lines

Rail Trail A community recently converted an old railroad corridor into a recreational trail. The graph at the right shows a map of the trail on a coordinate grid. They plan to construct a path to connect the trail to a parking lot. The new path will be perpendicular to the recreational trail.

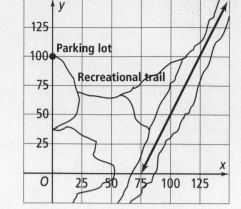

  a. Write an equation of the line representing the new path.

  b. What are the coordinates of the point at which the path will meet the recreational trail?

  c. If each grid space is 25 yd by 25 yd, how long is the path to the nearest yard?

1. How can you tell whether two lines are perpendicular, given their equations?

_____

_____

2. What is the slope of the line representing the existing trail?

3. What is the slope of the line representing the new path?

4. What is the y-intercept of the line representing the new path?

5. Write an equation for the line representing the new path, and then graph it.

6. Name the point at which the path meets the recreational trail.

7. How long is the path in units of the coordinate grid? (*Hint:* Use the distance formula.)

8. How long is the path in yards?

3-8

Practice

Form G

Slopes of Parallel and Perpendicular Lines

In Exercises 1 and 2, are lines m_1 and m_2 parallel? Explain.

1.

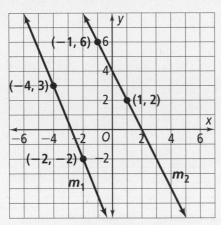

2.

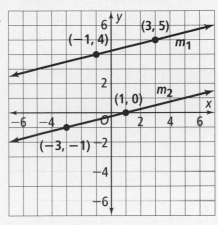

Write an equation of the line parallel to $\overleftrightarrow{AB}$ that contains point C.

3. $\overleftrightarrow{AB}: y = -5x + 12; C(-2, 1)$

4. $\overleftrightarrow{AB}: y = \frac{4}{7}x + 7\frac{2}{7}; C(7, 1)$

5. $\overleftrightarrow{AB}: y = \frac{1}{5}x + 8\frac{4}{5}; C(3, 6)$

6. $\overleftrightarrow{AB}: y = -\frac{2}{5}x + 5\frac{2}{5}; C(5, -2)$

In Exercises 7 and 8, are lines m_1 and m_2 perpendicular? Explain.

7.

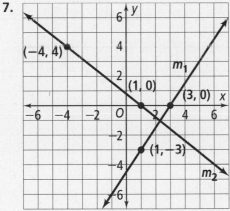

8.

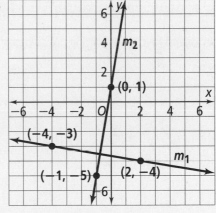

Write an equation of the line perpendicular to the given line that contains P.

9. $P(-6, 5); y = 2x - 3$

10. $P(4, 3); y = -3x - 15$

11. $P(-6, -3); y = x - 1$

12. $P(5, 5); y = -\frac{7}{4}x + 11\frac{1}{2}$

3-8 **Practice** (continued)   **Form G**

Slopes of Parallel and Perpendicular Lines

13. The line that represents the right boundary of a
street is shown on the grid at the right.
  a. What is the equation of the left boundary,
     which is parallel to the right boundary, and
     passes through point $L(200, 100)$?

  b. Graph the left boundary.

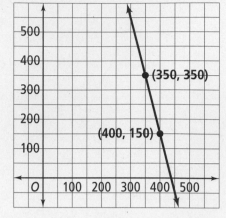

Rewrite each equation in slope intercept form. Then determine whether the
lines are parallel. Explain.

14. $2y = x + 15$ **15.** $10y + 130 = 50x$ **16.** $2y = 15 + 4x$
  $x = 2y + 5$ $-5y = 2x + 11$ $6y - 30 = 12x$

Rewrite each equation in slope-intercept form. Then determine whether the
lines are perpendicular. Explain.

17. $y - 1 = -x - 6$ **18.** $y - 6\frac{3}{4} = -\frac{1}{4}x$ **19.** $y - 6 = -\frac{5}{2}(x + 4)$
  $y - 3 = -\frac{5}{6}(x - 5)$ $2y = 8x + 18$ $5y = 2x + 6$

20. A town's building code states that stairs and
ramps must have a handrail. The sketch at the
right has a scale of 7 in. to each grid space.
  a. The handrail needs to be at least 35 in. above
     the ramp. Mark the point 35 in. above the top
     of the ramp. What are its coordinates?

  b. What is the equation of the line for the
     handrail?

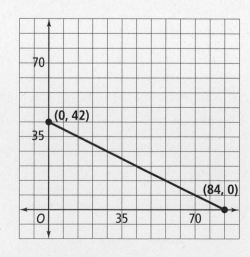

Name _____ Class _____ Date _____

3-8 Standardized Test Prep

Slopes of Parallel and Perpendicular Lines

Multiple Choice

For Exercises 1–4 choose the correct letter.

1. Which pair of slopes could represent perpendicular lines?

    Ⓐ $\frac{1}{7}, 7$ Ⓑ $\frac{1}{2}, \frac{2}{4}$ Ⓒ $-\frac{3}{4}, \frac{4}{3}$ Ⓓ $\frac{1}{3}, \frac{1}{3}$

2. The lines shown in the figure at the right are

    Ⓕ parallel.

    Ⓖ perpendicular.

    Ⓗ neither parallel nor perpendicular.

    Ⓘ both parallel and perpendicular.

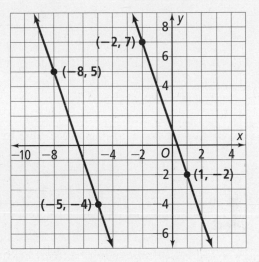

3. Two lines are perpendicular when

    Ⓐ the product of their slopes is −1.

    Ⓑ the product of their slopes is greater than 0.

    Ⓒ they have the same slope.

    Ⓓ their slopes are undefined.

4. Which is the equation for the line perpendicular to $y = -\frac{5}{3}x + 11\frac{1}{3}$ and containing $P(-2, 3)$?

    Ⓕ $y - 2 = -\frac{3}{5}(x - 3)$ Ⓖ $y = -\frac{5}{3}x + 4\frac{1}{3}$ Ⓗ $y = -\frac{3}{5}x + 4\frac{1}{5}$ Ⓘ $y = \frac{3}{5}x + 4\frac{1}{5}$

Extended Response

5. Graph the vertices of *ABCD* where $A(-1, 3)$, $B(-6, -2)$, $C(-1, -7)$, and $D(4, -2)$.

    a. Explain how you know the opposite sides of *ABCD* are parallel.

    b. Explain how you know the adjacent sides of *ABCD* are perpendicular.

    c. What is the length of each side, to the nearest inch, if each grid space is equal to 2 in.?

    d. What kind of figure is *ABCD*?

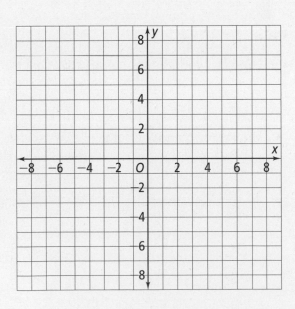

4-1   Think About a Plan

Congruent Figures

Algebra Find the values of the variables.

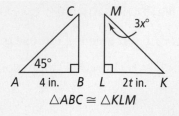

$\triangle ABC \cong \triangle KLM$

Know

1. What do you know about the measure of each of the non-right angles?

_____

2. What do you know about the length of each of the legs?

_____

3. What types of triangles are shown in the figure?

_____

Need

4. What information do you need to know to find the value of *x*?

_____

5. What information do you need to know to find the value of *t*?

_____

Plan

6. How can you find the value of *x*? What is its value?

_____

7. How do you find the value of *t*? What is its value?

_____

4-1

Practice

Form G

Congruent Figures

Each pair of polygons is congruent. Find the measures of the numbered angles.

1.

2.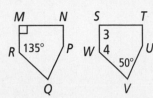

3.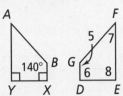

△CAT ≅ △JSD. **List each of the following.**

4. three pairs of congruent sides

5. three pairs of congruent angles

WXYZ ≅ JKLM. **List each of the following.**

6. four pairs of congruent sides

7. four pairs of congruent angles

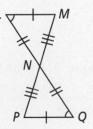

For Exercises 8 and 9, can you conclude that the triangles are congruent? Justify your answers.

8. △GHJ and △IHJ

9. △QRS and △TVS

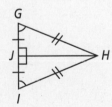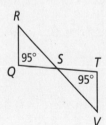

10. **Developing Proof** Use the information given in the diagram. Give a reason that each statement is true.

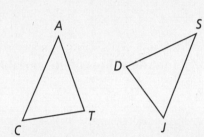

   a. ∠L ≅ ∠Q

   b. ∠LNM ≅ ∠QNP

   c. ∠M ≅ ∠P

   d. $\overline{LM} \cong \overline{QP}$, $\overline{LN} \cong \overline{QN}$, $\overline{MN} \cong \overline{PN}$

   e. △LNM ≅ △QNP

4-1

Practice (continued)

Congruent Figures

Form G

For Exercises 11 and 12, can you conclude that the figures are congruent? Justify your answers.

11. *AEFD* and *EBCF*

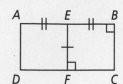

12. △*FGH* and △*JKH*

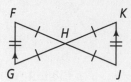

Algebra Find the values of the variables.

13.

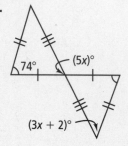

14.

Algebra *ABCD* ≅ *FGHJ*. Find the measures of the given angles or lengths of the given sides.

15. $m\angle B = 3y$, $m\angle G = y + 50$

16. $CD = 2x + 3$; $HJ = 3x + 2$

17. $m\angle C = 5z + 20$, $m\angle H = 6z + 10$

18. $AD = 5b + 4$; $FJ = 3b + 8$

19. *LMNP* ≅ *QRST*.

Find the value of *x*.

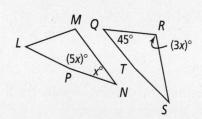

20. Given: $\overline{BD}$ is the angle bisector of $\angle ABC$.

$\overline{BD}$ is the perpendicular bisector of $\overline{AC}$.

Prove: △*ADB* ≅ △*CDB*

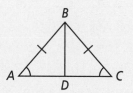

4-1

Standardized Test Prep
Congruent Figures

Multiple Choice

For Exercises 1–6, choose the correct letter.

1. The pair of polygons at the right is congruent. What is $m\angle J$?

   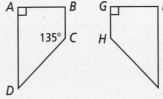

   Ⓐ 45   Ⓒ 135

   Ⓑ 90   Ⓓ 145

2. The triangles at the right are congruent. Which of the following statements must be true?

   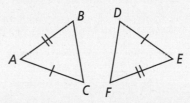

   Ⓕ $\angle A \cong \angle D$ Ⓗ $\overline{AB} \cong \overline{DE}$

   Ⓖ $\angle B \cong \angle E$ Ⓘ $\overline{BC} \cong \overline{FD}$

3. Given the diagram at the right, which of the following must be true?

   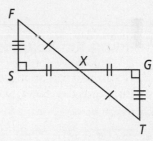

   Ⓐ $\triangle XSF \cong \triangle XTG$ Ⓒ $\triangle FXS \cong \triangle XGT$

   Ⓑ $\triangle SXF \cong \triangle GXT$ Ⓓ $\triangle FXS \cong \triangle GXT$

4. If $\triangle RST \cong \triangle XYZ$, which of the following need not be true?

   Ⓕ $\angle R \cong \angle X$ Ⓖ $\angle T \cong \angle Z$ Ⓗ $\overline{RT} \cong \overline{XZ}$ Ⓘ $\overline{SR} \cong \overline{YZ}$

5. If $\triangle ABC \cong \triangle DEF$, $m\angle A = 50$, and $m\angle E = 30$, what is $m\angle C$?

   Ⓐ 30   Ⓑ 50   Ⓒ 100   Ⓓ 120

6. If $ABCD \cong QRST$, $m\angle A = x - 10$, and $m\angle Q = 2x - 30$, what is $m\angle A$?

   Ⓕ 10   Ⓖ 20   Ⓗ 30   Ⓘ 40

Short Response

7. **Given:** $\overline{AB} \parallel \overline{DC}$, $\overline{AD} \parallel \overline{BC}$, $\overline{AB} \cong \overline{CD}$, $\overline{AD} \cong \overline{CB}$
   Prove: $\triangle ABD \cong \triangle CDB$

   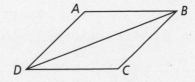

4-2 Think About a Plan

Triangle Congruence by SSS and SAS

Use the Distance Formula to determine whether $\triangle ABC$ and $\triangle DEF$ are congruent. Justify your answer.

$A(1, 4), B(5, 5), C(2, 2)$

$D(-5, 1), E(-1, 0), F(-4, 3)$

Understanding the Problem

1. You need to determine if $\triangle ABC \cong \triangle DEF$. What are the three ways you know to prove triangles congruent?

_____

_____

2. What information is given in the problem?

_____

Planning the Solution

3. If you use the SSS Postulate to determine whether the triangles are congruent, what information do you need to find?

_____

4. How can you find distances on a coordinate plane without measuring?

_____

5. In an ordered pair, which number is the *x*-coordinate? Which is the *y*-coordinate?

_____

Getting an Answer

6. Find the length of each segment using the Distance Formula, $D = \sqrt{(y_1 - y_2)^2 + (x_1 - x_2)^2}$. Your answers may be in simplest radical form.

$\overline{AB}$ [ ] $\overline{BC}$ [ ] $\overline{CA}$ [ ]

$\overline{DE}$ [ ] $\overline{EF}$ [ ] $\overline{FD}$ [ ]

7. Using the SSS Postulate, are the triangles congruent? Explain.

_____

4-2 Practice

Triangle Congruence by SSS and SAS

Form G

Draw △MGT. Use the triangle to answer the questions below.

1. What angle is included between $\overline{GM}$ and $\overline{MT}$?

2. Which sides include ∠T?

3. What angle is included between $\overline{GT}$ and $\overline{MG}$?

Would you use SSS or SAS to prove the triangles congruent? If there is not enough information to prove the triangles congruent by SSS or SAS, write *not enough information*. Explain your answer.

4.
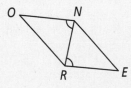

5.
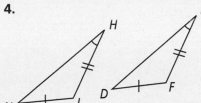

6.
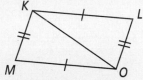

7.
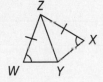

8.
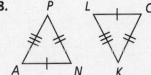

9.
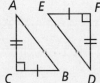

10.

11.
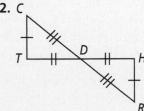

12.

4-2 Practice (continued) Form G
Triangle Congruence by SSS and SAS

13. Draw a Diagram A student draws △ABC and △QRS. The following sides and angles are congruent:

$$\overline{AC} \cong \overline{QS} \qquad \overline{AB} \cong \overline{QR} \qquad \angle B \cong \angle R$$

Based on this, can the student use either SSS or SAS to prove that △ABC ≅ △QRS? If the answer is no, explain what additional information the student needs. Use a sketch to help explain your answer.

14. Given: $\overline{BC} \cong \overline{DC}$, $\overline{AC} \cong \overline{EC}$
   Prove: △ABC ≅ △EDC

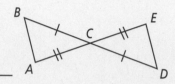

Statements	Reasons

15. Given: $\overline{WX} \parallel \overline{YZ}$, $\overline{WX} \cong \overline{YZ}$
   Prove: △WXZ ≅ △YZX

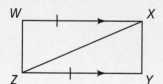

16. Error Analysis △FGH and △PQR are both equilateral triangles. Your friend says this means they are congruent by the SSS Postulate. Is your friend correct? Explain.

17. A student is gluing same-sized toothpicks together to make triangles. She plans to use these triangles to make a model of a bridge. Will all the triangles be congruent? Explain your answer.

4-2 Standardized Test Prep

Triangle Congruence by SSS and SAS

Multiple Choice

For Exercises 1–4, choose the correct letter.

1. Which pair of triangles can be proved congruent by SSS?

2. Which pair of triangles can be proved congruent by SAS?

   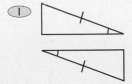

3. What additional information do you need to prove △NOP ≅ △QSR?

  Ⓐ $\overline{PN} \cong \overline{SQ}$ Ⓒ $\angle P \cong \angle S$

  Ⓑ $\overline{NO} \cong \overline{QR}$ Ⓓ $\angle O \cong \angle S$

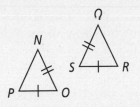

4. What additional information do you need to prove △GHI ≅ △DEF?

  Ⓕ $\overline{HI} \cong \overline{EF}$ Ⓗ $\angle F \cong \angle G$

  Ⓖ $\overline{HI} \cong \overline{ED}$ Ⓘ $\overline{GI} \cong \overline{DF}$

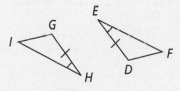

Short Response

5. Write a two-column proof.

  Given: M is the midpoint of $\overline{LS}$, $\overline{PM} \cong \overline{QM}$.

  Prove: △LMP ≅ △SMQ

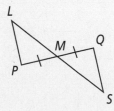

4-3 Think About a Plan

Triangle Congruence by ASA and AAS

Given: $\overline{AB} \parallel \overline{CD}$, $\overline{AD} \parallel \overline{CB}$

Prove: $\triangle ABC \cong \triangle CDA$

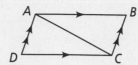

1. What do you need to find to solve the problem?

   _____

   _____

2. What are the corresponding parts of the two triangles?

   _____

   _____

3. What word would you use to describe $\overline{AC}$? _____

4. What can you show about angles in the triangles that can indicate congruency?

   _____

5. What do you know about a side or sides of the triangles that can be used to show congruency?

   _____

   _____

6. Write a proof in paragraph form.

   _____

   _____

   _____

   _____

4-3 Practice

Form G

Triangle Congruence by ASA and AAS

Name two triangles that are congruent by ASA.

1.

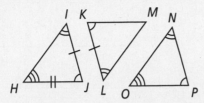

2.

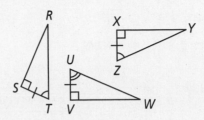

3. **Developing Proof** Complete the proof by filling in the blanks.

Given: $\angle HIJ \cong \angle KIJ$

$\angle IJH \cong \angle IJK$

Prove: $\triangle HIJ \cong \triangle KIJ$

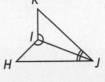

Proof: $\angle HIJ \cong \angle KIJ$ and $\angle IJH \cong \angle IJK$ are given.

$\overline{IJ} \cong \overline{IJ}$ by _?_.

So, $\triangle HIJ \cong \triangle KIJ$ by _?_.

4. **Given:** $\angle LOM \cong \angle NPM$, $\overline{LM} \cong \overline{NM}$

Prove: $\triangle LOM \cong \triangle NPM$

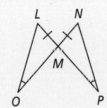

5. **Given:** $\angle B$ and $\angle D$ are right angles.

$\overline{AE}$ bisects $\overline{BD}$

Prove: $\triangle ABC \cong \triangle EDC$

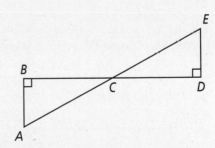

4-3

Practice (continued)   Form G

Triangle Congruence by ASA and AAS

6. Developing Proof Complete the proof.

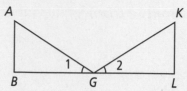

Given: $\angle 1 \cong \angle 2$, $\overline{AB} \perp \overline{BL}$, $\overline{KL} \perp \overline{BL}$, $\overline{AB} \cong \overline{KL}$

Prove: $\triangle ABG \cong \triangle KLG$

Proof:

```
┌──────────┐     ┌─────────────────┐        ┌──────────┐
│ AB ⊥ BL  │ ──> │ ∠B is a right ∠. │ ──┐    │ ∠1 ≅ ∠2  │ ──┐
└──────────┘     └─────────────────┘   │    └──────────┘   │
_____        _____       ┼──> ┌──────────┐   ┼──> ┌───────────────┐
                                        │    │ ∠B ≅ ∠L  │ ──────>│ △ABG ≅ △KLG   │
┌──────────┐     ┌─────────────────┐   │    └──────────┘   │    └───────────────┘
│ KL ⊥ BL  │ ──> │ ∠L is a right ∠. │ ──┘    ┌──────────┐   │    _____
└──────────┘     └─────────────────┘        │ AB ≅ KL  │ ──┘
_____        _____           └──────────┘
```

7. Write a flow proof.

Given: $\angle E \cong \angle H$

       $\angle HFG \cong \angle EGF$

Prove: $\triangle EGF \cong \triangle HFG$

8. Write a two-column proof.

Given: $\angle K \cong \angle M$

       $\overline{KL} \cong \overline{ML}$

Prove: $\triangle JKL \cong \triangle PML$

For Exercises 9 and 10, write a paragraph proof.

9. Given: $\angle D \cong \angle G$

       $\overline{HE} \cong \overline{FE}$

Prove: $\triangle EFG \cong \triangle EHD$

10. Given: $\overline{JM}$ bisects $\angle J$.

       $\overline{JM} \perp \overline{KL}$

Prove: $\triangle JMK \cong \triangle JML$

4-3 Standardized Test Prep

Triangle Congruence by ASA and AAS

Multiple Choice

For Exercises 1–4, choose the correct letter.

1. Which pair of triangles can be proven congruent by the ASA Postulate?

(A)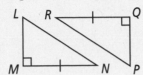

(C)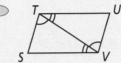

(B)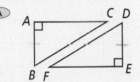

(D)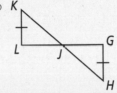

2. For the ASA Postulate to apply, which side of the triangle must be known?

(F) the included side

(H) the shortest side

(G) the longest side

(I) a non-included side

3. Which pair of triangles can be proven congruent by the AAS Theorem?

(A)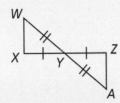

(C)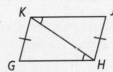

(B)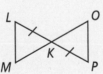

(D)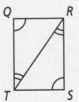

4. For the AAS Theorem to apply, which side of the triangle must be known?

(F) the included side

(H) the shortest side

(G) the longest side

(I) a non-included side

Short Response

5. Write a paragraph proof.

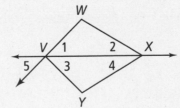

Given: $\angle 3 \cong \angle 5$, $\angle 2 \cong \angle 4$

Prove: $\triangle VWX \cong \triangle VYX$

4-4 Think About a Plan

Using Corresponding Parts of Congruent Triangles

Constructions The construction of $\angle B$ congruent to given $\angle A$ is shown. $\overline{AD} \cong \overline{BF}$ because they are the radii of the same circle. $\overline{DC} \cong \overline{FE}$ because both arcs have the same compass settings. Explain why you can conclude that $\angle A \cong \angle B$.

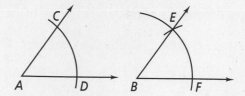

Understanding the Problem

1. What is the problem asking you to prove?

_____

2. Segments $\overline{DC}$ and $\overline{FE}$ are not drawn on the construction. Draw them in. What figures are formed by drawing these segments?

_____

3. What information do you need to be able to use corresponding parts of congruent triangles?

_____

Planning the Solution

4. To use corresponding parts of congruent triangles, which two triangles do you need to show to be congruent?

_____

5. What reason can you use to state that $\overline{AC} \cong \overline{BE}$?

_____

Getting an Answer

6. Write a paragraph proof that uses corresponding parts of congruent triangles to prove that $\angle A \cong \angle B$.

_____

_____

_____

4-4

Practice   *Form G*

Using Corresponding Parts of Congruent Triangles

For each pair of triangles, tell why the two triangles are congruent. Give the congruence statement. Then list all the other corresponding parts of the triangles that are congruent.

1.
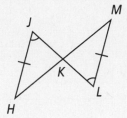

2.
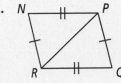

3. Complete the proof.

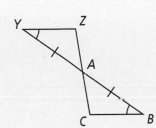

   Given: $\overline{YA} \cong \overline{BA}$, $\angle B \cong \angle Y$

   Prove: $\overline{AZ} \cong \overline{AC}$

Statements	Reasons
1) $\overline{YA} \cong \overline{BA}$, $\angle B \cong \angle Y$	1) _?_
2) $\angle YAZ$ and $\angle BAC$ are vertical angles.	2) Definition of vertical angles
3) $\angle YAZ \cong \angle BAC$	3) _?_
4) _?_	4) _?_
5) _?_	5) _?_

4. **Open-Ended** Construct a figure that involves two congruent triangles. Set up given statements and write a proof that corresponding parts of the triangles are congruent.

Name _____ Class _____ Date _____

4-4 Practice (continued)   Form G
Using Corresponding Parts of Congruent Triangles

5. Complete the proof.

Given: $\overline{BD} \perp \overline{AB}$, $\overline{BD} \perp \overline{DE}$, $\overline{BC} \cong \overline{DC}$

Prove: $\angle A \cong \angle E$

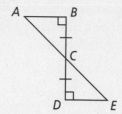

Statements	Reasons
1) $\overline{BD} \perp \overline{AB}$, $\overline{BD} \perp \overline{DE}$	1) __?__
2) $\angle CDE$ and $\angle CBA$ are right angles.	2) Definition of right angles
3) $\angle CDE \cong \angle CBA$	3) __?__
4) __?__	4) Vertical angles are congruent.
5) $\overline{BC} \cong \overline{DC}$	5) __?__
6) __?__	6) __?__
7) $\angle A \cong \angle E$	7) __?__

6. Construction Use a construction to prove that the two base angles of an isosceles triangle are congruent.

Given: Isosceles $\triangle ABC$ with base $\overline{AC}$

Prove: $\angle A \cong \angle C$

Statements	Reasons
1) $\triangle ABC$ is isosceles.	1) __?__
2) $\overline{AB} \cong \overline{CB}$	2) Definition of isosceles triangle.
3) Construct the midpoint of $\overline{AC}$ and call it D. Construct $\overline{DB}$.	3) Construction
4) __?__	4) Definition of midpoint
5) $\overline{BD} \cong \overline{BD}$	5) __?__
6) $\triangle ABD \cong \triangle CBD$	6) __?__
7) __?__	7) __?__

104

4-4

Standardized Test Prep

Using Corresponding Parts of Congruent Triangles

Multiple Choice

For Exercises 1–6, choose the correct letter.

1. Based on the given information in the figure at the right, how can you justify that $\triangle JHG \cong \triangle HJI$?

   Ⓐ ASA

   Ⓑ SSS

   Ⓒ AAS

   Ⓓ ASA

2. In the figure at the right the following is true: $\angle ABD \cong \angle CDB$ and $\angle DBC \cong \angle BDA$. How can you justify that $\triangle ABD \cong \triangle CDB$?

   Ⓕ SAS

   Ⓖ SSS

   Ⓗ ASA

   Ⓘ CPCTC

3. $\triangle BRM \cong \triangle KYZ$. How can you justify that $\overline{YZ} \cong \overline{RM}$?

   Ⓐ CPCTC   Ⓑ SAS   Ⓒ ASA   Ⓓ SSS

4. Which statement *cannot* be justified given only that $\triangle PBJ \cong \triangle TIM$?

   Ⓕ $\overline{PB} \cong \overline{TI}$ Ⓖ $\angle B \cong \angle I$ Ⓗ $\angle BJP \cong \angle IMT$ Ⓘ $\overline{JP} \cong \overline{MI}$

5. In the figure at the right, which theorem or postulate can you use to prove $\triangle ADM \cong \triangle ZMD$?

   Ⓐ ASA

   Ⓑ SSS

   Ⓒ SAS

   Ⓓ AAS

6. In the figure at the right, which theorem or postulate can you use to prove $\triangle KGC \cong \triangle FHE$?

   Ⓕ ASA

   Ⓖ SSS

   Ⓗ SAS

   Ⓘ AAS

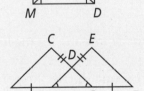

Short Response

7. What would a brief plan for the following proof look like?

   Given: $\overline{AB} \cong \overline{DC}$, $\angle ABC \cong \angle DCB$

   Prove: $\overline{AC} \cong \overline{DB}$

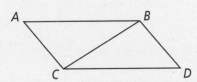

4-5 Think About a Plan

Isosceles and Equilateral Triangles

Algebra The length of the base of an isosceles triangle is x. The length of a leg is $2x - 5$. The perimeter of the triangle is 20. Find x.

Know

1. What is the perimeter of a triangle?

   _____

2. What is an isosceles triangle?

   _____

Need

3. What are the sides of an isosceles triangle called?

   _____

4. How many of each type of side are there?

   _____

5. The lengths of the base and one leg are given. What is the third side of the triangle called?

   _____

Plan

6. Write an expression for the length of the third side.

7. Write an equation for the perimeter of this isosceles triangle.

8. Solve the equation for x. Show your work.

4-5

Practice   Form G

Isosceles and Equilateral Triangles

Complete each statement. Explain why it is true.

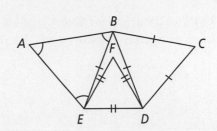

1. $\angle DBC \cong$ __?__ $\cong \angle CDB$

2. $\angle BED \cong$ __?__

3. $\angle FED \cong$ __?__ $\cong \angle DFE$

4. $\overline{AB} \cong$ __?__ $\cong \overline{BE}$

Algebra Find the values of x and y.

5.

6.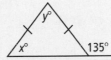

7.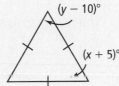

8.

9.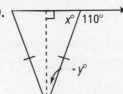

10.

Use the properties of isosceles and equilateral triangles to find the measure of the indicated angle.

11. $m\angle ACB$

12. $m\angle DBC$

13. $m\angle ABC$

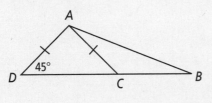

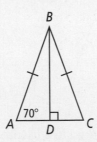

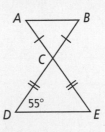

14. Equilateral $\triangle ABC$ and isosceles $\triangle DBC$ share side BC. If $m\angle BDC = 34$ and $BD = BC$, what is the measure of $\angle ABD$? (*Hint:* it may help to draw the figure described.)

4-5 Practice (continued)   Form G
Isosceles and Equilateral Triangles

Use the diagram for Exercises 15–17 to complete each congruence statement. Explain why it is true.

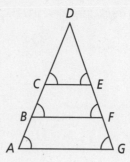

15. $\overline{DF} \cong$ __?__

16. $\overline{DG} \cong$ __?__

17. $\overline{DC} \cong$ __?__

18. The wall at the front entrance to the Rock and Roll Hall of Fame and Museum in Cleveland, Ohio, is an isosceles triangle. The triangle has a vertex angle of 102. What is the measure of the base angles?

19. Reasoning An exterior angle of an isosceles triangle has the measure 130. Find two possible sets of measures for the angles of the triangle.

20. Open-Ended Draw a design that uses three equilateral triangles and two isosceles triangles. Label the vertices. List all the congruent sides and angles.

Algebra Find the values of m and n.

21.

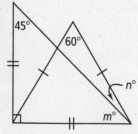

22.

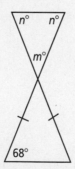

23.

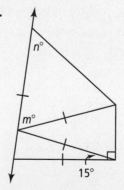

24. Writing Explain how a corollary is related to a theorem. Use examples from this lesson in making your comparison.

4-5 Standardized Test Prep

Isosceles and Equilateral Triangles

Gridded Response

Solve each exercise and enter your answer on the grid provided.

Refer to the diagram for Exercises 1–3.

1. What is the value of x?

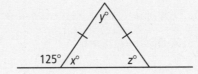

2. What is the value of y?

3. What is the value of z?

4. The measures of two of the sides of an equilateral triangle are $3x + 15$ in. and $7x - 5$ in. What is the measure of the third side in inches?

5. In $\triangle GHI$, $HI = GH$, $m\angle IHG = 3x + 4$, and $m\angle IGH = 2x - 24$. What is $m\angle HIG$?

Answers

1.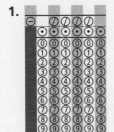
2.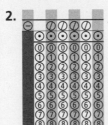
3.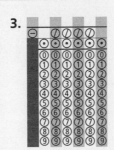
4.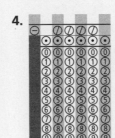
5.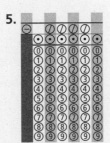

4-6 Think About a Plan

Congruence in Right Triangles

Algebra For what values of x and y are the triangles congruent by HL?

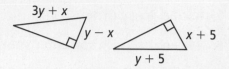

Know

1. For two triangles to be congruent by the Hypotenuse-Leg Theorem, there must be a

   _____, and the lengths of _____ and _____

   _____ must be equal.

2. The length of the hypotenuse of the triangle on the left is _____ and the

   hypotenuse of the triangle on the right is _____.

3. The length of the leg of the triangle on the left is _____ and the length of

   the leg of the triangle on the right is _____.

Need

4. To solve the problem you need to find _____.

Plan

5. What system of equations can you use to find the values of x and y?

6. What method(s) can you use to solve the system of equations?

   _____

   _____

7. What is the value of y? What is the value of x?

4-6

Practice

Form G

Congruence in Right Triangles

1. **Developing Proof** Complete the paragraph proof.

   Given: $\overline{RT} \perp \overline{SU}$, $\overline{RU} \cong \overline{RS}$.
   Prove: $\triangle RUT \cong \triangle RST$

   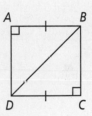

   Proof: It is given that $\overline{RT} \perp \overline{SU}$. So, _____ and _____ are _____ angles because perpendicular lines form _____ angles. _____ $\cong \overline{RT}$ by the Reflexive Property of Congruence. It is given that _____ $\cong \overline{RS}$. So, $\triangle RUT \cong \triangle RST$ by _____.

2. Look at Exercise 1. If $m\angle RST = 46$, what is $m\angle RUT$?

3. Write a flow proof. Use the information from the diagram to prove that $\triangle ABD \cong \triangle CDB$.

4. Look at Exercise 3. Can you prove that $\triangle ABD \cong \triangle CDB$ without using the Hypotenuse-Leg Theorem? Explain.

Construct a triangle congruent to each triangle by the Hypotenuse-Leg Theorem.

5.

6.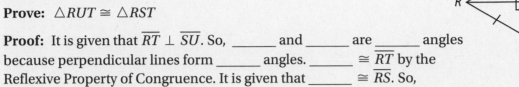

4-6 Practice (continued) Form G
Congruence in Right Triangles

Algebra For what values of x or x and y are the triangles congruent by HL?

7.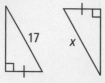

8.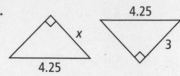

9.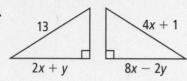

10.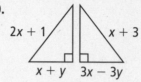

11. Write a paragraph proof.

Given: $\overline{AD}$ bisects $\overline{EB}$, $\overline{AB} \cong \overline{DE}$; $\angle ECD$, $\angle ACB$ are right angles.

Prove: $\triangle ACB \cong \triangle DCE$

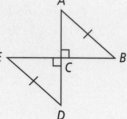

What additional information would prove each pair of triangles congruent by the Hypotenuse-Leg Theorem?

12.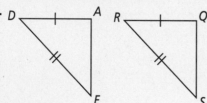

13.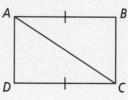

14.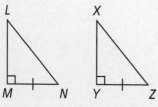

15.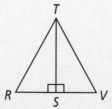

16. **Reasoning** Are the triangles congruent? Explain.

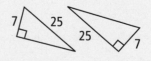

4-6 Standardized Test Prep

Congruence in Right Triangles

Multiple Choice

For Exercises 1–4, choose the correct letter.

1. Which additional piece of information would allow you to prove that the triangles are congruent by the HL theorem?

    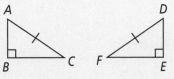

    Ⓐ $m\angle DFE = 40$ Ⓒ $\overline{AB} \cong \overline{DE}$

    Ⓑ $m\angle F = m\angle ABC$ Ⓓ $\overline{AC} \cong \overline{DF}$

2. For what values of x and y are the triangles shown congruent?

    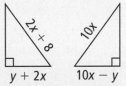

    Ⓕ $x = 1, y = 4$ Ⓗ $x = 4, y = 1$

    Ⓖ $x = 2, y = 4$ Ⓘ $x = 1, y = 3$

3. Two triangles have two pairs of corresponding sides that are congruent. What else must be true for the triangles to be congruent by the HL Theorem?

    Ⓐ The included angles must be right angles.

    Ⓑ They have one pair of congruent angles.

    Ⓒ Both triangles must be isosceles.

    Ⓓ There are right angles adjacent to just one pair of congruent sides.

4. Which of the following statements is true?

    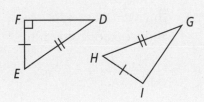

    Ⓕ $\triangle BAC \cong \triangle GHI$ by SAS.

    Ⓖ $\triangle DEF \cong \triangle GHI$ by SAS.

    Ⓗ $\triangle BAC \cong \triangle DEF$ by HL.

    Ⓘ $\triangle DEF \cong \triangle GHI$ by HL.

Extended Response

5. Are the given triangles congruent by the HL Theorem? Explain.

    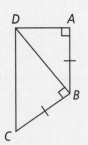

4-7 Think About a Plan

Congruence in Overlapping Triangles

Given: $\overline{QT} \perp \overline{PR}$, $\overline{QT}$ bisects $\overline{PR}$,
$\overline{QT}$ bisects $\angle VQS$

Prove: $\overline{VQ} \cong \overline{SQ}$

Know

1. What information are you given? What else can you determine from the given information and the diagram?

   _____

   _____

2. To solve the problem, what will you need to prove?

   _____

Need

3. For which two triangles are $\overline{VQ}$ and $\overline{SQ}$ corresponding parts?

   _____

4. You need to use corresponding parts to prove the triangles from Exercise 3 congruent. Which two triangles should you prove congruent first, using the given information? Which theorem or postulate should you use?

   _____

5. Which corresponding parts should you then use to prove that the triangles in Exercise 3 are congruent?

   _____

Plan

6. Use the space below to write the proof.

4-7 Practice

Form G

Congruence in Overlapping Triangles

For Exercises 1–6, separate and redraw the indicated triangles. Identify any common angles or sides.

1. △ABC and △DCB

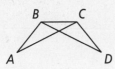

2. △EFG and △HGF

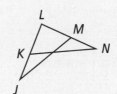

3. △JML and △NKL

4. △BYA and △CXA

5. △GEH and △FEH

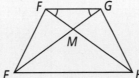

6. △MPN and △MOQ

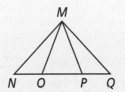

In each diagram in Exercises 7–12 the given triangles are congruent. Identify their common side or angle.

7. △ADC and △BCD

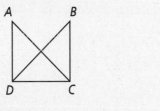

8. △KNJ and △KML

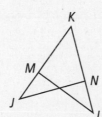

9. △UXV and △VWU

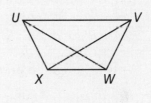

10. △QTR and △SRT

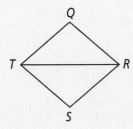

11. △EGH and △EGF

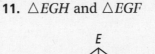

12. △YNI and △YPZ

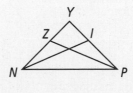

13. Open-Ended Draw a diagram of a pair of triangles that share a common angle and a common side.

4-7 Practice (continued)   Form G
Congruence in Overlapping Triangles

14. Complete the following proof.

Given: $\overline{RU} \cong \overline{TS}$, $\angle RUT$ and $\angle UTS$ are right angles, V is the midpoint of $\overline{US}$.

Prove: $\triangle RVU \cong \triangle TVS$

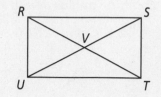

Statements	Reasons
1) $\overline{RU} \cong \overline{TS}$, $\angle RUT$ and $\angle UTS$ are right angles, V is the midpoint of $\overline{US}$.	1) _?_
2) $\overline{UT} \cong \overline{TU}$	2) _?_
3) _?_	3) All right angles are congruent
4) _?_	4) SAS
5) $\angle RUS$ and $\angle SUT$ are complementary angles.	5) _?_
6) _?_	6) Definition of complementary angles
7) $\angle SUT \cong \angle RTU$	7) _?_
8) $\angle RUS \cong \angle STR$	8) _?_
9) _?_	9) Definition of midpoint
10) $\angle RVU \cong \angle TVS$	10) _?_
11) $\triangle RVU \cong \triangle TVS$	11) _?_

15. Write a paragraph proof.

Given: P is the midpoint of $\overline{QN}$, $\overline{MP} \perp \overline{QN}$
Prove: $\triangle MRQ \cong \triangle MRN$

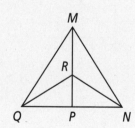

16. In the diagram at the right, $\angle A \cong \angle C$, $\overline{AB} \cong \overline{CE}$, and $\overline{DA} \cong \overline{FC}$. Which two triangles are congruent by SAS? Explain.

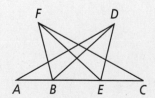

4-7 Standardized Test Prep

Congruence in Overlapping Triangles

Multiple Choice

For Exercises 1–5, choose the correct letter.

1. What is the common angle of $\triangle PQT$ and $\triangle RSQ$?

   (A) $\angle PQT$ (C) $\angle SRQ$

   (B) $\angle SPT$ (D) $\angle SUT$

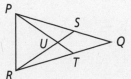

Use the following information for Exercises 2–5.

Given: $\triangle ZWX \cong \triangle YXW$, $\overline{ZW} \parallel \overline{YX}$

Prove: $\triangle ZWR \cong \triangle YRX$

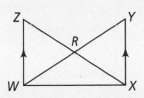

2. Which corresponding parts statement is needed to prove $\triangle ZWR \cong \triangle YRX$?

   (F) $\angle ZWR \cong \angle YXR$ (H) $ZW = YX$

   (G) $\angle Z \cong \angle R$ (I) $WX = WX$

3. A classmate writes the statement $\angle ZRW \cong \angle YRX$ to help prove the congruence of the triangles. What reason should the classmate give?

   (A) Given

   (B) Angles cut by a bisector are congruent.

   (C) Base angles of an isosceles triangle are congruent.

   (D) Vertical angles are congruent.

4. After using the congruence statements from Exercises 2 and 3, which statement can be used to prove the triangles congruent?

   (F) $\angle Z \cong \angle Y$ (H) $\overline{WX} \cong \overline{WX}$

   (G) $\angle ZWR \cong \angle RYX$ (I) $\overline{WR} \cong \overline{RX}$

5. Which theorem or postulate will prove $\triangle ZWR \cong \triangle YRX$?

   (A) SAS   (B) SSS   (C) ASA   (D) AAS

Short Response

6. In the diagram at the right, which two triangles should be proved congruent first to help prove $\triangle ABF \cong \triangle EDF$?

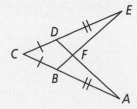

5-1 Think About a Plan

Midsegments of Triangles

Coordinate Geometry The coordinates of the vertices of a triangle are $E(1, 2)$, $F(5, 6)$, and $G(3, -2)$.

   a. Find the coordinates of H, the midpoint of $\overline{EG}$, and J, the midpoint of $\overline{FG}$.

   b. Show that $\overline{HJ} \parallel \overline{EF}$.

   c. Show that $HJ = \frac{1}{2}EF$.

1. In part (a), what formula would you use to find the midpoints of $\overline{EG}$ and $\overline{FG}$? Write this formula.

2. Substitute the x- and y-coordinates of E and G into the formula.

3. Simplify to find the coordinates of H, the midpoint of $\overline{EG}$.

4. Use the coordinates of F and G to find the coordinates of J, the midpoint of $\overline{FG}$.

5. In part (b), what information do you need to show $\overline{HJ} \parallel \overline{EF}$? Write the formula you would use.

6. Substitute the x- and y-coordinates of H and J into the formula.

7. Simplify to find the slope of $\overline{HJ}$.

8. Use the coordinates of E and F to find the slope of $\overline{EF}$.

9. Is $\overline{HJ} \parallel \overline{EF}$? Explain.

10. In part (c), what formula would you use to find HJ and EF? Write this formula.

11. Substitute the x- and y-coordinates of H and J into the formula.

12. Simplify to find HJ. Keep in simplest radical form.

13. Use the coordinates of E and F to find EF. Keep in simplest radical form.

14. What is the relationship between HJ and EF?

5-1 Practice

Form G

Midsegments of Triangles

Identify three pairs of triangle sides in each diagram.

1.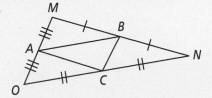

2.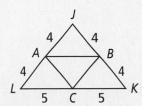

Name the triangle sides that are parallel to the given side.

3. $\overline{AB}$

4. $\overline{AC}$

5. $\overline{CB}$

6. $\overline{XY}$

7. $\overline{XZ}$

8. $\overline{ZY}$

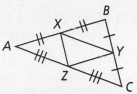
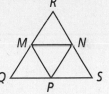

Points *M*, *N*, and *P* are the midpoints of the sides of △*QRS*.
$QR = 30$, $RS = 30$, and $SQ = 18$.

9. Find *MN*.

10. Find *MQ*.

11. Find *MP*.

12. Find *PS*.

13. Find *PN*.

14. Find *RN*.

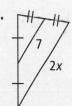

Algebra Find the value of *x*.

15.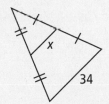

16.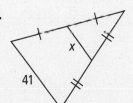

17.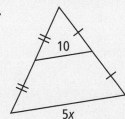

18.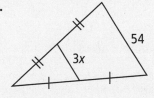

19.

20.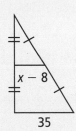

21.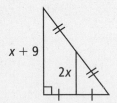

22.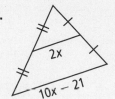

23.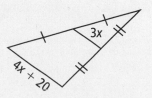

5-1

Practice (continued)   Form G

Midsegments of Triangles

D is the midpoint of $\overline{AB}$. *E* is the midpoint of $\overline{CB}$.

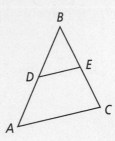

24. If $m\angle A = 70$, find $m\angle BDE$.

25. If $m\angle BED = 73$, find $m\angle C$.

26. If $DE = 23$, find AC.

27. If $AC = 83$, find DE.

Find the distance across the lake in each diagram.

28.
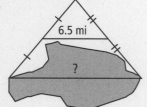

29.
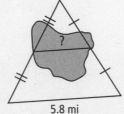

30.
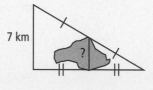

Use the diagram at the right for Exercises 31 and 32.

31. Which segment is shorter for kayaking across the lake, $\overline{AB}$ or $\overline{BC}$? Explain.

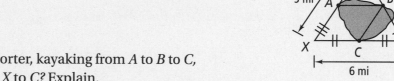

32. Which distance is shorter, kayaking from *A* to *B* to *C*, or walking from *A* to *X* to *C*? Explain.

33. Open-Ended Draw a triangle and all of its midsegments. Make a conjecture about what appears to be true about the four triangles that result. What postulates could be used to prove the conjecture?

34. Coordinate Geometry The coordinates of the vertices of a triangle are $K(2, 3)$, $L(-2, -1)$, and $M(5, 1)$.
   a. Find the coordinates of *N*, the midpoint of $\overline{KM}$, and *P*, the midpoint of $\overline{LM}$.

   b. Show that $\overline{NP} \parallel \overline{KL}$.

   c. Show that $NP = \frac{1}{2}KL$.

5-1 Standardized Test Prep

Midsegments of Triangles

Gridded Response

Solve each exercise and enter your answer on the grid provided.

In △*RST*, *U* is the midpoint of $\overline{RS}$, *V* is the midpoint of $\overline{ST}$, and *W* is the midpoint of $\overline{TR}$.

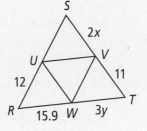

1. What is the length of $\overline{RS}$?

2. What is the value of *x*?

3. What is the value of *y*?

4. What is the length of $\overline{UW}$?

5. What is the length of $\overline{UV}$?

Answers

1. 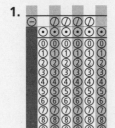 2. 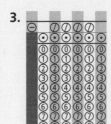 3. 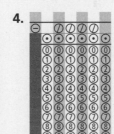 4. 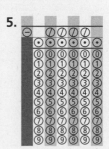 5.

Name _____ Class _____ Date _____

5-2 Think About a Plan

Perpendicular and Angle Bisectors

a. Constructions Draw a large acute scalene triangle, △PQR. Construct the perpendicular bisectors of each side.
b. Make a Conjecture What appears to be true about the perpendicular bisectors?
c. Test your conjecture with another triangle.

1. For part (a), what is an acute scalene triangle?

_____

2. Sketch a large acute scalene triangle. Use a protractor to make sure each angle is less than 90°. Label the vertices P, Q, and R. Check to make sure the triangle is scalene by comparing the side lengths.

3. To construct the perpendicular bisector for $\overline{PQ}$, set the compass to greater than _____. Draw two arcs, one from P and one from Q. The arcs _____ at two points. Draw a segment connecting the points. This segment is the _____.

4. Construct the perpendicular bisectors of $\overline{QR}$ and $\overline{RP}$.

5. For part (b), examine the three perpendicular bisectors. Write a conjecture about the perpendicular bisectors in all triangles.

_____

_____

_____

6. For part (c), repeat Steps 1–4 for an obtuse, equilateral, or isosceles triangle. Does the conjecture appear to be true for this triangle?

_____

_____

_____

5-2 Practice   Form G

Perpendicular and Angle Bisectors

Use the figure at the right for Exercises 1–4.

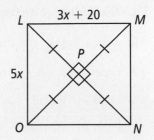

1. What is the relationship between $\overline{LN}$ and $\overline{MO}$?

2. What is the value of x?

3. Find LM.   4. Find LO.

Use the figure at the right for Exercises 5–8.

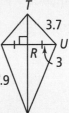

5. From the information given in the figure, how is $\overline{TV}$ related to $\overline{SU}$?

6. Find TS.   7. Find UV.   8. Find SU.

9. At the right is a layout for the lobby of a building placed on a coordinate grid.

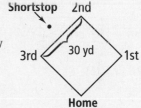

   a. At which of the labeled points would a receptionist chair be equidistant from both entrances?

   b. Is the statue equidistant from the entrances? How do you know?

10. In baseball, the baseline is a segment connecting the bases. A shortstop is told to play back 3 yd from the baseline and exactly the same distance from second base and third base. Describe how the shortstop could estimate the correct spot. There are 30 yd between bases. Assume that the shortstop has a stride of 36 in.

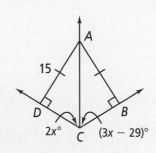

Use the figure at the right for Exercises 11–15.

11. According to the figure, how far is A from $\overline{CD}$? From $\overline{CB}$?

12. How is $\overrightarrow{CA}$ related to $\angle DCB$? Explain.

13. Find the value of x.

14. Find $m\angle ACD$ and $m\angle ACB$.

15. Find $m\angle DAC$ and $m\angle BAC$.

5-2 Practice (continued) Form G
Perpendicular and Angle Bisectors

Use the figure at the right for Exercises 16–19.

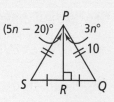

16. According to the diagram, what are the lengths of $\overline{PQ}$ and $\overline{PS}$?

17. How is $\overline{PR}$ related to $\angle SPQ$?

18. Find the value of n.

19. Find $m\angle SPR$ and $m\angle QPR$.

Algebra Find the indicated values of the variables and measures.

20. x, BA, DA

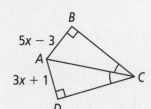

21. $x, m\angle DEF$

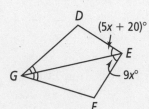

22. $x, m\angle DAB$

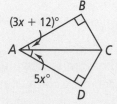

23. m, LO, NO

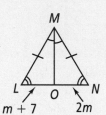

24. $x, m\angle QTS$

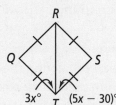

25. p, IJ, KJ

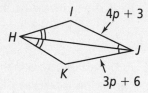

26. r, UW

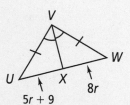

27. $y, m\angle DEF$

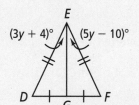

28. m, p

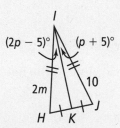

Writing Determine whether A must be on the bisector of $\angle LMN$. Explain.

29.

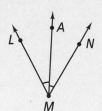

30.

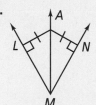

5-2 Standardized Test Prep

Perpendicular and Angle Bisectors

Multiple Choice

For Exercises 1–6, choose the correct letter.
Use the figure at the right.

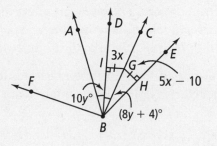

1. Which ray is a bisector of $\angle ABC$?

   Ⓐ $\overrightarrow{BC}$ Ⓒ $\overrightarrow{BA}$

   Ⓑ $\overrightarrow{BD}$ Ⓓ $\overrightarrow{BF}$

2. What is GH?

   Ⓕ 5   Ⓖ 10   Ⓗ 15   Ⓘ 25

3. What is the value of y?

   Ⓐ 2   Ⓑ 4   Ⓒ 16   Ⓓ 20

4. What is $m\angle DBE$?

   Ⓕ 20   Ⓖ 30   Ⓗ 40   Ⓘ 50

5. What is $m\angle ABE$?

   Ⓐ 20   Ⓑ 30   Ⓒ 40   Ⓓ 60

6. If $m\angle FBA = 7x + 6y$, what is $m\angle FBA$?

   Ⓕ 40   Ⓖ 44   Ⓗ 47   Ⓘ 60

Short Response

7. Construct the bisector of $\angle ABC$.

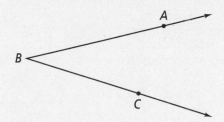

5-3 Think About a Plan

Bisectors in Triangles

Writing Ivars found an old piece of paper inside an antique book. It read:

From the spot I buried Olaf's treasure, equal sets of paces did I measure; each of three directions in a line, there to plant a seedling Norway pine. I could not return for failing health; now the hounds of Haiti guard my wealth. —Karl

After searching Caribbean islands for five years, Ivars found an island with three tall Norway pines. How might Ivars find where Karl buried Olaf's treasure?

Know

1. Make a sketch as you answer the questions.

2. *"From the spot I buried Olaf's treasure ..."* Mark a point *X* on your paper.

3. *"... equal sets of paces I did measure; each of the three directions in a line ..."* This tells you to draw segments that have an endpoint at *X*.

   a. Explain how you know these are segments. _____

   b. How many segments should you draw?

   c. What do you know about the length of the segments? _____

   d. What do you know about the endpoints of the segments?

   _____

4. You do not know in which direction to draw each segment, but you can choose three directions for your sketch. Mark the locations of the trees. Draw a triangle with the trees at its vertices. What is the name of the point where *X* is located? _____

Need

5. Look at your sketch. What do you need to find? _____

Plan

6. Describe how to find the treasure. The first step is done for you.

   Step 1 Find the midpoints of each side of the triangle.

   Step 2 _____

   Step 3 _____

   _____

5-3 Practice

Form G

Bisectors in Triangles

Coordinate Geometry Find the circumcenter of each triangle.

1.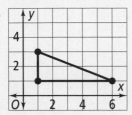

2.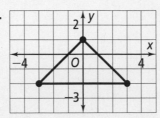

3.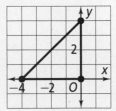

Coordinate Geometry Find the circumcenter of $\triangle ABC$.

4. $A(1, 3)$
$B(4, 3)$
$C(4, 2)$

5. $A(2, -3)$
$B(-4, -3)$
$C(-4, -7)$

6. $A(-5, -2)$
$B(1, -2)$
$C(1, 6)$

7. $A(5, 6)$
$B(0, 6)$
$C(0, -3)$

8. $A(1, 3)$
$B(5, 3)$
$C(5, 2)$

9. $A(2, -2)$
$B(-4, -2)$
$C(-4, -7)$

10. $A(-5, -3)$
$B(1, -3)$
$C(1, 6)$

11. $A(5, 2)$
$B(-1, 2)$
$C(-1, -3)$

Name the point of concurrency of the angle bisectors.

12.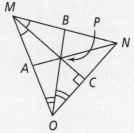

13.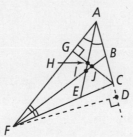

14.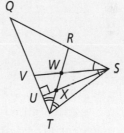

15.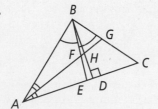

16.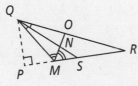

17.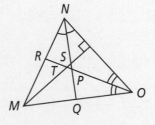

5-3 **Practice** (continued)   *Form G*
_____
Bisectors in Triangles

Find the value of *x*.

18.
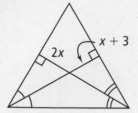

19.
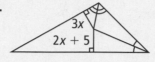

20.
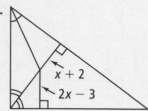

21.
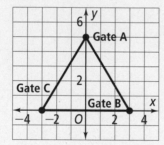

22.
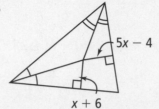

23.
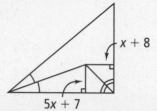

24. Where should the farmer place the hay bale so that it is equidistant from the three gates?

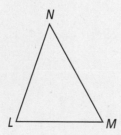

25. Where should the fire station be placed so that it is equidistant from the grocery store, the hospital, and the police station?

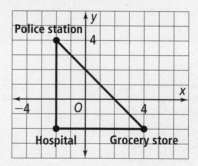

26. Construction Construct three perpendicular bisectors for △*LMN*. Then use the point of concurrency to construct the circumscribed circle.

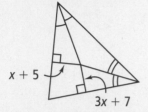

27. Construction Construct two angle bisectors for △*ABC*. Then use the point of concurrency to construct the inscribed circle.

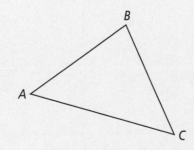

5-3 Standardized Test Prep

Bisectors in Triangles

Multiple Choice

For Exercises 1–5, choose the correct letter. Use the figure below.

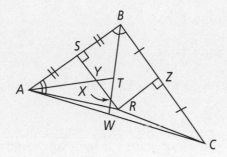

1. Which point is the incenter of $\triangle ABC$?

   Ⓐ X Ⓑ T Ⓒ R Ⓓ Y

2. Which point is the circumcenter of $\triangle ABC$?

   Ⓕ X Ⓖ T Ⓗ R Ⓘ Y

3. Which segment is an angle bisector of $\triangle ABC$?

   Ⓐ $\overline{BX}$ Ⓑ $\overline{SX}$ Ⓒ $\overline{AS}$ Ⓓ $\overline{RZ}$

4. Which segment is a perpendicular bisector of $\triangle ABC$?

   Ⓕ $\overline{BW}$ Ⓖ $\overline{SB}$ Ⓗ $\overline{AS}$ Ⓘ $\overline{RZ}$

5. If $RC = x + 3$ and $RA = 3x - 3$, what is the value of x?

   Ⓐ 3   Ⓑ 6   Ⓒ 7   Ⓓ 9

Extended Response

6. Draw $\triangle ABC$. Construct three angle bisectors. Use the point of concurrency to construct the inscribed circle.

Name _____ Class _____ Date _____

5-4 | **Think About a Plan**
Medians and Altitudes

Coordinate Geometry $\triangle ABC$ has vertices $A(0, 0)$, $B(2, 6)$, and $C(8, 0)$. Define the points L, M, and N such that $AL = LB$, $BM = MC$, and $CN = NA$. Complete the following steps to verify the Concurrency of Medians Theorem for $\triangle ABC$.

  a. Find the coordinates of midpoints L, M, and N.

  b. Find equations of $\overleftrightarrow{AM}$, $\overleftrightarrow{BN}$, and $\overleftrightarrow{CL}$.

  c. Find the coordinates of P, the intersection of $\overleftrightarrow{AM}$ and $\overleftrightarrow{BN}$. This is the centroid.

  d. Show that point P is on $\overleftrightarrow{CL}$.

  e. Use the Distance Formula to show that point P is two-thirds of the distance from each vertex to the midpoint of the opposite side.

 1. Write the midpoint formula.

 2. Use the formula to find the coordinates of L, M, and N.

 3. Find the slopes of $\overleftrightarrow{AM}$, $\overleftrightarrow{BN}$, and $\overleftrightarrow{CL}$.

 4. Write the general point-slope form of a linear equation.

 5. Write the point-slope form equations of $\overleftrightarrow{AM}$, $\overleftrightarrow{BN}$, and $\overleftrightarrow{CL}$.

 6. Solve the system of equations for $\overleftrightarrow{AM}$ and $\overleftrightarrow{BN}$ to find the point of intersection.

 7. Show that the coordinates of point P satisfy the equation of $\overleftrightarrow{CL}$.

 8. Use the distance formula to find AM, BN, and CL. Use a calculator and round to the nearest hundredth.

 9. Use the distance formula to find AP, BP, and CP.

10. Check to see that $AP = \frac{2}{3}AM$, $BP = \frac{2}{3}BN$, and $CP = \frac{2}{3}CL$.

5-4

Practice

Form G

Medians and Altitudes

In △ABC, X is the centroid.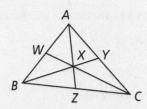

1. If CW = 15, find CX and XW.

2. If BX = 8, find BY and XY.

3. If XZ = 3, find AX and AZ.

Is $\overline{AB}$ a *median,* an *altitude,* or *neither?* Explain.

4.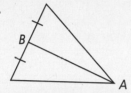

5.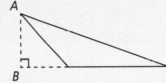

6.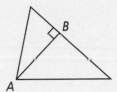

7.

Coordinate Geometry Find the orthocenter of △ABC.

8. A(2, 0), B(2, 4), C(6, 0)

9. A(1, 1), B(3, 4), C(6, 1)

10. Name the centroid.

11. Name the orthocenter.

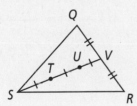

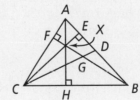

Draw a triangle that fits the given description. Then construct the centroid and the orthocenter.

12. equilateral △CDE

13. acute isosceles △XYZ

5-4

Practice (continued)

Medians and Altitudes

Form G

In Exercises 14–18, name each segment.

14. a median in $\triangle ABC$

15. an altitude for $\triangle ABC$

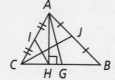

16. a median in $\triangle AHC$

17. an altitude for $\triangle AHB$

18. an altitude for $\triangle AHG$

19. $A(0, 0)$, $B(0, -2)$, $C(-3, 0)$. Find the orthocenter of $\triangle ABC$.

20. Cut a large isosceles triangle out of paper. Paper-fold to construct the medians and the altitudes. How are the altitude to the base and the median to the base related?

21. In which kind of triangle is the centroid at the same point as the orthocenter?

22. P is the centroid of $\triangle MNO$. $MP = 14x + 8y$. Write expressions to represent PR and MR.

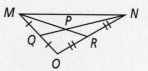

23. F is the centroid of $\triangle ACE$. $AD = 15x^2 + 3y$. Write expressions to represent AF and FD.

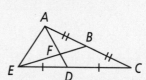

24. Use coordinate geometry to prove the following statement.
   Given: $\triangle ABC$; $A(c, d)$, $B(c, e)$, $C(f, e)$
   Prove: The circumcenter of $\triangle ABC$ is a point on the triangle.

Name _____ Class _____ Date _____

5-4 Standardized Test Prep
Medians and Altitudes

Multiple Choice

For Exercises 1–5, choose the correct letter.

1. Z is the centroid of $\triangle ABC$. If $AZ = 12$, what is ZY?

   Ⓐ 6   Ⓒ 12

   Ⓑ 9   Ⓓ 18

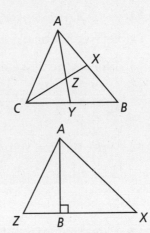

2. What is the best description of $\overline{AB}$?

   Ⓕ altitude

   Ⓖ perpendicular bisector

   Ⓗ median

   Ⓘ angle bisector

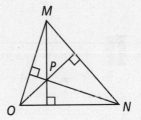

3. What is the best description of P?

   Ⓐ incenter

   Ⓑ centroid

   Ⓒ circumcenter

   Ⓓ orthocenter

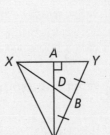

Use $\triangle XYZ$ for Exercises 4 and 5.

4. Which is an altitude of $\triangle XYZ$?

   Ⓕ $\overline{AZ}$ Ⓗ $\overline{XB}$

   Ⓖ $\overline{XY}$ Ⓘ $\overline{ZY}$

5. Which is a median of $\triangle XYZ$?

   Ⓐ $\overline{AZ}$ Ⓒ $\overline{XY}$

   Ⓑ $\overline{BX}$ Ⓓ $\overline{YZ}$

Short Response

6. M is the centroid of $\triangle QRS$, and $QM = 22x + 10y$.
   What expressions can you write for MV and QV?

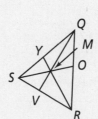

5-5 Think About a Plan

Indirect Proof

Write an indirect proof.

Given: $\triangle XYZ$ is isosceles.

Prove: Neither base angle is a right angle.

1. What is the first step in writing an indirect proof?

   _____

2. Write the first step for this indirect proof.

   _____

3. What is the second step in writing an indirect proof?

   _____

4. Find the contradiction:

   a. How are the base angle measures of an isosceles triangle related?

   _____

   b. What must be the measure of each base angle?

   _____

   c. What is the sum of the angle measures in a triangle? _____

   d. If both base angles of $\triangle XYZ$ are right angles, and the non-base angle has a measure greater than 0, what must be true of the sum of the angle measures?

   _____

   e. What does your assumption contradict?

   _____

5. What is your conclusion?

   _____

   _____

$5\text{-}5$ **Practice**   Form G

Indirect Proof

Write the first step of an indirect proof of the given statement.

1. A number g is divisible by 2.

2. There are more than three red houses on the block.

3. $\triangle ABC$ is equilateral.

4. $m\angle B < 90$

5. $\angle C$ is not a right angle.

6. There are less than 15 pounds of apples in the basket.

7. If the number ends in 4, then it is not divisible by 5.

8. If $\overline{MN} \cong \overline{NO}$, then point N is on the perpendicular bisector of $\overline{MO}$.

9. If two right triangles have congruent hypotenuses and one pair of congruent legs, then the triangles are congruent.

10. If two parallel lines are intersected by a transversal, then alternate interior angles are congruent.

11. **Developing Proof** Fill in the blanks to prove the following
    statement: In right $\triangle ABC$, $m\angle B + m\angle C = 90$.
    Given: right $\triangle ABC$
    Prove: $m\angle B + m\angle C = 90$
    Assume temporarily that $m\angle B + m\angle C$ _____. If $m\angle B + m\angle C$ _____,
    then $m\angle A + m\angle B + m\angle C$ _____. According to the Triangle Angle-Sum
    Theorem, $m\angle A + m\angle B + m\angle C =$ _____. This contradicts the previous
    statement, so the temporary assumption is _____.
    Therefore, _____.

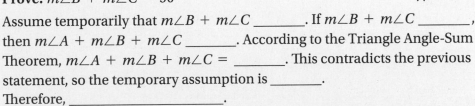

12. Use indirect reasoning to eliminate all but one of the following answers.
    In what year was Barack Obama born?
    (A) 1809   (B) 1909   (C) 1961   (D) 2000

5-5 Practice (continued) Form G
Indirect Proof

Identify the two statements that contradict each other.

13. I. $\triangle ABC$ is acute.   **II.** $\triangle ABC$ is scalene.   **III.** $\triangle ABC$ is equilateral.

14. I. $m\angle B \leq 90$ **II.** $\angle B$ is acute.   **III.** $\angle B$ is a right angle.

15.   I. $\overline{FA} \parallel \overline{AC}$
   II. $\overline{FA}$ and $\overline{AC}$ are skew.
   III. $\overline{FA}$ and $\overline{AC}$ do not intersect.

16.   I. Victoria has art class from 9:00 to 10:00 on Mondays.
   II. Victoria has math class from 10:30 to 11:30 on Mondays.
   III. Victoria has math class from 9:00 to 10:00 on Mondays.

17.   I. $\triangle MNO$ is acute.
   II. The centroid and the orthocenter for $\triangle MNO$ are at different points.
   III. $\triangle MNO$ is equilateral.

18.   I. $\triangle ABC$ such that $\angle A$ is obtuse.
   II. $\triangle ABC$ such that $\angle B$ is obtuse.
   III. $\triangle ABC$ such that $\angle C$ is acute.

19.   I. The orthocenter for $\triangle ABC$ is outside the triangle.
   II. The median for $\triangle ABC$ is inside the triangle.
   III. $\triangle ABC$ is an acute triangle.

Write an indirect proof.

20. Given: $m\angle XCD = 30$, $m\angle BCX = 60$, $\angle XCD \cong \angle XBC$
   Prove: $\overline{CX} \perp \overline{BD}$

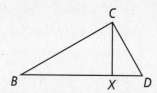

21. It is raining outside. Show that the temperature must be greater than 32°F.

5-5 Standardized Test Prep

Indirect Proof

Multiple Choice

For Exercises 1–5, choose the correct letter.

1. Which two statements contradict each other?
   I. $\triangle ABC$ is scalene.
   II. $\triangle ABC$ is isosceles.
   III. $\triangle ABC$ is right.
   IV. $\triangle ABC$ is acute.

   (A) I and II   (B) I and IV   (C) II and III   (D) II and IV

2. $\triangle MNO$ is equilateral. Which is a contradiction to this statement?
   (F) $\triangle MON$ is equilateral.
   (G) $\triangle MNO$ is acute.
   (H) $m\angle M = 120$
   (I) $m\angle M = 60$

3. What is the first step of the following indirect proof?
   Given: The side lengths of a triangle are 4, 4, and 6.
   Prove: The triangle is not a right triangle.

   (A) Assume the triangle is a right triangle.

   (B) Assume the triangle is obtuse.

   (C) Assume the side lengths are not 4, 4, and 6.

   (D) Assume the side lengths are 4, 5, and 6.

4. $MN = PQ$. Which is a contradiction to this statement?
   (F) $\overline{MN} \parallel \overline{PQ}$
   (G) $\overline{MN} \perp \overline{PQ}$
   (H) $\overline{MN} \cong \overline{PQ}$
   (I) $\overline{MN}$ is not congruent to $\overline{PQ}$.

5. What is the first step of an indirect proof of the statement: A number x is not divisible by 5?
   (A) Assume x is not divisible by 5.
   (B) Assume x is divisible by 5.
   (C) Assume x is divisible by 2.
   (D) Assume x is prime.

Short Response

6. What is the first step of an indirect proof of the following statement? Explain.
   If a number ends in 0, then it is divisible by 5.

5-6 Think About a Plan

Inequalities in One Triangle

Prove this corollary to Theorem 5-11: The perpendicular segment from a point to a line is the shortest segment from the point to the line.

Given: $\overline{PT} \perp \overline{TA}$

Prove: $PA > PT$

1. What is $m\angle T$? Explain how you know this.

_____

2. What is $m\angle P + m\angle A + m\angle T$? Explain how you know this.

_____

3. What is $m\angle P + m\angle A$? Explain how you know this.

_____

_____

4. Write an inequality to show $m\angle A$.

5. Write an inequality to show the relationship between $m\angle A$ and $m\angle T$.

6. Which side lies opposite $\angle A$ and which side lies opposite $\angle T$?

_____

7. What is Theorem 5-11?

_____

_____

8. What can you conclude about PA and PT?

_____

5-6   **Practice**   Form G

Inequalities in One Triangle

Explain why m∠1 > m∠2.

1.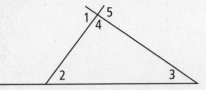

2.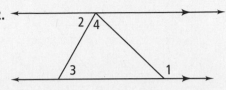

For Exercises 3–6, list the angles of each triangle
in order from smallest to largest.

3.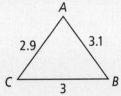

4.

5.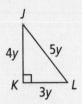

6.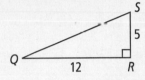

For Exercises 7–10, list the sides of each triangle in order from
shortest to longest.

7.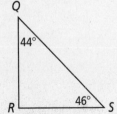

8.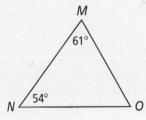

9. $\triangle ABC$, with $m\angle A = 99$, $m\angle B = 44$, and $m\angle C = 37$

10. $\triangle ABC$, with $m\angle A = 122$, $m\angle B = 22$, and $m\angle C = 36$

For Exercises 11 and 12, list the angles of each triangle in order from
smallest to largest.

11. $\triangle ABC$, where $AB = 17$, $AC = 13$, and $BC = 29$

12. $\triangle MNO$, where $MN = 4$, $NO = 12$, and $MO = 10$

5-6 **Practice** (continued)   Form G

Inequalities in One Triangle

Determine which side is shortest in the diagram.

13.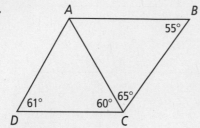

14.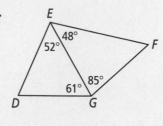

Can a triangle have sides with the given lengths? Explain.

15. 8 cm, 7 cm, 9 cm

16. 7 ft, 13 ft, 6 ft

17. 20 in., 18 in., 16 in.

18. 3 m, 11 m, 7 m

Algebra The lengths of two sides of a triangle are given. Describe the possible lengths for the third side.

19. 5, 11

20. 12, 12

21. 25, 10

22. 6, 8

23. Algebra List the sides in order from shortest to longest in $\triangle PQR$, with $m\angle P = 45$, $m\angle Q = 10x + 30$, and $m\angle R = 5x$.

24. Algebra List the sides in order from shortest to longest in $\triangle ABC$, with $m\angle A = 80$, $m\angle B = 3x + 5$, and $m\angle C = 5x - 1$.

25. Error Analysis A student draws a triangle with a perimeter 36 cm. The student says that the longest side measures 18 cm. How do you know that the student is incorrect? Explain.

Prentice Hall Gold Geometry • Practice and Problem Solving Workbook
140

5-6 Standardized Test Prep

Inequalities in One Triangle

Multiple Choice

For Exercises 1–6, choose the correct letter.

1. Which of the following could be lengths of sides of a triangle?

    (A) 11, 15, 27   (B) 13, 14, 32   (C) 16, 19, 34   (D) 33, 22, 55

2. △ABC has the following angle measures: $m\angle A = 120$, $m\angle B = 40$, and $m\angle C = 20$. Which lists the sides in order from shortest to longest?

    (F) $\overline{CB}, \overline{BA}, \overline{AC}$ (H) $\overline{AC}, \overline{BA}, \overline{CB}$

    (G) $\overline{BA}, \overline{AC}, \overline{CB}$ (I) $\overline{CB}, \overline{AC}, \overline{BA}$

3. △RST has the following side lengths: $RS = 7$, $ST = 13$, and $RT = 19$. Which lists the angles in order from smallest to largest?

    (A) $\angle R, \angle S, \angle T$ (C) $\angle S, \angle T, \angle R$

    (B) $\angle T, \angle S, \angle R$ (D) $\angle T, \angle R, \angle S$

4. A triangle has side lengths 21 and 17. Which is a possible length for the third side?

    (F) 2   (G) 4   (H) 25   (I) 39

5. Look at △LMN. Which lists the angles in order from the smallest to the largest?

    (A) $\angle L, \angle M, \angle N$ (C) $\angle N, \angle M, \angle L$

    (B) $\angle M, \angle N, \angle L$ (D) $\angle M, \angle L, \angle N$

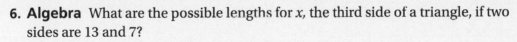

6. **Algebra** What are the possible lengths for x, the third side of a triangle, if two sides are 13 and 7?

    (F) $6 < x < 20$ (G) $7 < x < 13$ (H) $6 \le x \le 20$ (I) $7 \le x \le 13$

Short Response

7. What is the relationship between a and y? Explain.

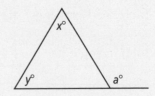

5-7 Think About a Plan

Inequalities in Two Triangles

Reasoning The legs of a right isosceles triangle are congruent to the legs of an isosceles triangle with an 80° vertex angle. Which triangle has a greater perimeter? How do you know?

1. How can you use a sketch to help visualize the problem?
Draw a sketch.

2. The triangles have two pairs of congruent sides. For the right triangle, what is the measure of the included angle? How do you know this?

_____

3. For the second triangle, what is the measure of the included angle? How do you know this?

_____

4. How could you find the perimeter of each triangle?

_____

5. How does the sum of the lengths of the legs in the right triangle compare to the sum of the lengths of the legs in the other triangle?

_____

6. Write formulas for the perimeters of each triangle. Use the variable ℓ for leg length, b_1 for base length of the right triangle, and b_2 for base length of the second triangle.

7. What values do you need to compare to find the triangle with the greater perimeter?

_____

8. How can you use the Hinge Theorem to find which base length is longer?

_____

9. Which base length is longer? _____

10. Which triangle has the greater perimeter? _____

5-7 Practice   Form G

Inequalities in Two Triangles

Write an inequality relating the given side lengths. If there is not enough information to reach a conclusion, write *no conclusion*.

1. *ST* and *MN*

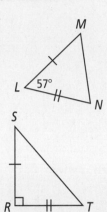

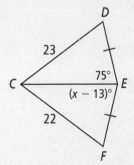

2. *BA* and *BC*

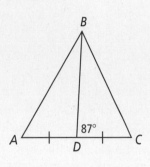

3. *CD* and *CF*

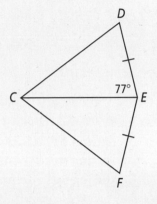

4. A crocodile opens his jaws at a 30° angle. He closes his jaws, then opens them again at a 36° angle. In which case is the distance between the tip of his upper jaw and the tip of his lower jaw greater? Explain.

5. At which time is the distance between the tip of the hour hand and the tip of the minute hand greater, 2:20 or 2:25?

Find the range of possible values for each variable.

6.

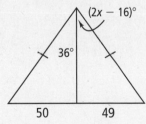

7.

8.

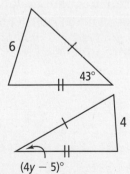

9. In the triangles at the right, *AB* = *DC* and *m∠ABC* < *m∠DCB*. Explain why *AC* < *BD*.

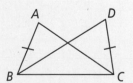

Name _____ Class _____ Date _____

5-7
Practice (continued)   Form G
Inequalities in Two Triangles

Copy and complete with > or <. Explain your reasoning.

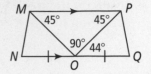

10. $m\angle POQ$ __?__ $m\angle MON$

11. MN __?__ PQ

12. MP __?__ OP

13. Jogger A and Jogger B start at the same point. Jogger A travels 0.9 mi due east, then turns 120° clockwise, then travels another 3 mi. Jogger B travels 0.9 mi due west, then turns 115° counterclockwise, then travels another 3 mi. Do the joggers end in the same place? Explain.

14. In the diagram at the right, in which position are the tips of the scissors farther apart?

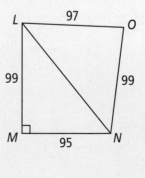

Position A   Position B

15. The legs of an isosceles triangle with a 65° vertex angle are congruent with the sides of an equilateral triangle. Which triangle has a greater perimeter? How do you know?

Write an inequality relating the given angle measures. If there is not enough information to reach a conclusion, write *no conclusion*.

16. $m\angle A$ and $m\angle F$

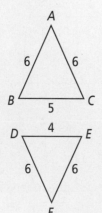

17. $m\angle L$ and $m\angle R$

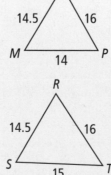

18. $m\angle MLN$ and $m\angle ONL$

5-7 Standardized Test Prep

Inequalities in Two Triangles

Multiple Choice

For Exercises 1–5, choose the correct letter.

1. At which time is the distance between the tip of the hour hand and the tip of the minute hand on a clock the greatest?

   Ⓐ 12:00   Ⓑ 12:10   Ⓒ 1:30   Ⓓ 5:25

2. What is the range of possible values for *x*?

   Ⓕ $\frac{2}{3} < x < 24$ Ⓗ $0 < x < 48$

   Ⓖ $\frac{3}{2} < x < 24$ Ⓘ $x > 24$

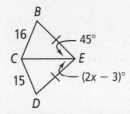

3. Which inequality relates *BC* and *XY*?

   Ⓐ $BC < XY$ Ⓒ $BC = XY$

   Ⓑ $BC > XY$ Ⓓ $BC \geq XY$

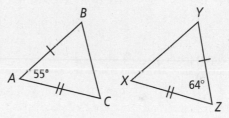

4. Four pairs of identical scissors lie on a table. Scissors 1 is opened 30°, scissors 2 is opened 29°, scissors 3 is opened 59°, and scissors 4 is opened 74°. In which pair of scissors is the distance between the tips of the scissor blades greatest?

   Ⓕ scissors 1   Ⓖ scissors 2   Ⓗ scissors 3   Ⓘ scissors 4

5. In △*ABC* and △*DEF*, *AB* = *DE*, *CA* = *FD*, and *BC* < *EF*. Which of the following must be true?

   Ⓐ $m\angle B < m\angle E$ Ⓒ $m\angle C < m\angle F$

   Ⓑ $m\angle A < m\angle D$ Ⓓ $m\angle B = m\angle E$

Short Response

6. What value must *x* be greater than, and what value must *x* be less than?

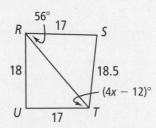

6-1 Think About a Plan

The Polygon Angle-Sum Theorems

Reasoning Your friend says she has another way to find the sum of the angle measures of a polygon. She picks a point inside the polygon, draws a segment to each vertex, and counts the number of triangles. She multiplies the total by 180, and then subtracts 360 from the product. Does her method work? Explain.

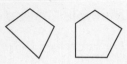

Understanding the Problem

1. According to the Polygon Angle-Sum Theorem, what is the relationship between the number of sides of a polygon and the sum of the measures of the interior angles of a polygon?

   _____

2. How can you write this relationship as an expression in which *n* is the number of sides?

Planning the Solution

3. Mark a point near the center of each figure. Then draw a segment from that point to each vertex as described in the problem.

4. What is the relationship between the number of sides in a polygon and the number of triangles in that polygon?

   _____

5. What expression can you write to represent multiplying the number of triangles by 180 and then subtracting 360? Let *n* represent the number of sides. Explain how this expression relates to the picture you drew.

   _____

   _____

   _____

Getting an Answer

6. Can you show that the two expressions you wrote are equal? Explain.

   _____

$6\text{-}1$ **Practice**   *Form G*

The Polygon Angle-Sum Theorems

Find the sum of the angle measures of each polygon.

1.

2.

3.

4. 12-gon

5. 18-gon

6. 25-gon

7. 60-gon

8. 102-gon

9. 17-gon

10. 36-gon

11. 90-gon

12. 11-gon

Find the measure of one angle in each regular polygon. Round to the nearest tenth if necessary.

13.

14.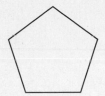

15.

16. regular 15-gon

17. regular 11-gon

18. regular 13-gon

19. regular 24-gon

20. regular 360-gon

21. regular 18-gon

22. regular 36-gon

23. regular 72-gon

24. regular 144-gon

Algebra Find the missing angle measures.

25.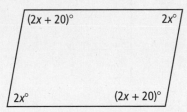

26.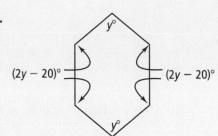

27.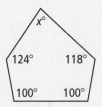

28.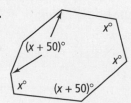

29.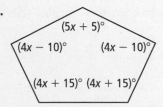

Prentice Hall Gold Geometry • Practice and Problem Solving Workbook

6-1

Practice (continued)   Form G

The Polygon Angle-Sum Theorems

Algebra Find the missing angle measures.

30.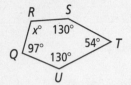

31.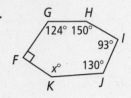

32.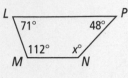

33.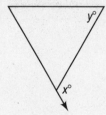

34.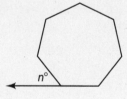

35.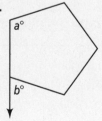

Find the measure of an exterior angle of each regular polygon. Round to the nearest tenth if necessary.

36. decagon   **37.** 16-gon   **38.** hexagon

39. 20-gon   **40.** 72-gon   **41.** square

42. 15-gon   **43.** 25-gon   **44.** 80-gon

Find the values of the variables for each regular polygon. Round to the nearest tenth if necessary.

45.

46.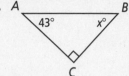

47.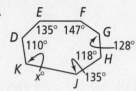

48. Reasoning Can a quadrilateral have no obtuse angles? Explain.

The measure of an exterior angle of a regular polygon is given. Find the measure of an interior angle. Then find the number of sides.

49. 12   **50.** 6   **51.** 45

52. 40   **53.** 24   **54.** 18

55. 9   **56.** 14.4   **57.** 7.2

6-1 Standardized Test Prep

The Polygon Angle-Sum Theorems

Gridded Response

Solve each exercise and enter your answer on the grid provided.

1. What is the sum of the interior angle measures of a regular octagon?

2. What is the measure of one interior angle of a regular 12-gon?

3. What is the value of x in the regular polygon at the right?

$3x°$

4. What is the measure of an exterior angle of a regular octagon?

5. If the measure of an exterior angle of a regular polygon is 24, how many sides does the polygon have?

Answers

1. 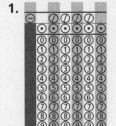 **2.**  **3.**  **4.** 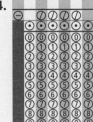 **5.**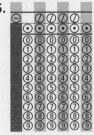

6-2 Think About a Plan

Properties of Parallelograms

Algebra The perimeter of $\square ABCD$ is 92 cm. AD is 7 cm more than twice AB. Find the lengths of all four sides of $\square ABCD$.

1. What is perimeter? _____

2. Write a formula to find the perimeter of $\square ABCD$ with side lengths AB, BC, CD, and DA.

3. What is the relationship between opposite sides of a parallelogram?

   _____

4. Mark the vertices of the parallelogram at the right so it is $\square ABCD$. Then mark the appropriate sides congruent.

5. How could you use the relationship between opposite sides of a parallelogram to rewrite the formula you wrote in Step 2?

   _____

6. Now look back at the relationship between the sides as described in the problem. Let x represent AB. What expression can you write to represent AD?

7. Write the side lengths from Step 6 on the parallelogram above.

8. How can you use these expressions in the perimeter formula you wrote in Step 5?

   _____

9. Rewrite the perimeter formula using the expressions and the value of the perimeter given in the problem.

10. What property can you use to simplify the equation? Rewrite the simplified equation and then solve for x.

    _____

11. Now substitute the value of x back into the expression to find AD. What is the length of each of the four sides of $ABCD$?

Prentice Hall Geometry • Practice and Problem Solving Workbook
150

6-2

Practice
Properties of Parallelograms

Form G

Find the value of x in each parallelogram.

1.

2.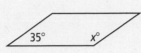

3.

4.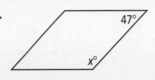

5. 27°

6.

Developing Proof Complete this two-column proof.

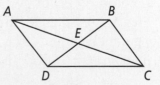

7. **Given:** □EFGH, with diagonals $\overline{EG}$ and $\overline{HF}$

Prove: $\triangle EFK \cong \triangle GHK$

Statements	Reasons
1) _?_	1) Given
2) _?_	2) The diagonals of a parallelogram bisect each other.
3) $\overline{EF} \cong \overline{GH}$	3) _?_
4) _?_	4) _?_

Algebra Find the values for x and y in □ABCD.

8. $AE = 3x$, $EC = y$, $DE = 4x$, $EB = y + 1$

9. $AE = x + 5$, $EC = y$, $DE = 2x + 3$, $EB = y + 2$

10. $AE = 3x$, $EC = 2y - 2$, $DE = 5x$, $EB = 2y + 2$

11. $AE = 2x$, $EC = y + 4$, $DE = x$, $EB = 2y - 1$

12. $AE = 4x$, $EC = 5y - 2$, $DE = 2x$, $EB = y + 14$

6-2

Practice (continued)   Form G

Properties of Parallelograms

In the figure, *TU* = *UV*. Find each length.

13. *NM*   **14.** *QR*

15. *LN*   **16.** *QS*

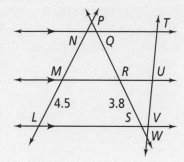

Find the measures of the numbered angles for each parallelogram.

17.

18.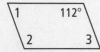

19.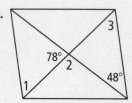

20.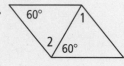

21.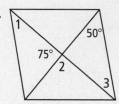

22.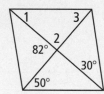

23.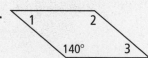

24.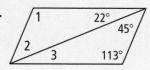

25. Developing Proof A rhombus is a parallelogram with four congruent sides. Write a plan for the following proof that uses SSS and a property of parallelograms.

Given: Rhombus *ABCD* with diagonals $\overline{AC}$ and $\overline{BD}$ intersecting at *E*

Prove: $\overline{AC} \perp \overline{BD}$

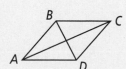

6-2 Standardized Test Prep
Properties of Parallelograms

Multiple Choice

For Exercises 1–5, choose the correct letter.

1. In $\square ABCD$, $m\angle A = 53$. What is $m\angle C$?

   (A) 37   (B) 53   (C) 127   (D) 307

2. What is the value of x in $\square QRST$?

   (F) 16   (H) 8

   (G) 12   (I) 4

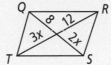

3. What is the value of y in $\square LMNO$?

   (A) 4   (C) 12

   (B) 6   (D) 24

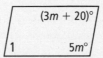

4. What is $m\angle 1$ in this parallelogram?

   (F) 20   (H) 80

   (G) 60   (I) 100

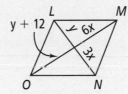

5. What is $m\angle 2$ in this parallelogram?

   (A) 115   (C) 15

   (B) 50   (D) 2

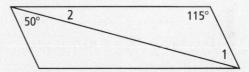

Extended Response

6. Figure $ABCD$ is a parallelogram. What are four geometric attributes you know because $ABCD$ is a parallelogram?

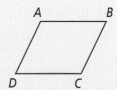

6-3 Think About a Plan

Proving That a Quadrilateral Is a Parallelogram

Prove Theorem 6-8.

Given: $\overline{AB} \cong \overline{CD}$ and $\overline{BC} \cong \overline{DA}$

Prove: *ABCD* is a parallelogram.

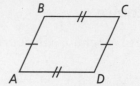

1. What is the definition of a parallelogram?

   _____

2. What are some of the ways that you can prove that two lines are parallel using a transversal?

   _____

   _____

3. Draw a transversal on *ABCD* above. This will help you prove that $\overline{BC} \parallel \overline{AD}$.

4. How can you prove that the triangles formed by the diagonal are congruent?

   _____

   _____

5. If $\overline{BD}$ is a transversal between lines $\overline{BC}$ and $\overline{AD}$, which angles represent the alternate interior angles?

6. How can you prove $\angle CBD \cong \angle ADB$?

7. What can you conclude about $\overline{BC}$ and $\overline{AD}$?

   _____

8. Draw a transversal to help prove that $\overline{AB} \parallel \overline{DC}$.

9. How can you prove that $\angle BAC \cong \angle DCA$?

   _____

   _____

10. What can you conclude about $\overline{AB}$ and $\overline{CD}$? Why?

    _____

11. How can you conclude that *ABCD* is a parallelogram?

    _____

6-3

Practice

Form G

Proving That a Quadrilateral Is a Parallelogram

Algebra For what values of *x* and *y* must each figure be a parallelogram?

1.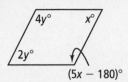

2.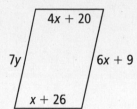

3.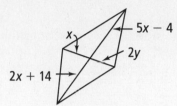

4.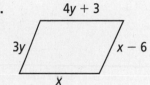

5.

6.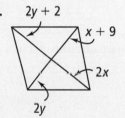

7.

8.

Can you prove that the quadrilateral is a parallelogram based on the given information? Explain.

9.

10.

11.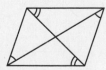

12.

6-3 Practice (continued)   Form G
Proving That a Quadrilateral Is a Parallelogram

13. Developing Proof Complete the two-column proof. Remember, a rectangle is a parallelogram with four right angles.

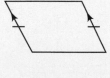

Given: $\square ABCD$, with $\overline{AC} \cong \overline{BD}$

Prove: $ABCD$ is a rectangle.

Statements	Reasons
1) $\square ABCD$, with $\overline{AC} \cong \overline{BD}$	1) Given
2) __?__	2) Opposite sides of a $\square$ are congruent.
3) $\overline{DC} \cong \overline{CD}$	3) __?__
4) __?__	4) SSS
5) $\angle ADC$ and $\angle BCD$ are supplementary.	5) __?__
6) $\angle ADC \cong \angle BCD$	6) CPCTC
7) __?__	7) Congruent supplementary angles are right angles.
8) $\angle DAB$ and $\angle CBA$ are right angles.	8) __?__
9) __?__	9) Definition of a rectangle

Can you prove that the quadrilateral is a parallelogram based on the given information? Explain.

14. $\overline{FG} \parallel \overline{IH}$, $\overline{FI} \parallel \overline{GH}$

15.

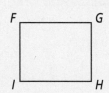

16.

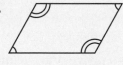

17.

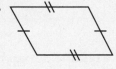

18. $\overline{AE} \cong \overline{EC}$, $\overline{BE} \cong \overline{ED}$

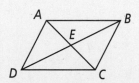

19.

20. Error Analysis It is given that $\overline{MO} \cong \overline{TR}$ and $\overline{NP} \cong \overline{QS}$, where $MNOP$ and $TQRS$ are parallelograms. A student has said that if those statements are true, then $MNOP \cong TQRS$. Why is this student incorrect?

6-3 Standardized Test Prep

Proving That a Quadrilateral Is a Parallelogram

Multiple Choice

For Exercises 1–4, choose the correct letter.

1. For what value of x must $ABCD$ be a parallelogram?

   (A) 5   (C) 15

   (B) 10   (D) 20

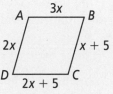

2. For what value of y must $QRST$ be a parallelogram?

   (F) 0.5   (H) 2

   (G) 1   (I) 3

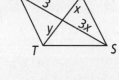

3. Which reason can be used to conclude that $DFGH$ is a parallelogram?

   (A) There are two pairs of congruent opposite angles.

   (B) The diagonals bisect each other.

   (C) There are two pairs of congruent opposite sides.

   (D) There are two pairs of opposite parallel sides.

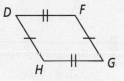

4. Which reason can be used to conclude that $LMNO$ is a parallelogram?

   (F) There are two pairs of congruent opposite angles.

   (G) There are two pairs of congruent opposite sides.

   (H) There are two pairs of opposite parallel sides.

   (I) There is one pair of congruent and parallel sides.

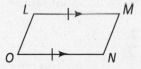

Short Response

5. What additional pieces of information could be supplied to make $ABCD$ a parallelogram?

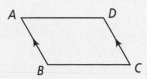

6-4 Think About a Plan

Properties of Rhombuses, Rectangles, and Squares

Algebra Find the angle measures and the side lengths of the rhombus at the right.

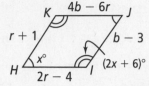

1. What do you know about the sum of the angle measures of a quadrilateral?

_____

2. Write an equation to represent the sum of the measures of each angle in this rhombus.

3. Based on the diagram, which pairs of angles are congruent? _____

4. What is the value of $m\angle H$ given in the diagram? Explain how you can use this value to rewrite the equation from Step 2. Rewrite the equation using this value.

_____

5. What is the value of $m\angle I$ given in the diagram? Explain how you can use this value to rewrite the equation from Step 4. Rewrite the equation using this value.

_____

_____

6. In the space at the right, simplify and solve the equation.

7. $m\angle H = m\angle J = x =$ ☐   8. $m\angle I = m\angle K = 2x + 6 =$ ☐

9. How can you check that your answer is correct?

_____

10. What do you know about the sides of a rhombus? _____

11. What does your answer to Step 10 tell you about the expressions for the sides of the rhombus shown in the diagram? _____

12. Which two expressions in the figure contain the same variable?

13. How do these expressions relate to each other? Explain how you can use this relationship to find the value of r. Find the value of r.

_____

14. How can you find the length of each side of the rhombus? What is the length of each side? _____

6-4   **Practice**   *Form G*

Properties of Rhombuses, Rectangles, and Squares

Decide whether the parallelogram is a *rhombus,* a *rectangle,* or a *square*. Explain.

1. 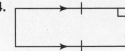   **2.**   **3.**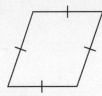

4. 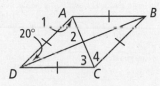   **5.**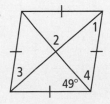

Find the measures of the numbered angles in each rhombus.

6. 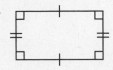   **7.**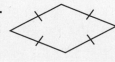

8. 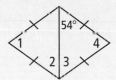   **9.**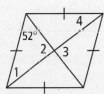

10. 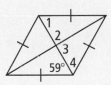   **11.**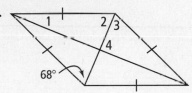

12. 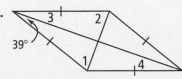   **13.**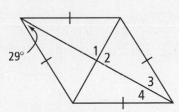

Algebra *HIJK* is a rectangle. Find the value of x and the length of each diagonal.

14. $HJ = x$ and $IK = 2x - 7$ **15.** $HJ = 3x + 5$ and $IK = 5x - 9$

16. $HJ = 3x + 7$ and $IK = 6x - 11$ **17.** $HJ = 19 + 2x$ and $IK = 3x + 22$

6-4 Practice (continued) Form G
Properties of Rhombuses, Rectangles, and Squares

Algebra *HIJK* is a rectangle. Find the value of *x* and the length of each diagonal.

18. $HJ = 4x$ and $IK = 7x - 12$

19. $HJ = x + 40$ and $IK = 5x$

Determine the most precise name for each quadrilateral.

20.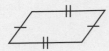

21.

22.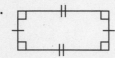

23.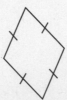

Algebra Find the values of the variables. Then find the side lengths.

24. square *WXYZ*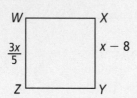

25. rhombus *ABCD*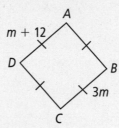

26. rectangle *QRST*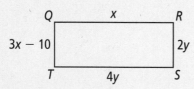

27. square *LMNO*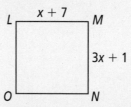

28. Solve using a paragraph proof.

 Given: Rectangle *DVEO* with diagonals $\overline{DE}$ and $\overline{OV}$

 Prove: $\triangle OVE \cong \triangle DEV$

6-4 Standardized Test Prep

Properties of Rhombuses, Rectangles, and Squares

Multiple Choice

For Exercises 1–6, choose the correct letter.

Use rhombus *TQRS* for Exercises 1–4.

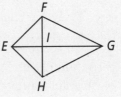

1. What is the measure of $\angle 1$?
   - Ⓐ 47
   - Ⓒ 74
   - Ⓑ 37
   - Ⓓ 53

2. What is the measure of $\angle 2$?
   - Ⓕ 47
   - Ⓖ 74
   - Ⓗ 37
   - Ⓘ 53

3. What is the value of *x*?
   - Ⓐ 2
   - Ⓑ 1
   - Ⓒ 5
   - Ⓓ 4

4. What is the value of *y*?
   - Ⓕ 4
   - Ⓖ 3
   - Ⓗ 2
   - Ⓘ 1

5. What statement would be sufficient to prove that a quadrilateral is a rhombus?
   - Ⓐ The quadrilateral has four congruent angles.
   - Ⓑ The quadrilateral has two pairs of parallel sides.
   - Ⓒ The quadrilateral has four congruent sides.
   - Ⓓ The quadrilateral has two pairs of congruent angles.

6. *EFGH* is a kite. To prove that the diagonals of a kite are perpendicular, which pair of angles must you prove congruent using CPCTC?
   - Ⓕ $\angle EFI$ and $\angle EHI$
   - Ⓗ $\angle EIF$ and $\angle EIH$
   - Ⓖ $\angle GFI$ and $\angle GHI$
   - Ⓘ $\angle FIE$ and $\angle HIG$

Short Response

7. Why is it that the statement "all rhombuses are squares" is false, but the statement "all squares are rhombuses" is true? Explain.

6-5 Think About a Plan

Conditions for Rhombuses, Rectangles, and Squares

Prove Theorem 6-18.

Given: $\square ABCD$, $\overline{AC} \cong \overline{DB}$

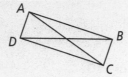

Prove: *ABCD* is a rectangle.

Understanding the Problem

1. What must you prove in order to show that parallelogram *ABCD* is a rectangle?

   _____

Planning the Solution

2. Using the properties of parallelograms, prove $\triangle BAD \cong \triangle CDA$. Show the steps of this proof below.

Statement	Reason
_____	_____
_____	_____
_____	_____
_____	_____

3. If $\triangle BAD \cong \triangle CDA$, which angles are congruent?

   _____

4. To prove that the angles are right angles you need to use the properties of parallel lines. When a transversal intersects parallel lines, which angles are supplementary?

   _____

5. Given that $\overline{AB} \parallel \overline{CD}$, which angles in $\triangle BAD$ and $\triangle CDA$ are supplementary?

   _____

6. If these angles are both congruent and supplementary, what must the measure of each angle be?

7. How can you prove that the other angles of the parallelogram are right angles?

   _____

Name _____ Class _____ Date _____

6-5 Practice   Form G

Conditions for Rhombuses, Rectangles, and Squares

Can you conclude that the parallelogram is a *rhombus*, a *rectangle*, or a *square*? Explain.

1.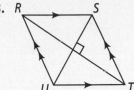

2.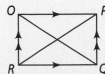

3.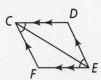

4. $\overline{NP} \cong \overline{OQ}$

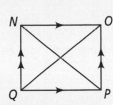

For what value of x is the figure the given special parallelogram?

5. rhombus

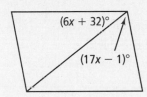

6. rhombus

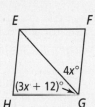

7. rectangle

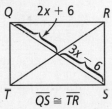

$\overline{QS} \cong \overline{TR}$

8. rhombus

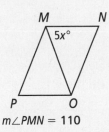

$m\angle PMN = 110$

9. rectangle

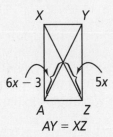

$AY = XZ$

10. rectangle

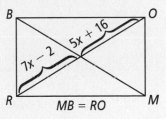

$MB = RO$

Open-Ended Given two segments with lengths x and y $(x \neq y)$, what special parallelograms meet the given conditions? Show each sketch.

11. One diagonal has length x, the other has length y. The diagonals intersect at right angles.

12. Both diagonals have length y and do not intersect at right angles.

6-5

Practice (continued)   Form G

Conditions for Rhombuses, Rectangles, and Squares

For Exercises 13–16, determine whether the parallelogram is a *rhombus*, a *rectangle*, or a *square*. Give the most precise description in each case.

13. A parallelogram has perpendicular diagonals and angle measures of 45, 135, 45, and 135.

14. A parallelogram has perpendicular and congruent diagonals.

15. A parallelogram has perpendicular diagonals and angle measures that are all 90.

16. A parallelogram has congruent diagonals.

17. A woman is plotting out a garden bed. She measures the diagonals of the bed and finds that one is 22 ft long and the other is 23 ft long. Could the garden bed be a rectangle? Explain.

18. A man is making a square frame. How can he check to make sure the frame is square, using only a tape measure?

19. A girl cuts out rectangular pieces of cardboard for a project. She checks to see that they are rectangular by determining if the diagonals are perpendicular. Will this tell her whether a piece is a rectangle? Explain.

20. **Reasoning** Explain why drawing both diagonals on any rectangle will always result in two pairs of nonoverlapping congruent triangles.

6-5 Standardized Test Prep

Conditions for Rhombuses, Rectangles, and Squares

Multiple Choice

For Exercises 1–4, choose the correct letter.

1. Which is the most precise name of this figure?

   Ⓐ parallelogram   Ⓒ rectangle

   Ⓑ rhombus   Ⓓ square

   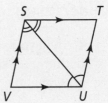

2. Which of the following conditions or set of conditions must be met for a parallelogram to be a rectangle?

   Ⓕ Diagonals are perpendicular.

   Ⓖ Diagonals are congruent.

   Ⓗ All sides are congruent.

   Ⓘ The length of a diagonal is equal to the length of a side.

3. Which of the following conditions or set of conditions is sufficient for a parallelogram to be a square?

   Ⓐ Diagonals are perpendicular and diagonals are congruent.

   Ⓑ Diagonals are congruent.

   Ⓒ All sides are congruent.

   Ⓓ The length of a diagonal is equal to the length of a side.

4. For what value of x is ▱$XYZA$ a rectangle?

   Ⓕ 2   Ⓗ 4

   Ⓖ 3   Ⓘ 5

Short Response

5. The diagonals of a parallelogram are 2.3 cm and 3.2 cm long. Can you tell if the parallelogram is a rhombus? Explain.

6-6 Think About a Plan

Trapezoids and Kites

Prove the converse of Theorem 6-19: If a trapezoid has a pair of congruent base angles, then the trapezoid is isosceles.

Understanding the Problem

1. To help you solve this problem, draw trapezoid *ABCD* in the space to the right. Mark the base angles congruent and label the vertices so that $\overline{AB} \parallel \overline{CD}$.

2. Which two sides of the trapezoid do you need to prove congruent? _____

Planning the Solution

3. What type of polygons can you construct inside the trapezoid to prove that $\overline{AD} \cong \overline{BC}$? _____

4. What makes a set of lines parallel? Describe the relationship between two segments that are perpendicular to a pair of parallel lines and have endpoints on the lines.

   _____

5. In your diagram draw $\overline{AE} \perp \overline{DC}$ and $\overline{BF} \perp \overline{DC}$. What must be true about the length of these segments? Mark the diagram appropriately.

   _____

   _____

6. What must be true of $\angle AED$ and $\angle BFC$? Explain your answer, and then mark the diagram appropriately.

   _____

   _____

Getting an Answer

7. How can you prove that $\triangle AED \cong \triangle BFC$? Explain.

   _____

   _____

   _____

8. How does this allow you to prove that $\overline{AD} \cong \overline{BC}$? _____

Practice

Form G

Trapezoids and Kites

Find the measures of the numbered angles in each isosceles trapezoid.

1.

96° ∠1 ∠2

2.
∠1 ∠2 79°

3.
∠1 ∠2 67°

4.
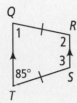
A ∠1 B ∠2
55° D C ∠3

5.
L ∠1 M ∠2
135° O N ∠3

6.
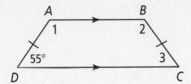
Q ∠1 R ∠2 ∠3
85° S T

7.
K ∠1 L ∠2
47° N M ∠3

Algebra Find the value(s) of the variable(s) in each isosceles trapezoid.

8.
$3x - 3$
$x - 1$
$x + 5$

9.
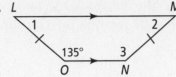
$(6x + 20)°$
$y°$
$4x°$

10.
L M
$7x$ $2x + 5$
O N

Find XY in each trapezoid.

11.
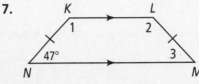
B X C
5   2.5
F Y E

12.
H 16 I
X   Y
M 8 L

13.
S 15 T
X   Y
V 6 U

Algebra Find the lengths of the segments with variable expressions.

14.
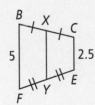
F $2x - 5.5$ G
A $2x + 0.75$ B
X $x + 16$ W

15.
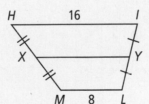
L $2x - 4$ M
T $2x + 4$ U
Q $3x + 2$ P

16.
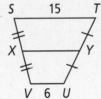
B $8x + 3$ C
T $4x + 7.5$ U
K $4x$ H

6-6

Practice (continued)   Form G

Trapezoids and Kites

17. $\overline{CD}$ is the midsegment of trapezoid *WXYZ*.

   a. What is the value of *x*?

   b. What is *XY*?

   c. What is *WZ*?

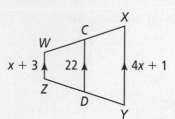

18. Reasoning The diagonals of a quadrilateral form two acute and two obtuse angles at their intersection. Is this quadrilateral a kite? Explain.

19. Reasoning The diagonals of a quadrilateral form right angles and its side lengths are 4, 4, 6, and 6. Could this quadrilateral be a kite? Explain.

Find the measures of the numbered angles in each kite.

20.

21.

22.

23.

24.

25.
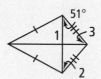

Algebra Find the value(s) of the variable(s) in each kite.

26.
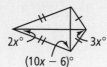

27.

28.
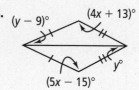

For which value of *x* is each figure a kite?

29.
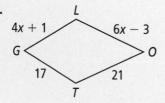

30.
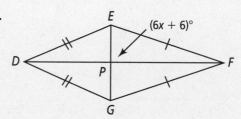

6-6 Standardized Test Prep

Trapezoids and Kites

Multiple Choice

For Exercises 1–5, choose the correct letter.

1. In the isosceles trapezoid at the right, what is the measure of ∠L?

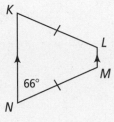

   A) 24   C) 114

   B) 66   D) 132

2. What is true about the diagonals in an isosceles trapezoid?

   F) They are congruent.

   G) They are perpendicular.

   H) They are congruent and perpendicular.

   I) The length of each diagonal is equal to half the sum of the bases.

3. $\overline{LM}$ is the midsegment of trapezoid *RSXY*. What is *LM*?

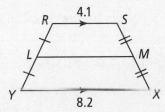

   A) 4.1   C) 6.15

   B) 6   D) 12.3

4. For which value of *x* is *ABCD* a kite?

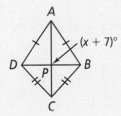

   F) 23   H) 73

   G) 33   I) 83

5. **Algebra** What is the value of *x* in kite *ABCD* at the right?

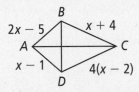

   A) 2   C) 8

   B) 4   D) 16

Short Response

6. A quadrilateral has diagonals that are congruent and bisect opposite pairs of angles. Could this quadrilateral be a kite? Explain.

6-7 Think About a Plan

Polygons in the Coordinate Plane

$\overline{DE}$ is a midsegment of $\triangle ABC$ at the right. Show that the Triangle Midsegment Theorem holds true for $\triangle ABC$.

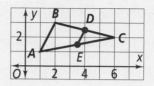

Understanding the Problem

1. What does the Triangle Midsegment Theorem state?

_____

_____

2. What do you need to prove to show that the Triangle Midsegment Theorem holds true for $\triangle ABC$? _____

Planning the Solution

3. What is always true of the slope of parallel lines? _____

4. Which formula can you use to find the length of a segment on the coordinate plane? _____

5. What are the coordinates for D and E? _____

Getting an Answer

6. Find the slope of segments $\overline{DE}$ and $\overline{BA}$ below.

Slope of $\overline{DE}$: $m = \dfrac{\square - \square}{\square - \square} = \dfrac{\square}{\square} = \square$

Slope of $\overline{BA}$: $m = \dfrac{\square - \square}{\square - \square} = \dfrac{\square}{\square} = \square$

7. Are segments $\overline{DE}$ and $\overline{BA}$ parallel? _____

8. Find the length of segments $\overline{DE}$ and $\overline{BA}$ below.

Length of $\overline{DE}$: $\sqrt{\left(\square - \square\right)^2 + \left(\square - \square\right)^2} = \square$

Length of $\overline{BA}$: $\sqrt{\left(\square - \square\right)^2 + \left(\square - \square\right)^2} = \square$

9. Does the Triangle Midsegment Theorem hold true for $\triangle ABC$? Explain.

_____

6-7

Practice

Polygons in the Coordinate Plane

Form G

Determine whether △XYZ is *scalene, isosceles,* or *equilateral.*

1.

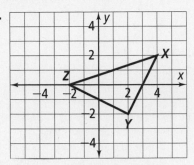

2.

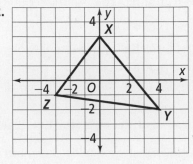

3.

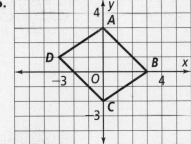

4.

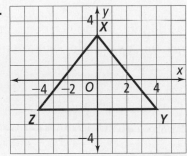

What is the most precise classification of the quadrilateral formed by connecting in order the midpoints of each figure below?

5.

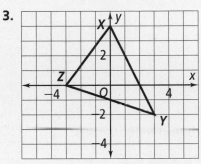

6.

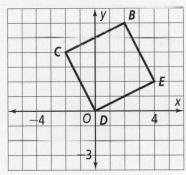

7.

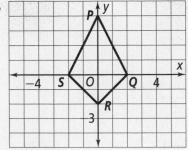

8.

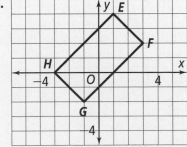

6-7

Practice (continued)

Polygons in the Coordinate Plane

Form G

9. **Writing** Describe two ways in which you can show whether a parallelogram in the coordinate plane is a rectangle.

10. **Writing** Describe how you can show whether a quadrilateral in the coordinate plane is a kite.

Use the trapezoid at the right for Exercises 11 and 12.

11. Is the trapezoid an isosceles trapezoid? Explain.

12. Is the quadrilateral formed by connecting the midpoints of the trapezoid a parallelogram, rhombus, rectangle, or square? Explain.

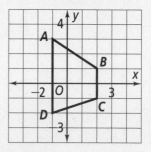

Determine the most precise name for each quadrilateral. Then find its area.

13. $A(-6, 3)$, $B(-2, 0)$, $C(-2, -5)$, $D(-6, -2)$

14. $A(1, 8)$, $B(4, 6)$, $C(1, -2)$, $D(-2, 0)$

15. $A(3, 4)$, $B(8, 1)$, $C(2, -9)$, $D(-3, -6)$

16. $A(0, -1)$, $B(1, 4)$, $C(4, 3)$, $D(3, -2)$

17. $A(-5, 14)$, $B(-2, 11)$, $C(-5, 8)$, $D(-8, 11)$

Determine whether the triangles are congruent. Explain.

18.

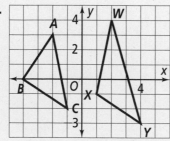

19.

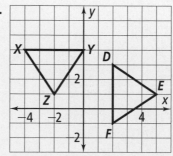

6-7 Standardized Test Prep

Polygons in the Coordinate Plane

Multiple Choice

For Exercises 1–4, choose the correct letter.

1. What kind of triangle is this?

   Ⓐ right

   Ⓑ equilateral

   Ⓒ isosceles

   Ⓓ scalene

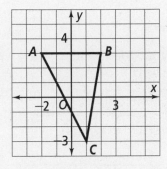

2. What is the most accurate description of the polygon at the right?

   Ⓕ rhombus

   Ⓖ square

   Ⓗ rectangle

   Ⓘ parallelogram

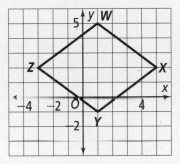

3. What is the most accurate description of the polygon at the right?

   Ⓐ rhombus   Ⓒ kite

   Ⓑ trapezoid   Ⓓ quadrilateral

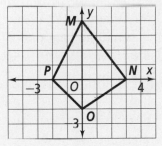

4. What kind of triangle is made by connecting the points $A(0, -6)$, $B(3, -6)$, and $C(3, -2)$?

   Ⓕ equilateral   Ⓗ isosceles

   Ⓖ right   Ⓘ right and isosceles

Short Response

5. What type of quadrilateral is formed by connecting the points $(0, 9)$, $(3, 6)$, $(0, 1)$, and $(-3, 6)$? Explain.

6-8

Think About a Plan

Applying Coordinate Geometry

Plan the coordinate proof of the statement.

The diagonals of a rectangle bisect each other.

Know

1. What does it mean when we say that the diagonals bisect each other?

_____

2. If the diagonals do bisect each other, what should the point of intersection be for each diagonal?

_____

Need

3. Which formula will you need to use to prove that the diagonals bisect each other?

_____

4. Based on the formula you need to use, what type of number should you use for the coordinates of the vertices?

_____

5. Draw rectangle *WXYZ* on the coordinate plane at the right. Include diagonals that intersect at point *Q*. Use variables to write the coordinates for each point.

6. What information is given?

_____

7. What must you prove?

_____

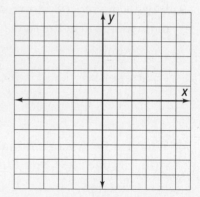

Plan

8. How will you go about proving this?

_____

_____

6-8 Practice   Form G

Applying Coordinate Geometry

Algebra **What are the coordinates of the vertices of each figure?**

1. rectangle with base *b* and height *h*

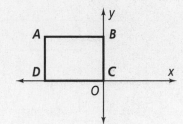

2. rectangle centered at the origin with base 2*b* and height 2*h*

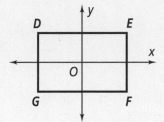

3. square with height *x*

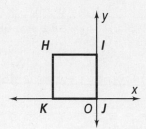

4. parallelogram with height *m* and point *Z* distance *j* from the origin

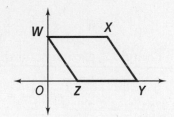

5. kite *MNOP* where $PN = 4s$ and the *y*-axis bisects $\overline{PN}$

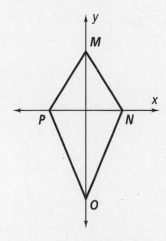

6. isosceles $\triangle ABC$ where $AB = 2n$ and the *y*-axis is the median

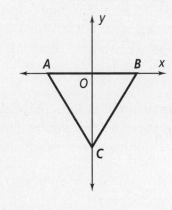

7. How can you determine if a triangle on a coordinate grid is an isosceles triangle?

8. How can you determine if a parallelogram on a coordinate grid is a rhombus?

9. How can you determine if a parallelogram on a coordinate grid is a rectangle?

6-8 Practice (continued)

Applying Coordinate Geometry

Form G

10. In the triangle at the right, A is at $(m + r, s)$, B is at $(2m, -p)$, and C is at $(2r, -p)$. Is this an isosceles triangle? Explain.

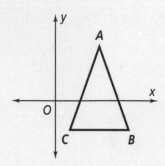

11. Is the trapezoid shown at the right an isosceles trapezoid? Explain.

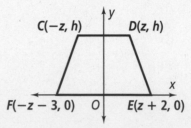

For Exercises 12 and 13, give the coordinates for point X without using any new variables.

12. Kite

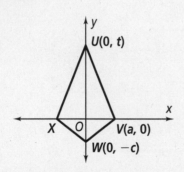

13. $TX = UV$

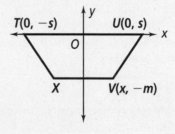

14. Plan a coordinate proof to show that either diagonal of a parallelogram divides the parallelogram into two congruent triangles.
   a. Name the coordinates of parallelogram $ABCD$ at the right.

   b. What do you need to do to show that $\triangle ACD$ and $\triangle CAB$ are congruent?

   c. How will you determine that those parts are congruent?

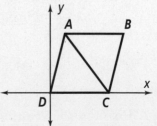

Classify each quadrilateral as precisely as possible.

15. $A(-3a, 3a)$, $B(3a, 3a)$, $C(3a, -3a)$, $D(-3a, -3a)$

16. $A(c, d + e)$, $B(2c, d)$, $C(c, d - 2e)$, $D(0, d)$

6-8 Standardized Test Prep

Applying Coordinate Geometry

Multiple Choice

For Exercises 1–5, choose the correct letter.

1. Rectangle *RECT* is shown at the right. What are the coordinates of point *E*?

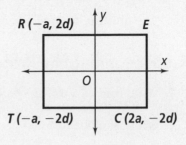

   Ⓐ $(2a, d)$ Ⓒ $(-2a, d)$

   Ⓑ $(a, 2d)$ Ⓓ $(2a, 2d)$

2. Isosceles trapezoid *TRAP* is shown at the right. What are the coordinates of point *T*?

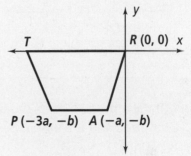

   Ⓕ $(-4a, 0)$ Ⓗ $(0, -4a)$

   Ⓖ $(-b, 0)$ Ⓘ $(-3b, 0)$

3. What type of triangle is shown at the right?

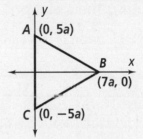

   Ⓐ equilateral   Ⓒ isosceles

   Ⓑ right   Ⓓ scalene

4. What is the most precise description of a quadrilateral with coordinates $A(-a, b)$, $B(3a, b)$, $C(3a, -b)$, $D(-a, -b)$?

   Ⓕ kite   Ⓖ rectangle   Ⓗ rhombus   Ⓘ square

5. Given the parallelogram at the right, what coordinates for point *A* can you write without using any new variables?

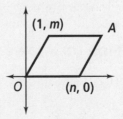

   Ⓐ (n, m) Ⓒ $(n + m, 1)$

   Ⓑ $(1 + n, m)$ Ⓓ $(m, n + 1)$

Short Response

6. What type of quadrilateral is formed by connecting the points $(0, 0)$, $(3x, b)$, $(18x, b)$, and $(15x, 0)$? Explain.

6-9 Think About a Plan

Proofs Using Coordinate Geometry

Use coordinate geometry to prove the following statement.

The altitude to the base of an isosceles triangle bisects the base.

Understanding the Problem

1. What makes a triangle isosceles? _____

2. What is an altitude?

_____

3. What does it mean when we say that the altitude bisects the base?

_____

4. If the altitude bisects the base, what should the point of intersection between the altitude and the base represent? _____

Planning the Solution

5. Which formula will you need to use to prove that the altitude bisects the base?

_____

6. Based on the formula you chose, what type of numbers should the coordinates be? _____

7. Think about how you can draw the triangle on the coordinate plane so that the altitude will intersect $\overline{YZ}$ at $(0, 0)$. Draw isosceles triangle XYZ such that $\overline{XY} \cong \overline{XZ}$. Draw altitude $\overline{XP}$. Use variables to write the coordinates for each point.

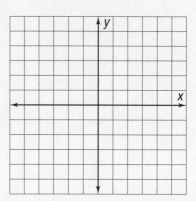

Getting an Answer

8. Use the Midpoint Formula to find the midpoint of $\overline{YZ}$.

$$M = \left(\frac{? + ?}{2}, \frac{? + ?}{2} \right)$$

9. Does the altitude to the base of an isosceles triangle bisect the base? Explain.

_____

_____

6-9   **Practice**   *Form G*

Proofs Using Coordinate Geometry

Use coordinate geometry to prove each statement. Follow the outlined steps.

1. Either diagonal of a parallelogram divides the parallelogram
   into two congruent triangles.

   Given: $\square ABCD$

   Prove: $\triangle ACD \cong \triangle CAB$

   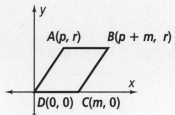

   a. Use the figure at the right. Draw $\overline{AC}$.

   b. Which theorem should you use to show that $\triangle ACD$ and
       $\triangle CAB$ are congruent? Explain.

   c. Which formula(s) will you need to use?

   d. Show that $\triangle ACD$ and $\triangle CAB$ are congruent.

2. The diagonals of a parallelogram bisect one another.

   Given: $\square ABCD$

   Prove: The midpoints of the diagonals are the same.

   a. How will you place the parallelogram in the coordinate plane?

   b. Find the midpoints of $\overline{AC}$ and $\overline{BD}$. What are the coordinates
       of the midpoints?

   c. Are the midpoints the same? Do the diagonals bisect one another?

   d. Reasoning Would using a different parallelogram or labeling the vertices
       differently change your answer? Explain.

3. How can you use coordinate geometry to prove that if the midpoints of a
   square are joined to form a quadrilateral, then the quadrilateral is a
   square? Explain.

6-9

Practice (continued)

Proofs Using Coordinate Geometry

Form G

Tell whether you can reach each conclusion below using coordinate methods. Give a reason for each answer.

4. A triangle is isosceles.

5. The midpoint of the hypotenuse of a right triangle is equidistant from the three vertices.

6. If the midpoints of the sides of an isosceles trapezoid are connected, they will form a parallelogram.

7. The diagonals of a rhombus bisect one another.

Use coordinate geometry to prove each statement.

8. The segments joining the midpoints of a rhombus form a rectangle.

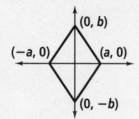

9. The median to the base of an isosceles triangle is perpendicular to the base.

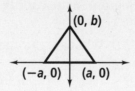

10. The segments joining the midpoints of a quadrilateral form a parallelogram.

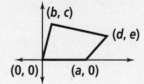

6-9 Standardized Test Prep

Proofs Using Coordinate Geometry

Multiple Choice

For Exercises 1–4, choose the correct letter.

1. Which of the following could you conclude using coordinate geometry?

    A. $\triangle EFG$ is an equilateral triangle.

    B. $m\angle E = 60$

    C. $m\angle F = 99$

    D. $m\angle E = m\angle F$

2. Quadrilateral *TRAP* is shown at the right. Which of the following could you use to show that *TRAP* is a trapezoid?

    F. Prove $RA = TP$.

    G. Prove $\overline{RA} \perp \overline{AP}$.

    H. Prove $\overline{TR} \parallel PA$.

    I. Prove that there are no right angles formed by the line segments.

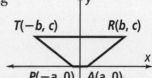

3. Which formula or formulas do you need to use to prove that if the segments connecting the midpoints of a trapezoid are joined they form a parallelogram?

    A. Slope Formula

    B. Distance Formula

    C. Distance Formula and Slope Formula

    D. Slope Formula and Midpoint Formula

4. Which formula or formulas do you need to use to prove that a quadrilateral is an isosceles trapezoid?

    F. Slope Formula

    G. Distance Formula

    H. Distance Formula and Slope Formula

    I. Slope Formula and Midpoint Formula

Short Response

5. How would you use coordinate geometry to prove that two line segments are perpendicular?

7-1
Think About a Plan
Ratios and Proportions

Reasoning The means of a proportion are 4 and 15. List all possible pairs of positive integers that could be the extremes of the proportion.

Understanding the Problem

1. What is a proportion? _____

2. What are some of the forms in which a proportion can be written?

   _____

3. Explain the difference between the means and the extremes of a proportion. Use an example in your explanation.

   _____

   _____

   _____

Planning the Solution

4. How can you write the proportion described in the problem, using variables for the extremes? Should you use the same variable for the extremes or different variables?

   _____

5. How can you rewrite the proportion as equivalent fractions? _____

6. How do you solve for variables in a proportion? Apply this to the proportion you wrote in Step 5. _____

Getting an Answer

7. Look at the equation you wrote in Step 6. How do the two variables on the one side of the equation relate to the value on the other side?

   _____

8. How can you use factoring to find all the positive integers that could represent the values of the variables?

   _____

9. Find the solution to the problem.

   _____

7-1 Practice Form G

Ratios and Proportions

Write the ratio of the first measurement to the second measurement.

1. diameter of a salad plate: 8 in.   diameter of a dinner plate: 1 ft

2. weight of a cupcake: 2 oz   weight of a cake: 2 lb 2 oz

3. garden container width: 2 ft 6 in.   garden container length: 8 ft

4. width of a canoe: 28 in.   length of a canoe: 12 ft 6 in.

5. height of a book: 11 in.   height of a bookshelf: 3 ft 3 in.

6. The perimeter of a rectangle is 280 cm. The ratio of the width to the length is 3 : 4. What is the length of the rectangle?

7. The ratio of country albums to jazz albums in a music collection is 2 : 3. If the music collection has 45 albums, how many are country albums?

8. The lengths of the sides of a triangle are in the extended ratio 3 : 6 : 8. The triangle's perimeter is 510 cm. What are the lengths of the sides?

Algebra Solve each proportion.

9. $\dfrac{x}{4} = \dfrac{13}{52}$

10. $\dfrac{x}{2x + 1} = \dfrac{16}{40}$

11. $\dfrac{9}{10} = \dfrac{9x}{70}$

12. $\dfrac{2}{7} = \dfrac{b + 1}{56}$

13. $\dfrac{11}{y} = \dfrac{9}{27}$

14. $\dfrac{3}{34} = \dfrac{m}{51}$

Use the proportion $\dfrac{x}{z} = \dfrac{6}{5}$. Complete each statement. Justify your answer.

15. $\dfrac{x}{6} = \dfrac{\square}{\square}$

16. $\dfrac{x + z}{z} = \dfrac{\square}{\square}$

17. $\dfrac{z}{x} = \dfrac{\square}{\square}$

18. $5x = \square$

19. The measures of two consecutive angles in a parallelogram are in the ratio 4 : 11. What are the measures of the four angles of the parallelogram?

7-1

Practice (continued)   Form G

Ratios and Proportions

Coordinate Geometry Use the graph. Write each ratio in simplest form.

20. $\dfrac{AB}{BD}$

21. $\dfrac{AE}{EC}$

22. $\dfrac{EC}{BC}$

23. $\dfrac{\text{slope of } \overline{BE}}{\text{slope of } \overline{AE}}$

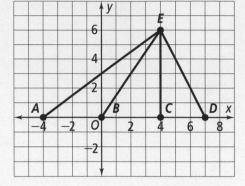

24. A band director needs to purchase new uniforms. The ratio of small to medium to large uniforms is 3 : 4 : 6.

   a. If there are 260 total uniforms to purchase, how many will be small?

   b. How many of these uniforms will be medium?

   c. How many of these uniforms will be large?

25. The measures of two complementary angles are in the ratio 2 : 3. What is the measure of the smaller angle?

26. The measures of two supplementary angles are in the ratio 4 : 11. What is the measure of the larger angle?

27. The means of a proportion are 4 and 17. List all possible pairs of positive integers that could be the extremes of the proportion.

28. The extremes of a proportion are 5 and 14. List all possible pairs of positive integers that could be the means of the proportion.

Algebra Solve each proportion.

29. $\dfrac{(x-1)}{(x+1)} = \dfrac{10}{14}$

30. $\dfrac{7}{50} = \dfrac{x}{30}$

31. **Writing** Explain why solving proportions is an important skill for solving geometry problems.

32. Draw a triangle that satisfies this condition: The ratio of the interior angles is 7 : 11 : 12.

7-1 Standardized Test Prep

Ratios and Proportions

Gridded Response

Solve each exercise and enter your answer on the grid provided.

Use the graph at the right for Exercises 1 and 2.

1. What is $\frac{AD}{AB}$ in simplest form?

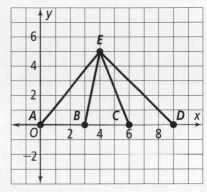

2. What is $\dfrac{\text{slope of } \overline{BE}}{\text{slope of } \overline{AE}}$ in simplest form?

3. What is the value of x in the proportion $\dfrac{(x-1)}{5} = \dfrac{(4x+2)}{35}$?

4. What is the value of x in the proportion $\dfrac{x+1}{x+3} = \dfrac{15}{21}$?

5. The lengths of the sides of a triangle are in the extended ratio $3 : 10 : 12$. The perimeter is 400 cm. What is the length of the longest side in centimeters?

Answers

1.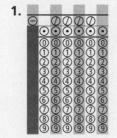
2.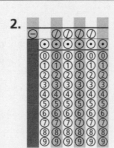
3.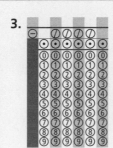
4.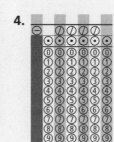
5.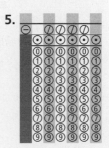

7-2

Think About a Plan

Similar Polygons

Sports Choose a scale and make a scale drawing of a rectangular soccer field that is 110 yd by 60 yd.

1. What is a scale drawing? How does a figure in a scale drawing relate to an actual figure?

   _____

   _____

2. What is a scale? What will the scale of your drawing compare? Write a ratio to represent this.

   _____

   _____

3. To select a scale you need to choose a unit for the drawing. Assuming you are going to make your drawing on a typical sheet of paper, which customary unit of length should you use?_____

4. You have to choose how many yards each unit you chose in Step 3 will represent. The soccer field is 110 yd long. What is the least number of yards each unit can represent and still fit on an 8.5 in.-by-11 in. sheet of paper? Explain. Does this scale make sense for your scale drawing?

   _____

   _____

   _____

5. Choose the scale of your drawing. _____

6. How can you use the scale to write a proportion to find the length of the field in the scale drawing? Write and solve a proportion to find the length of the soccer field in the scale drawing.

   _____

   _____

7. Write and solve a proportion to find the width of the soccer field in the scale drawing.

8. Use a ruler to create the scale drawing on a separate piece of paper.

7-2 **Practice**   Form G
     Similar Polygons

List the pairs of congruent angles and the extended proportion that relates the corresponding sides for the similar polygons.

1. $ABCD \sim WXYZ$

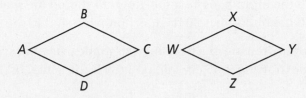

2. $\triangle MNO \sim \triangle RST$

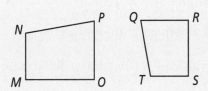

3. $NPOM \sim TQRS$

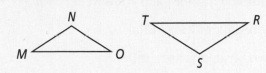

Determine whether the polygons are similar. If so, write a similarity statement and give the scale factor. If not, explain.

4.

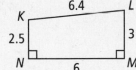

5.

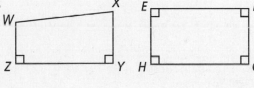

6.

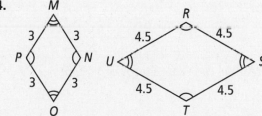

Determine whether the polygons are similar.

7. an equilateral triangle with side length 6 and an equilateral triangle with side length 15

8. a square with side length 4 and a rectangle with width 8 and length 8.5

9. a triangle with side lengths 3 cm, 4 cm, and 5 cm, and a triangle with side lengths 18 cm, 19 cm, and 20 cm

10. a rhombus with side lengths 8 and consecutive angles 50° and 130°, and a rhombus with side lengths 13 and consecutive angles 50° and 130°

7-2

Practice (continued)

Similar Polygons

Form G

11. An architect is making a scale drawing of a building. She uses the scale
1 in. = 15 ft.
   a. If the building is 48 ft tall, how tall should the scale drawing be?
   b. If the building is 90 ft wide, how wide should the scale drawing be?

12. A scale drawing of a building was made using the scale 15 cm = 120 ft. If the
scale drawing is 45 cm tall, how tall is the actual building?

Determine whether each statement is *always*, *sometimes*, or *never* true.

13. Two squares are similar.

14. Two hexagons are similar.

15. Two similar triangles are congruent.

16. A rhombus and a pentagon are similar.

Algebra Find the value of *y*. Give the scale factor of the polygons.

17. $ABCD \sim TSVU$

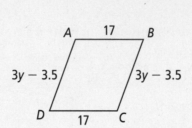
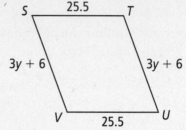

18. The scale factor of *RSTU* to *VWXY* is 14 : 3. What is the scale factor of *VWXY*
to *RSTU*?

In the diagram below, $\triangle PRQ \sim \triangle DEF$. Find each of the following.

19. the scale factor of $\triangle PRQ$ to $\triangle DEF$

20. $m\angle D$

21. $m\angle R$

22. $m\angle P$

23. *DE*

24. *FE*

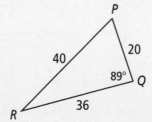
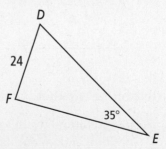

25. Writing Explain why all isosceles right triangles are similar, but not all
scalene right triangles are similar.

7-2

Standardized Test Prep

Similar Polygons

Multiple Choice

For Exercises 1–5, choose the correct letter.

1. You make a scale drawing of a tree using the scale 5 in. = 27 ft. If the tree is 67.5 ft tall, how tall is the scale drawing?

   Ⓐ 10 in.   Ⓑ 11.5 in.   Ⓒ 12 in.   Ⓓ 12.5 in.

2. You make a scale drawing of a garden plot using the scale 2 in. = 17 ft. If the length of a row of vegetables on the drawing is 3 in., how long is the actual row?

   Ⓕ 17 ft   Ⓖ 25.5 ft   Ⓗ 34 ft   Ⓘ 42.5 ft

3. The scale factor of $\triangle RST$ to $\triangle DEC$ is $3 : 13$. What is the scale factor of $\triangle DEC$ to $\triangle RST$?

   Ⓐ 3 : 13   Ⓑ 1 : 39   Ⓒ 39 : 1   Ⓓ 13 : 3

4. $\triangle ACB \sim \triangle FED$. What is the value of x?

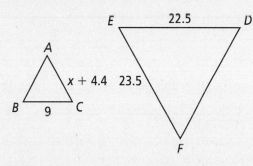

   Ⓕ 4   Ⓖ 4.2   Ⓗ 4.5   Ⓘ 5

5. $MNOP \sim QRST$ with a scale factor of $5 : 4$. $MP = 85$ mm. What is the value of QT?

   Ⓐ 60 mm   Ⓑ 68 mm   Ⓒ 84 mm   Ⓓ 106.25 mm

Short Response

6. Are the triangles at the right similar? Explain.

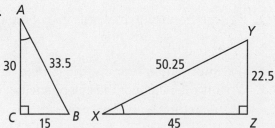

7-3 Think About a Plan

Proving Triangles Similar

Indirect Measurement A 2-ft vertical post casts a 16-in. shadow at the same time a nearby cell phone tower casts a 120-ft shadow. How tall is the cell phone tower?

Know

1. Draw a sketch of the situation described in the problem. Label the sketch with information from the problem and assign a variable to represent the unknown.

2. If you connect the top of each figure to the end of its shadow, what kind of polygons have you formed? How are these polygons related?

   _____

3. Which parts of the polygons are corresponding?

   _____

   _____

Need

4. In your diagram, which corresponding parts have different units?

   _____

5. What must you do so that corresponding parts have the same units? Which unit does it make the most sense to change? Explain.

   _____

   _____

6. Change the units and update your diagram.

Plan

7. Write a proportion in words that compares the corresponding parts.

8. Use information from the diagram to write and solve a numerical proportion. What is the height of the cell phone tower?

7-3

Practice

Form G

Proving Triangles Similar

Determine whether the triangles are similar. If so, write a similarity statement and name the postulate or theorem you used. If not, explain.

1.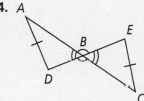

2.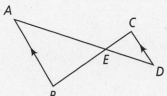

3.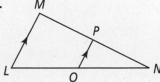

4.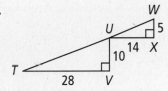

5.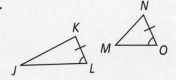

6.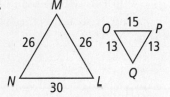

7. **Given:** $\overline{RM} \parallel \overline{SN}$, $\overline{RM} \perp \overline{MS}$, $\overline{SN} \perp \overline{NT}$

   Prove: $\triangle RSM \sim \triangle STN$

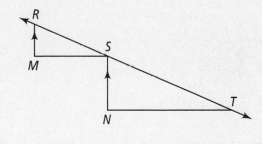

8. **Given:** A bisects $\overline{JK}$, C bisects $\overline{KL}$, B bisects $\overline{JL}$

   Prove: $\triangle JKL \sim \triangle CBA$

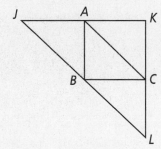

9. A 1.4-m tall child is standing next to a flagpole. The child's shadow is 1.2 m long. At the same time, the shadow of the flagpole is 7.5 m long. How tall is the flagpole?

7-3

Practice (continued)
Proving Triangles Similar

Form G

Explain why the triangles are similar. Then find the value of x.

10. $\overline{OP} \cong \overline{NP}$, $KN = 15$,
$LO = 20$, $JN = 9$,
$MO = 12$

11.

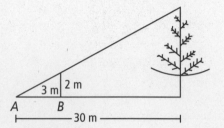

12. A stick 2 m long is placed vertically at point B. The top of the stick is in line with the top of a tree as seen from point A, which is 3 m from the stick and 30 m from the tree. How tall is the tree?

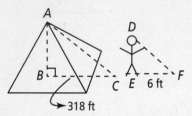

13. Thales was an ancient philosopher familiar with similar triangles. One story about him says that he found the height of a pyramid by measuring its shadow and his own shadow at the same time. If the person is 5-ft tall, what is the height of the pyramid in the drawing?

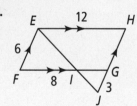

Identify the similar triangles in each figure. Explain.

14.

15.

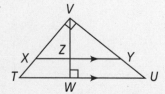

16.

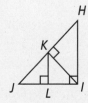

17.

7-3 Standardized Test Prep
Proving Triangles Similar

Multiple Choice

For Exercises 1–3, choose the correct letter.

1. Which pair of triangles can be proven similar by the AA ~ Postulate?

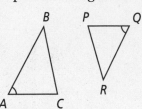
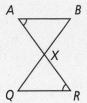

Ⓐ
Ⓒ
Ⓑ
Ⓓ

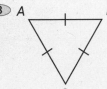

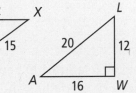

2. △AXY ~ △ABC. What is the value of x?

Ⓕ $10\frac{1}{5}$ Ⓗ $11\frac{1}{3}$

Ⓖ 19   Ⓘ $28\frac{1}{3}$

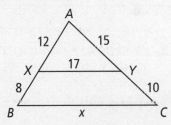

3. △LMN ~ △PON. What is the value of x?

Ⓐ 36   Ⓒ 25

Ⓑ 20   Ⓓ $28\frac{1}{3}$

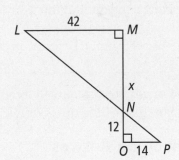

Short Response

4. Irene places a mirror on the ground 24 ft from the base of an oak tree. She walks backward until she can see the top of the tree in the middle of the mirror. At that point, Irene's eyes are 5.5 ft above the ground, and her feet are 4 ft from the mirror. How tall is the oak tree? Explain.

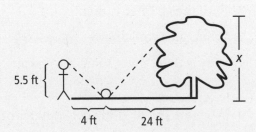

7-4

Think About a Plan

Similarity in Right Triangles

Coordinate Geometry $\overline{CD}$ is the altitude to the hypotenuse of right $\triangle ABC$. The coordinates of A, D, and B are $(4, 2)$, $(4, 6)$, and $(4, 15)$, respectively. Find all possible coordinates of point C.

Understanding the Problem

1. What is an altitude? _____

   _____

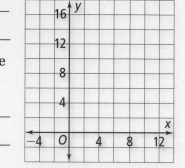

2. Plot the points given in the problem on the grid. Which side of the triangle must $\overline{AB}$ be? Explain.

   _____

   _____

3. What is the special relationship between the altitude to a hypotenuse of a right triangle and the lengths of the segments it creates? _____

   _____

4. What does the phrase "Find all possible coordinates of point C" tell you about the problem? _____

Planning the Solution

5. How can you find the geometric mean of a pair of numbers?

   _____

   _____

6. For which numbers or lengths are you finding the geometric mean? How can you determine the geometric mean? _____

Getting an Answer

7. Find the geometric mean.

8. What does your answer represent?

9. Why is there more than one possible correct answer?

   _____

10. What are the possible coordinates of point C?

7-4 Practice   Form G
Similarity in Right Triangles

Identify the following in right △QRS.

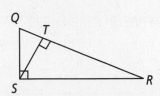

1. the hypotenuse

2. the segments of the hypotenuse

3. the altitude

4. the segment of the hypotenuse adjacent to leg $\overline{QS}$

Write a similarity statement relating the three triangles in the diagram.

5.

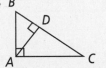

6.

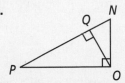

7.

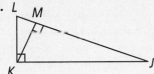

8.

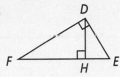

9.

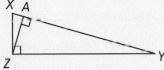

10.

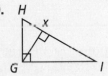

Algebra Find the geometric mean of each pair of numbers.

11. 9 and 4   **12.** 14 and 6   **13.** 9 and 30

14. 25 and 49   **15.** 4 and 120   **16.** 9 and 18

17. 16 and 64   **18.** 5 and 25   **19.** 12 and 16

Use the figure at the right to complete each proportion.

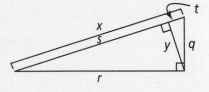

20. $\dfrac{q}{r} = \dfrac{\square}{y}$ **21.** $\dfrac{s}{y} = \dfrac{\square}{t}$ **22.** $\dfrac{t}{q} = \dfrac{q}{\square}$

23. $\dfrac{q}{x} = \dfrac{t}{\square}$ **24.** $\dfrac{s}{r} = \dfrac{\square}{q}$ **25.** $\dfrac{\square}{r} = \dfrac{r}{x}$

7-4

Practice (continued)   Form G

Similarity in Right Triangles

Algebra Solve for the value of the variables in each right triangle.

26.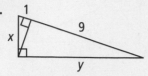

27.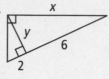

28.

29.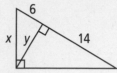

30.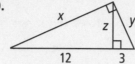

31.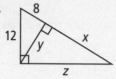

The diagram shows the parts of a right triangle with an altitude to the hypotenuse. For the two given measures, find the other four. Use simplest radical form.

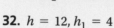

32. $h = 12, h_1 = 4$

33. $a = 6, h_2 = 9$

34. $\ell_1 = 6\sqrt{3}, h_2 = 3$

35. $h_1 = 5, \ell_2 = 2\sqrt{51}$

36. The altitude of the hypotenuse of a right triangle divides the hypotenuse into 45 in. and 5 in. segments. What is the length of the altitude?

37. **Error Analysis** A classmate writes an incorrect proportion to find x. Explain and correct the error.

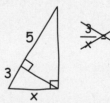

38. **Draw a Diagram** The sides of a right triangle measure $6\sqrt{3}$ in., 6 in., and 12 in. If an altitude is drawn from the right angle to the hypotenuse, what is the length of the segment of the hypotenuse adjacent to the shorter leg? What is the length of the altitude?

7-4 | Standardized Test Prep

Similarity in Right Triangles

Multiple Choice

For Exercises 1–5, choose the correct letter.

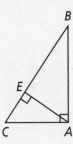

1. Which segment of the hypotenuse is adjacent to $\overline{AB}$?

   (A) $\overline{EC}$ (B) $\overline{AC}$ (C) $\overline{AE}$ (D) $\overline{BE}$

2. What is the geometric mean of 7 and 12?

   (F) $1\frac{5}{7}$ (G) 9.5   (H) $2\sqrt{21}$ (I) $4\sqrt{21}$

3. Which similarity statement is true?

   (A) $\triangle WYZ \sim \triangle XZW \sim \triangle XYZ$

   (B) $\triangle WYZ \sim \triangle WZX \sim \triangle ZYX$

   (C) $\triangle YZW \sim \triangle XZW \sim \triangle XZY$

   (D) $\triangle YZW \sim \triangle ZXW \sim \triangle ZYX$

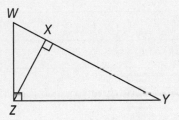

4. What is the value of x?

   (F) $2\sqrt{3}$ (H) 4

   (G) $4\sqrt{3}$ (I) 6

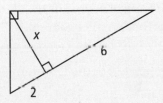

5. The altitude of the hypotenuse of a right triangle divides the hypotenuse into segments of lengths 14 and 8. What is the length of the altitude?

   (A) $2\sqrt{77}$ (B) $4\sqrt{7}$ (C) $4\sqrt{11}$ (D) 11

Extended Response

6. What is the perimeter of the large triangle shown at the right? Show your work.

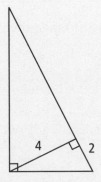

7-5 Think About a Plan

Proportions in Triangles

An angle bisector of a triangle divides the opposite side of the triangle into segments 5 cm and 3 cm long. A second side of the triangle is 7.5 cm long. Find all possible lengths for the third side of the triangle.

1. What is the Triangle-Angle-Bisector Theorem? What relationships does it specifically describe?

_____

_____

_____

2. What information is given in this problem? What information is not given?

_____

_____

_____

3. What does the phrase "all possible lengths" tell you about the problem?

_____

4. In the space below, draw all the possible representations of the triangle described in the problem.

5. How can proportions be used to solve this problem?

_____

6. How many proportions will you need to set up? Explain.

_____

_____

7. Use the space below to write and solve the proportions.

8. What are the possible lengths for the third side of the triangle?

7-5

Practice

Form G

Proportions in Triangles

Use the figure at the right to complete each proportion.

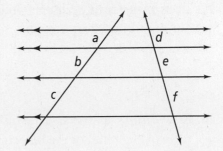

1. $\dfrac{a}{c} = \dfrac{\square}{f}$ 2. $\dfrac{f}{e} = \dfrac{c}{\square}$ 3. $\dfrac{\square}{c} = \dfrac{e}{f}$

4. $\dfrac{a}{\square} = \dfrac{b}{e}$ 5. $\dfrac{a}{b} = \dfrac{\square}{e}$ 6. $\dfrac{e}{\square} = \dfrac{f}{c}$

Algebra Solve for *x*.

7.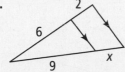

8.

9.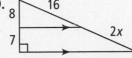

10.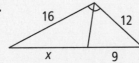

11.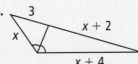

12.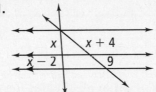

13.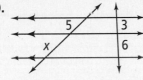

14.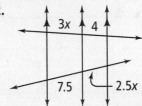

15.

16.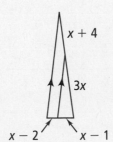

17.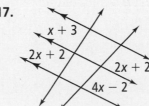

18.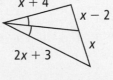

7-5

Practice (continued)   Form G

Proportions in Triangles

19. Compare and Contrast How is the Triangle-Angle-Bisector Theorem similar to Corollary 2 of Theorem 7-3? How is it different?

20. Reasoning In $\triangle FGH$, the bisector of $\angle F$ also bisects the opposite side. The ratio of each half of the bisected side to each of the other sides is $1 : 2$. What type of triangle is $\triangle FGH$? Explain.

21. Error Analysis Your classmate says you can use the Triangle-Angle-Bisector Theorem to find the value of x in the diagram. Explain what is wrong with your classmate's statement.

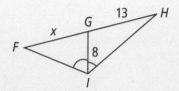

22. Reasoning An angle bisector of a triangle divides the opposite side of the triangle into segments 3 in. and 6 in. long. A second side of the triangle is 5 in. long. Find the length of the third side of the triangle. Explain how you arrived at the correct length.

23. The flag of Antigua and Barbuda is like the image at the right. In the image, $\overline{DE} \parallel \overline{CF} \parallel \overline{BG}$.

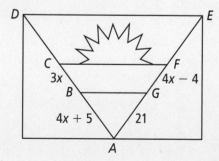

   a. An artist has made a sketch of the flag for a mural. The measures indicate the length of the lines in feet. What is the value of x?

   b. What type of triangle is $\triangle ACF$? Explain.

   c. Given: $\overline{DE} \parallel \overline{CF} \parallel \overline{BG}$

       Prove: $\triangle ABG \sim \triangle ACF \sim \triangle ADE$

7-5 Standardized Test Prep

Proportions in Triangles

Multiple Choice

For Exercises 1–5, choose the correct letter.

For Exercises 1 and 2, use the diagram at the right.

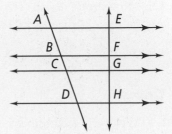

1. Which makes the proportion true? $\dfrac{AB}{\square} = \dfrac{EF}{GH}$

    Ⓐ AD Ⓒ CD

    Ⓑ DH Ⓓ BC

2. Which proportion is *not* true?

  Ⓕ $\dfrac{BC}{CD} = \dfrac{FG}{GH}$ Ⓖ $\dfrac{AC}{CD} = \dfrac{EG}{GH}$ Ⓗ $\dfrac{BD}{FH} = \dfrac{AD}{EH}$ Ⓘ $\dfrac{AB}{AE} = \dfrac{EF}{BF}$

3. What is the value of y?

    Ⓐ 2   Ⓒ 3

    Ⓑ 4   Ⓓ 6

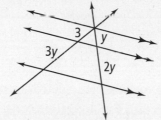

4. What is the value of x?

    Ⓕ 3   Ⓗ 6

    Ⓖ 8   Ⓘ 12

5. In $\triangle DEF$, the bisector of $\angle F$ divides the opposite sides into segments that are 4 and 9 in. long. The side of the triangle adjacent to the 4 in. segment is 6 in. long. To the nearest tenth of an inch, how long is the third side of the triangle?

    Ⓐ 2.7 in.   Ⓑ 6 in.   Ⓒ 13 in.   Ⓓ 13.5 in.

Short Response

6. In $\triangle QRS$, $\overline{XY} \parallel \overline{SR}$. $\overline{XY}$ divides $\overline{QR}$ and $\overline{QS}$ into segments as follows: $\overline{SX} = 3$, $\overline{XQ} = 2x$, $\overline{RY} = 4.5$, and $\overline{YQ} = 7.5$. Write a proportion to find x. What is the length of $\overline{QS}$?

8-1 Think About a Plan

The Pythagorean Theorem and Its Converse

Astronomy The Hubble Space Telescope orbits 600 km above Earth's surface. Earth's radius is about 6370 km. Use the Pythagorean Theorem to find the distance x from the telescope to Earth's horizon. Round your answer to the nearest ten kilometers. (Diagram is not to scale.)

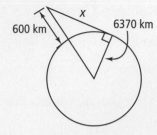

Know

1. Write the Pythagorean Theorem.

2. Look at the diagram. What could replace a and b in the Pythagorean Theorem?

_____

Need

3. How can you find the value of c, the hypotenuse of the right triangle?

_____

4. What is the value of c?

5. Substitute the known and unknown values for a, b, and c.

Plan

6. How can you find the value of x^2?

_____

7. What is the value of x^2?

8. How can you find the value of x?

_____

9. What is the value of x, to the nearest 10 kilometers?

10. Is your answer reasonable? Explain.

_____

8-1 Practice   Form G

The Pythagorean Theorem and Its Converse

Algebra Find the value of *y*. Express in simplest radical form.

1.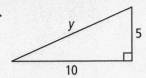

2.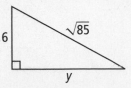

3.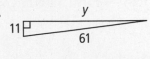

4.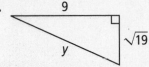

5.

6.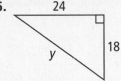

The lengths of the sides of a triangle are given. Classify each triangle as *acute,*
right, or *obtuse.*

7. 3, 8, 10   **8.** 4, 5, 7   **9.** 12, 15, 19

10. 10, 24, 26   **11.** 20, 21, 28   **12.** 20, 48, 52

13. A square has side length 10 yd. What is the length of a diagonal of the square?
Express in simplest radical form.

14. A square has diagonal length 9 m. What is the side length of the square, to the
nearest centimeter?

15. A repairman leans the top of an 8-ft ladder against the top of a stone wall. The
base of the ladder is 5.5 ft from the wall. About how tall is the wall? Round to
the nearest tenth of a foot.

16. Writing When field archeologists plan an excavation,
or digging site, they place a rectangular grid over the
surface to be dug up. An archeologist decides that the
dimensions of such a grid will be 11 m by 15 m. She will
place stakes at the corners of the grid. How can she make
sure that she places the stakes in the correct location? Explain.

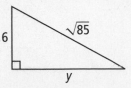

Corner 1   Corner 2

Corner 4   Corner 3

17. A river runs straight through the center of a park. A man stands on one bank
of the river, and his daughter stands across the river and 22 ft upstream. The
man's son swims from the man to his daughter. If the river is 11 ft wide, how
far does the son swim? Round to the nearest foot.

8-1

Practice (continued)   Form G

The Pythagorean Theorem and Its Converse

For each pair of numbers, find a third whole number such that the three numbers form a Pythagorean triple.

18. 13, 84

19. 16, 12

20. 32, 60

21. 80, 18

22. 99, 20

23. 75, 100

Is each triangle a right triangle? Explain.

24.
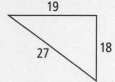

25.

26.
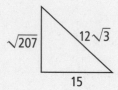

27.

28. A square is drawn inside a circle so that its vertices touch the circle. If the radius of the circle is 15 cm, what is the perimeter of the square?

29. The playing surface of a football field is 300 ft long and 160 ft wide. If a player runs from one corner of the field to the opposite corner, how many feet does he run?

30. A line of roses forms the diagonal of a rectangular flower garden. The line of roses is 18.4 m long, and one side of the garden is 13 m long. To the nearest tenth of a meter, what is the length of a perpendicular side of the garden?

31. $\triangle ABC$ is an acute triangle. Two of its sides measure 11 cm and 14 cm. What is the range of possible values for its third side?

32. $\triangle EFG$ is an obtuse triangle. Two of its sides measure 13 cm and 7 cm. What is the range of possible values for its third side to the nearest tenth of a centimeter?

33. The International Space Station orbits 350 km above Earth's surface. Earth's radius is about 6370 km. Use the Pythagorean Theorem to find the distance from the space station to Earth's horizon. Round your answer to the nearest 10 kilometers. (Diagram is not to scale.)

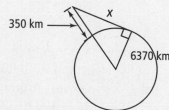

8-1 Standardized Test Prep

The Pythagorean Theorem and Its Converse

Gridded Response

Solve each exercise and enter your answer on the grid provided.
What is the value of *x*?

1.
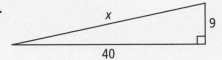

2.
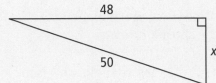

3.
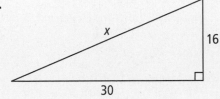

4.
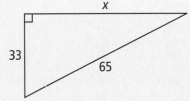

5. An acute triangle has sides that are 14 mm and 97 mm long,
respectively. The third side of the triangle must be greater than
what whole number of millimeters?

Answers

1.
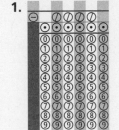

2.

3.

4.
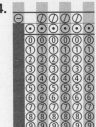

5.

8-2 Think About a Plan

Special Right Triangles

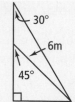

House Repair After heavy winds damaged a house, workers placed a 6-m brace against its side at a 45° angle. Then, at the same spot on the ground, they placed a second, longer brace to make a 30° angle with the side of the house.

   a. How long is the longer brace? Round to the nearest tenth of a meter.

   b. About how much higher does the longer brace reach than the shorter brace?

1. In a 45°-45°-90° triangle, how is the length of the hypotenuse related to the length of each leg? Write this information in an equation. _____

 _____

2. What is the distance from the bottom of the brace to the house? Round to the nearest tenth of a meter.

3. In a 30°-60°-90° triangle, how are the hypotenuse and leg lengths related? Write this information in two equations. _____

 _____

4. What do the legs and hypotenuse of the 30°-60°-90° triangle represent with respect to the brace, the house, and the ground? Which of these lengths do you know? _____

 _____

 _____

5. What is the length of the longer brace? Round to the nearest tenth of a meter.

6. What is the distance from the top of the shorter brace to the ground? Round to the nearest tenth of a meter.

7. How can you find the distance from the top of the longer brace to the ground? What is this distance? Round to the nearest tenth of a meter. _____

 _____

8. How can you find how much higher the longer brace reaches than the shorter brace? What is this distance? _____

 _____

8-2 Practice

Special Right Triangles

Form G

Find the value of each variable. If your answer is not an integer, express it in simplest radical form.

1.
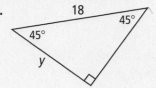

2.
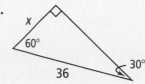

3.
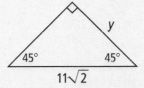

4.

5.

6.
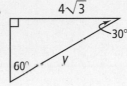

The side lengths of a triangle are given. Determine if the triangle is a 45°-45°-90° triangle, a 30°-60°-90° triangle, or neither.

7. 40, 50, 80

8. $31, 31\sqrt{2}, 62$

9. $6\sqrt{2}, 6\sqrt{2}, 12$

10. $11, 11\sqrt{3}, 22$

11. A square has side length 95. What is the length of the diagonal of the square? Express your answer in simplest radical form.

12. A square has diagonal length 13 m. What is the side length of the square, to the nearest centimeter?

13. A professional baseball diamond is a square. The distance from base to base is 90 ft. To the nearest foot, how far does a catcher standing at home plate throw the ball across the diagonal of the square to second base?

14. Children climb 8 ft to get to the top of a slide. The end of the slide is 1 ft above the ground and the slide rises at a 45° angle. If the slide makes a straight line from the top to the bottom, how far does a child travel down the slide? Round to the nearest foot.

8-2

Practice (continued)   Form G

Special Right Triangles

15. You set up a makeshift greenhouse by leaning a square pane of glass against a building. The glass is 4.5 ft long, and it makes a 30° angle with the ground. How much horizontal distance between the building and the glass is there to grow plants? Round to the nearest inch.

16. A square tablecloth has a line of embroidered flowers along the diagonal. The tablecloth is 48 in. on each side. How long is the embroidery line? Round to the nearest inch.

17. An equilateral triangle has height 26 cm. What is the length of each side of the triangle, to the nearest centimeter?

Find the value of each variable. If your answer is not an integer, express it in simplest radical form.

18.

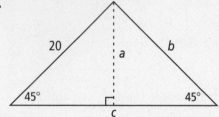

19.

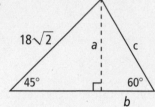

20.

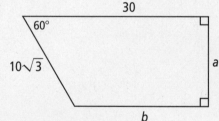

21.

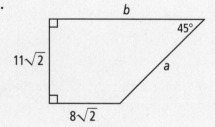

22. Right triangle *ABC* has area $32\sqrt{3}$ cm². The measure of $\angle A = 30$, $m\angle B = 90$. What is the length of *BC*? *AB*? *AC*? Express all answers in simplest radical form.

23. An equilateral triangle has perimeter 120 in. What is the area of the triangle? Express your answer in simplest radical form.

24. Open-Ended Write a real-life problem that you can solve using a 45°-45°-90° triangle with an 18-ft hypotenuse. Show your solution.

8-2

Standardized Test Prep

Special Right Triangles

Multiple Choice

For Exercises 1–5, choose the correct letter.

1. What is the value of *s*?

   Ⓐ 8   Ⓒ $16\sqrt{2}$

   Ⓑ 16   Ⓓ 32

   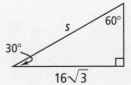

2. What are the angle measures of the triangle?

   Ⓕ 30°, 60°, and 90°   Ⓗ 60°, 60°, and 60°

   Ⓖ 45°, 45°, and 90°   Ⓘ They cannot be determined.

   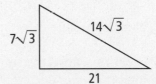

3. What is the value of *p*?

   Ⓐ 22   Ⓒ 44

   Ⓑ $22\sqrt{2}$ Ⓓ $44\sqrt{3}$

   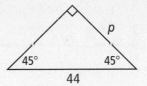

4. In the center of town there is a square park with side length 30 ft. If a person walks from one corner of the park to the opposite corner, how far does the person walk? Round to the nearest foot.

   Ⓕ 21 ft   Ⓖ 42 ft   Ⓗ 52 ft   Ⓘ 60 ft

5. An equilateral triangle has an altitude of 15 m. What is the perimeter of the triangle?

   Ⓐ $30\sqrt{2}$ m   Ⓑ 45 m   Ⓒ $30\sqrt{3}$ m   Ⓓ $60\sqrt{3}$ m

Short Response

6. The hypotenuse of a 30°-60°-90° triangle is 24.2 ft. Explain how to find the lengths of the legs of the triangle.

8-3 Think About a Plan

Trigonometry

Find the values of *w* and then *x*. Round lengths to the nearest tenth and angle measures to the nearest degree.

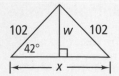

1. What type of triangle is the largest triangle? Explain.

_____

2. The measure of one of the base angles is given. What is the measure of the other base angle? Explain.

_____

3. What is the sine of an angle?

4. Focus on one of the smaller triangles. Write an equation relating sin 42° and *w*.

5. How can you find the value of *w*? What is this value? Round to the nearest tenth.

_____

6. Look at one of the smaller triangles. What is the measure of the angle between side *w* and the side with length 102? Explain.

_____

_____

7. What is the length of the third side (the base) of one of the small triangles in terms of *x*? Explain.

_____

8. Focus on one of the smaller triangles. Write an equation for the length of the third side, in terms of *x*, using the sine function.

9. How can you find the value of *x*? What is this value? Round to the nearest tenth.

_____

_____

10. How could you use tan 48° to check your answer?

_____

_____

8-3

Practice

Form G

Trigonometry

Write the ratios for sin _X_, cos _X_, and tan _X_.

1.

2.

3.

Find the value of _x_. Round to the nearest tenth.

4.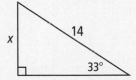

5.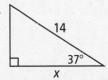

6.

7.

8. An escalator at a shopping center is 200 ft 9 in. long, and rises at an angle of 15°. What is the vertical rise of the escalator? Round to the nearest inch.

9. A 12-ft-long ladder is leaning against a wall and makes a 77° angle with the ground. How high does the ladder reach on the wall? Round to the nearest inch.

10. A straight ramp rises at an angle of 25.5° and has a base 30 ft long. How high is the ramp? Round to the nearest foot.

Find the value of _x_. Round to the nearest degree.

11.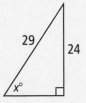

12.

13.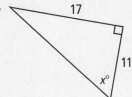

14.

8-3

Practice (continued)   *Form G*

Trigonometry

15. The lengths of the diagonals of a rhombus are 4 in. and 7 in. Find the measures of the angles of the rhombus to the nearest degree.

16. The lengths of the diagonals of a rhombus are 5 in. and 8 in. Find the measures of the angles of the rhombus to the nearest degree.

Find the values of *w* and then *x*. Round lengths to the nearest tenth and angle measures to the nearest degree.

17.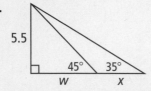

18.

19. Writing Explain why tan 45° = 1.

The sine, cosine, and tangent ratios each have a reciprocal ratio. The reciprocal ratios are cosecant (csc), secant (sec), and cotangent (cot). Use $\triangle DEF$ and the definitions below to write each ratio.

$$\csc X = \frac{1}{\sin X} \qquad\qquad \sec X = \frac{1}{\cos X} \qquad\qquad \cot X = \frac{1}{\tan X}$$

```
        F
       |
   18 /| 16
     / |
    /  |
  D  8  E
```

20. csc *D*   **21.** sec *D*   **22.** cot *D*

23. csc *F*   **24.** sec *F*   **25.** cot *F*

26. An *identity* is an equation that is true for all the allowed values of the variable. Use what you know about trigonometric ratios to show that the equation $\cot X = \dfrac{\cos X}{\sin X}$ is an identity.

27. Reasoning Does sin *A* + sin *B* = sin (*A* + *B*) when 0 < *A* + *B* < 90? Explain your reasoning.

28. A right triangle has a hypotenuse of length 10 and one leg of length 7. Find the length of the other leg and the measures of the acute angles in the triangle. Round your answers to the nearest tenth

29. A right triangle has an angle that measures 28. The leg opposite the 28° angle measures 13. Find the length of the other leg and the hypotenuse. Round your answers to the nearest tenth.

8-3

Standardized Test Prep

Trigonometry

Multiple Choice

For Exercises 1–6, choose the correct letter.

1. What is the value of sin *N*?

   Ⓐ $\frac{1}{2}$ Ⓒ $\frac{\sqrt{3}}{2}$

   Ⓑ $\frac{\sqrt{3}}{3}$ Ⓓ $\sqrt{3}$

2. What is the value of *x* to the nearest tenth?

   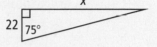

   Ⓕ 5.7   Ⓗ 30.3

   Ⓖ 21.2   Ⓘ 82.1

3. What is the value of *x* to the nearest degree?

   Ⓐ 18   Ⓒ 71

   Ⓑ 19   Ⓓ 72

4. A 14-ft-long ramp rises at an angle of 22.2°. How long is the base of the ramp to the nearest foot?

   Ⓕ 11 ft   Ⓖ 13 ft   Ⓗ 17 ft   Ⓘ 22 ft

5. What is the value of *w* to the nearest degree?

   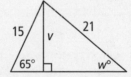

   Ⓐ 25   Ⓒ 40

   Ⓑ 35   Ⓓ 45

6. A right triangle has an angle that measures 34 and the adjacent side measures 17. What is the length of the hypotenuse to the nearest tenth?

   Ⓕ 20.5   Ⓖ 25.2   Ⓗ 30.4   Ⓘ 34

Short Response

7. A 12-ft-long ladder is leaning against a wall and makes an 80° angle with the ground. How high up the wall does the ladder reach, and how far is the base of the ladder from the base of the wall? Round to the nearest inch.

Name _____ Class _____ Date _____

8-4 Think About a Plan

Angles of Elevation and Depression

The world's tallest unsupported flagpole is a 282-ft-tall steel pole in Surrey, British Columbia. The shortest shadow cast by the pole during the year is 137 ft long. To the nearest degree, what is the angle of elevation of the sun when casting the flagpole's shortest shadow?

Know

1. Draw a sketch using the information given in the problem. Draw an arrow pointing to the angle of elevation.

2. Describe the triangle in your drawing. In general terms, what are the lengths of the legs and the hypotenuse?

_____

_____

_____

Need

3. Where is the angle of elevation?

_____

4. What is the tangent ratio?

Plan

5. Assign the variable x to the angle of elevation. What is the tangent of the angle of elevation?

6. How can you use the inverse tangent to find the angle of elevation?

_____

8-4 Practice   Form G
Angles of Elevation and Depression

Describe each angle as it relates to the situation in the diagram.

1. ∠1   **2.** ∠2   **3.** ∠3   **4.** ∠4

5. ∠5   **6.** ∠6   **7.** ∠7   **8.** ∠8

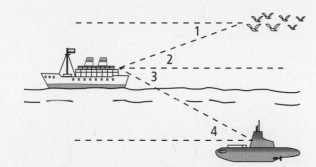

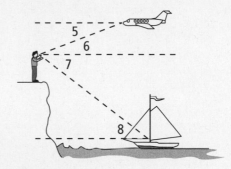

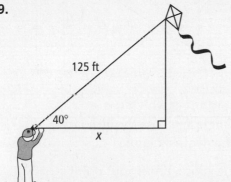

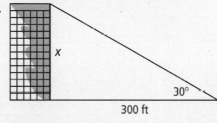

Find the value of x. Round to the nearest tenth of a unit.

9.

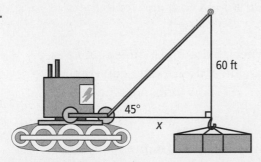

10.

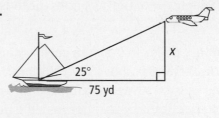

11.

12.

13. A person is standing 40 ft from a flagpole and can see the top of the pole at a 35° angle of elevation. The person's eye level is 4 ft from the ground. What is the height of the flagpole to the nearest foot?

14. An eagle perched 40 ft up in a tree looks down at a 35° angle and spots a vole. How far is the vole from the eagle to the nearest tenth of a foot?

8-4

Practice (continued)   *Form G*

Angles of Elevation and Depression

15. You stand 40 ft from a tree. The angle of elevation from your eyes (5 ft above the ground) to the top of the tree is 47°. How tall is the tree? Round your answer to the nearest foot.

Find the value of *x*. Round to the nearest tenth of a unit.

16.

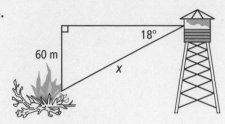

17.

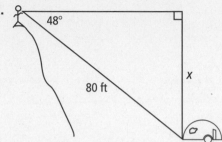

18.

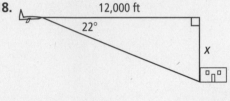

19.

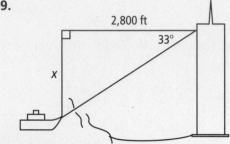

20. An airplane is flying at an altitude of 10,000 ft. The airport at which it is scheduled to land is 50 mi away. Find the average angle at which the airplane must descend for landing. Round your answer to the nearest degree.

21. A lake measures 600 ft across. A lodge stands on one shore. From your point on the opposite shore, the angle of elevation to the top of the lodge is 4°. How high above the lake does the lodge stand? Round your answer to the nearest foot.

22. A library needs to build an access ramp for wheelchairs. The main entrance to the library is 8 ft above sidewalk level. If the architect designs the slope of the ramp in such a way that the angle of elevation is 5°, how long must the access ramp be? Round your answer to the nearest foot.

Algebra The angle of elevation *e* from *A* to *B* and the angle of depression *d* from *B* to *A* are given. Find the measure of each angle.

23. *e*: $(3x + 6)°$, *d*: $(x + 20)°$

24. *e*: $(6x + 3)°$, *d*: $3(x + 6)°$

25. *e*: $(3x - 4)°$, *d*: $2(x + 7)°$

26. *e*: $(5x - 8)°$, *d*: $3(x + 4)°$

8-4 Standardized Test Prep

Angles of Elevation and Depression

Multiple Choice

For Exercises 1–5, choose the correct letter.

1. A person can see the top of a building at an angle of 65°. The person is standing 50 ft away from the building and has an eye level of 5 ft. How tall is the building to the nearest tenth of a foot?

   A 26.1 ft   B 50.3 ft   C 107.2 ft   D 112.2 ft

2. A fire ranger on a 150-ft-tall tower spots a fire at a 30° angle of depression. How many feet away from the tower is the fire to the nearest tenth?

   F 86.6 ft   G 129.9 ft   H 259.8 ft   I 300 ft

3. What is the value of *x* to the nearest foot?

   A 6713 ft   C 10,443 ft

   B 9534 ft   D 12,445 ft

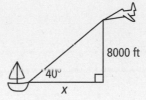

4. What is the value of *x* to the nearest foot?

   F 2097 ft   H 3108 ft

   G 2529 ft   I 6706 ft

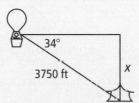

5. A wildlife biologist looks up at a 78° angle of elevation to see a flock of geese in the air. The biologist is standing 200 ft away from a place directly underneath the geese. How high are the geese flying, to the nearest tenth of a foot?

   A 195.6 ft   B 204.5 ft   C 940.9 ft   D 961.9 ft

Extended Response

6. Two buildings stand 90 ft apart at their closest points. At those points, the angle of depression from the top of the taller building to the top of the shorter building is 12°. How much taller is the taller building? Draw a diagram to support your answer. Round your answer to the nearest foot. Explain.

8-5 | Think About a Plan

Law of Sines

A zipline is constructed over a ravine as shown in the diagram below. What is the horizontal distance x from the bottom of the ladder to the platform where the zipline ends? Round your answer to the nearest tenth of a foot.

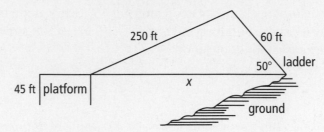

1. Based on the diagram provided for this problem, which measures in the triangle do you know?

   _____

   _____

2. What are the values of these measures?

   _____

   _____

3. Describe the part of the triangle you need to find.

   _____

   _____

4. Can you find the measure of this part of the triangle directly using the Law of Sines? If not, what can you find?

   _____

   _____

5. What steps do you need to take to find the measure of this part of the triangle?

   _____

   _____

   _____

6. What is the horizontal distance, x?

   _____

8-5

Practice

Form G

Law of Sines

Use the information given to solve.

1. In $\triangle ABC$, $m\angle A = 40$, $m\angle C = 70$, and $BC = 8.5$. To the nearest tenth, what is AB?

2. In $\triangle PQR$, $m\angle P = 33$, $m\angle Q = 82$, and $PR = 14.2$. To the nearest tenth, what is the length of $\overline{QR}$?

3. In $\triangle GHK$, $m\angle G = 105$, $m\angle K = 32$, and $GH = 10.2$. To the nearest tenth, what is GK?

4. In $\triangle XYZ$, $m\angle Y = 76$, $XY = 15$, and $XZ = 19$. To the nearest tenth, what is $m\angle Z$?

5. In $\triangle ABC$, $m\angle B = 93$, $AC = 15$, and $BC = 10$. To the nearest tenth, what is $m\angle A$?

6. In $\triangle DEF$, $m\angle D = 35$, $DE = 6.3$, and $EF = 7.5$. To the nearest tenth, what is $m\angle F$?

Use the Law of Sines to find the values of x and y. Round to the nearest tenth.

7.

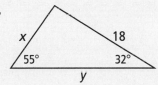

8.

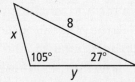

9.

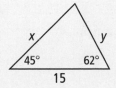

10.

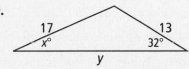

11.

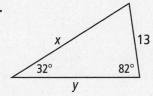

12.

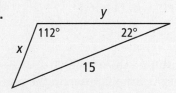

13.

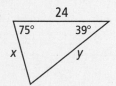

14.

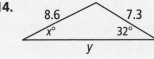

8-5

Practice (continued)

Form G

Law of Sines

15. A hot-air balloon is observed from two points, *A* and *B*, on the ground 800 feet apart as shown in the diagram. The angle of elevation of the balloon is 65° from point *A* and 37° from point *B*. What is the distance from point *A* to the balloon? Round your answer to the nearest foot.

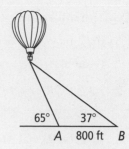

16. Two searchlights on the shore of a lake are located 3020 yards apart as shown in the diagram. A ship in distress is spotted from each searchlight. The beam from the first searchlight makes an angle of 38° with the shoreline. The beam from the second light makes an angle of 57° with the shoreline. What is the ship's distance from each searchlight? Round your answers to the nearest yard.

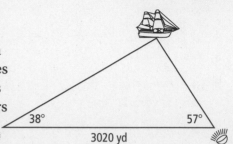

17. An airplane is flying between two airports that are 35 miles apart. The radar in one airport registers a 27° angle between the horizontal and the airplane. The radar system in the other airport registers a 69° angle between the horizontal and the airplane. How far is the airplane from each airport, to the nearest tenth of a mile?

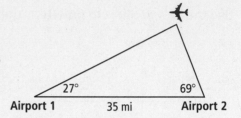

In $\triangle ABC$, $m\angle A = 25$ and $m\angle B = 50$. Find each value to the nearest tenth.

18. If $BC = 6.2$, what is AC?   **19.** If $AC = 14.9$, what is BC?

20. If $AB = 53.7$, what is AC?   **21.** If $AB = 27.3$, what is BC?

22. Writing Suppose you know the measures of two sides of a triangle and the measure of the angle between the two sides. Can you use the Law of Sines to find the remaining side and angle measures? Explain.

23. Reasoning Two angles of a triangle measure 40° and one side measures 10 inches. How many possible triangles are there? What are the missing measures of each possible triangle?

8-5 Standardized Test Prep

Law of Sines

Multiple Choice

For Exercises 1–5, choose the correct letter.

1. In $\triangle ABC$, $m\angle A = 45$, $m\angle C = 60$, and $BC = 10$. To the nearest tenth, what is AB?

   Ⓐ 6.1   Ⓑ 8.2   Ⓒ 12.2   Ⓓ 16.3

2. In $\triangle GHK$, $m\angle G = 102$, $GH = 12$, and $HK = 28$. To the nearest tenth, what is $m\angle K$?

   Ⓕ 52.0   Ⓖ 53.2   Ⓗ 26.0   Ⓘ 24.8

3. Use the Law of Sines. What is the value of x rounded to the nearest tenth?

   Ⓐ 9.8   Ⓒ 12.1

   Ⓑ 10.6   Ⓓ 14.0

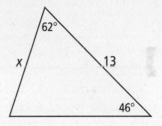

4. Use the Law of Sines. What is the perimeter of the triangle to the nearest tenth?

   Ⓕ 5.4   Ⓗ 13.1

   Ⓖ 7.7   Ⓘ 23.1

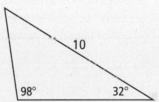

5. A ship has been spotted by two lighthouses as shown in the figure. What is the distance from the ship to Lighthouse A, to the nearest tenth?

   Ⓐ 37.3 mi   Ⓒ 41.9 mi

   Ⓑ 39.1 mi   Ⓓ 42.9 mi

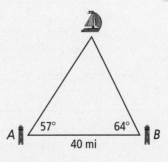

Short Response

6. In $\triangle XYZ$, $m\angle X = 35$, $m\angle Y = 58$, and $YZ = 12$. To the nearest tenth, what are XY and XZ?

8-6 Think About a Plan

Law of Cosines

A commuter plane flies from City A to City B, a distance of 90 mi due north. Due to bad weather, the plane is redirected at take-off to a heading N 60° W (60° west of north). After flying 57 mi, the plane is directed to turn northeast and fly directly toward City B. To the nearest tenth, how many miles did the plane fly on the last leg of the trip?

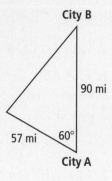

City B

90 mi

57 mi 60°

City A

1. Based on the diagram provided for this problem, which measures of the triangle do you know?

   _____

   _____

2. What are the values of these measures?

   _____

   _____

3. Describe the part of the triangle you need to find.

   _____

   _____

4. What concept will you use to write an equation? What is the equation?

   _____

   _____

5. Solve the equation. What is the distance of the last leg of the trip?

   _____

Prentice Hall Geometry • Practice and Problem Solving Workbook
222

8-6

Practice

Form G

Law of Cosines

Use the information given to solve.

1. In △ABC, m∠A = 40, AB = 9.2, and AC = 8.5. To the nearest tenth, what is BC?

2. In △PQR, m∠Q = 112, PQ = 12.5, and QR = 14.2. To the nearest tenth, what is the length of $\overline{PR}$?

3. In △GHK, GH = 11, HK = 21, and GK = 15. To the nearest tenth, what is m∠K?

4. In △XYZ, XY = 23, YZ = 15, and XZ = 19. To the nearest tenth, what is m∠Z?

5. In △ABC, m∠B = 53, AB = 9.2, and BC = 7.3. To the nearest tenth, what is AC?

6. In △DEF, DE = 12.1, EF = 5.8, and DF = 10.2. To the nearest tenth, what is m∠F?

Use the Law of Cosines to find the values of *x* and *y*. Round to the nearest tenth.

7.
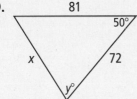

8.
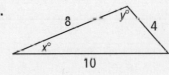

9.
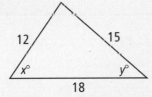

10.
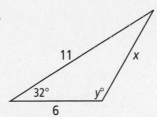

11.
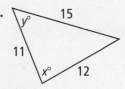

12.
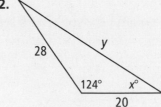

8-6 Practice (continued)
Law of Cosines

Form G

13. One airplane is 78 miles due south of a control tower. Another airplane is 52 miles from the tower at a heading of N 38° E (38° east of north). To the nearest tenth of a mile, how far apart are the two airplanes?

14. A coach sets up a triangular race course. One corner is 100 feet from the start/finish and the other corner is 85 feet from the start/finish. If the angle at the start/finish measures 55°, what is the total length of the course? Round to the nearest tenth of a foot.

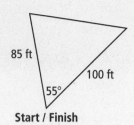

For each triangle shown below, determine whether you would use the Law of Sines or Law of Cosines to find the value of x. Explain. Then find the value of x to the nearest tenth.

15.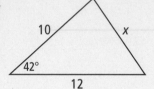

16.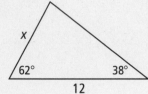

17.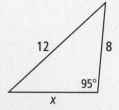

18.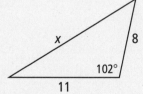

19. Writing Describe two situations in which you can use the Law of Cosines to solve for unknown measures of a triangle.

20. Reasoning Explain how you would find the measure of the smallest angle of a triangle if you are given the measures of all three sides.

8-6 Standardized Test Prep

Law of Cosines

Multiple Choice

For Exercises 1–5, choose the correct letter.

1. To the nearest tenth, what is the value of *x*?

    (A) 10.7   (C) 39.8

    (B) 21.9   (D) 113.9

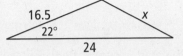

2. To the nearest tenth, what is the value of *x*?

    (F) 7.7   (H) 59.9

    (G) 50.1   (I) 70.0

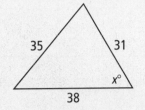

3. To the nearest tenth, what is the value of *x*?

    (A) 27.2   (C) 13.4

    (B) 17.3   (D) 12.3

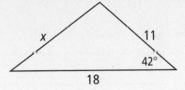

4. To the nearest tenth, what is the value of *x*?

    (F) 36.5   (H) 56.3

    (G) 49.1   (I) 74.6

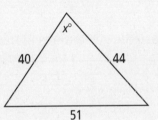

5. In $\triangle ABC$, $a = 20$, $b = 12$, and $c = 30$. What is the measure of the largest angle to the nearest tenth?

    (A) 15.6°   (C) 42.1°

    (B) 26.6°   (D) 137.9°

Short Response

6. To the nearest tenth, what are the measures of the remaining side and angles in the triangle?

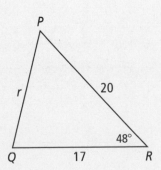

9-1 Think About a Plan

Translations

Coordinate Geometry Quadrilateral *PLAT* has vertices $P(-2, 0)$, $L(-1, 1)$, $A(0, 1)$, and $T(-1, 0)$. $T_{<2, -3>}(PLAT) = P'L'A'T'$. Show that $\overline{PP'}$, $\overline{LL'}$, $\overline{AA'}$, and $\overline{TT'}$ are all parallel.

Understanding the Problem

1. How can you use the three sentences of the problem to help you break the problem down into manageable pieces?

_____

_____

_____

Planning the Solution

2. How can you use a diagram to help you solve the problem?

_____

_____

3. Use the given translation to find the image points.

_____

4. Graph $\overline{PP'}$, $\overline{LL'}$, $\overline{AA'}$, and $\overline{TT'}$. What theorems about parallel lines come to mind when you look at the graph?

_____

Getting an Answer

5. Find the slopes of the lines that connect each original point to its image.

_____

6. How can you use the slopes to establish that $\overline{PP'}$, $\overline{LL'}$, $\overline{AA'}$, and $\overline{TT'}$ are all parallel?

_____

9-1

Practice

Form G

Translations

Tell whether the transformation appears to be a rigid motion. Explain.

1.
Preimage   Image

2.
Preimage   Image

3.
Preimage   Image

4.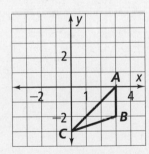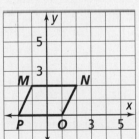
Preimage   Image

In each diagram, the dashed-line figure is an image of the solid-line figure.
(a) Choose an angle or point from the preimage and name its image.
(b) List all pairs of corresponding sides.

5.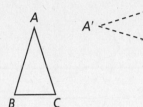

6.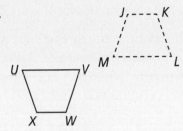

Graph the image of each figure under the given translation.

7. $T_{<-1,\,4>}(\triangle ABC)$

8. $T_{<3,\,3>}(MNOP)$

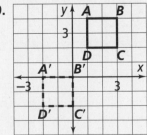

The dashed-line figure is a translation image of the solid-line figure. Write a rule to describe each translation.

9.

10.

9-1

Practice (continued)

Form G

Translations

11. You are visiting Washington, D.C. From the American History Museum you walk 5 blocks east and 1 block south to the Air and Space Museum. Then you walk 8 blocks west to the Washington Monument. Where is the Washington Monument in relation to the American History Museum?

12. You and some friends go to a book fair where booths are set out in rows. You buy drinks at the refreshment stand and then walk 8 rows north and 2 rows east to the science fiction booth. Then you walk 1 row south and 2 rows west to the children's book booth. Where is the children's book booth in relation to the refreshment stand?

13. **Reasoning** If $T_{<10, 15>}(PQRS) = P'Q'R'S'$, what translation maps $P'Q'R'S'$ onto $PQRS$?

14. $\triangle XYZ$ has coordinates $X(2, 3)$, $Y(1, 4)$, and $Z(8, 9)$. A translation maps X to $X'(4, 7)$. What are the coordinates for Y' and Z' for this translation?

15. Use the graph at the right. Write three different translation rules for which the image of $\triangle RST$ has a vertex at the origin.

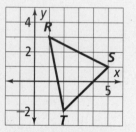

16. Use the graph at the right. Write three different translation rules for which the image of $\triangle BCD$ has a vertex at the origin.

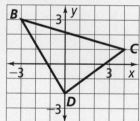

Graph the image of each figure under the given translation.

17. $T_{<-3, 4>}(\triangle DEF)$

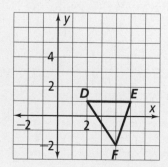

18. $T_{<-5, 1>}(KLMN)$

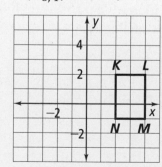

9-1 Standardized Test Prep

Translations

Multiple Choice

For Exercises 1–4, choose the correct letter.

1. In the diagram, $\triangle A'B'C'$ is an image of $\triangle ABC$. Which rule describes this translation?

    Ⓐ $T_{<-5,\,-3>}(\triangle ABC)$

    Ⓑ $T_{<5,\,3>}(\triangle ABC)$

    Ⓒ $T_{<-3,\,-5>}(\triangle ABC)$

    Ⓓ $T_{<3,\,5>}(\triangle ABC)$

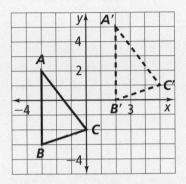

2. If $T_{<3,\,-7>}(TUVW) = T'U'V'W'$, what translation maps $T'U'V'W'$ onto $TUVW$?

    Ⓕ $T_{<3,\,-7>}(T'U'V'W')$ Ⓗ $T_{<7,\,-3>}(T'U'V'W')$

    Ⓖ $T_{<-7,\,3>}(T'U'V'W')$ Ⓘ $T_{<-3,\,7>}(T'U'V'W')$

3. Which of the following is true for a rigid motion?

    Ⓐ The preimage and the image have the same measurements.

    Ⓓ The preimage is larger than the image.

    Ⓒ The preimage is smaller than the image.

    Ⓓ The preimage is in the same position as the image.

4. $\triangle RSV$ has coordinates $R(2, 1)$, $S(3, 2)$, and $V(2, 6)$. A translation maps point R to R' at $(-4, 8)$. What are the coordinates for S' for this translation?

    Ⓕ $(-6, -4)$ Ⓖ $(-3, 2)$ Ⓗ $(-3, 9)$ Ⓘ $(-4, 13)$

Short Response

5. $\triangle LMP$ has coordinates $L(3, 4)$, $M(6, 6)$, and $P(5, 5)$. A translation maps point L to L' at $(7, -4)$. What are the coordinates for M' and for P' for this translation?

9-2 Think About a Plan

Reflections

Copy the pair of figures. Then draw the line of reflection you can use to map one figure onto the other.

1. Designate one figure to be the preimage and one to be its reflection. Label two points A and B on the preimage and label their images (A' and B') on the reflection.

2. Sketch $\overline{AA'}$ and $\overline{BB'}$. This step is optional, but provides a frame of reference for later steps.

3. Open your compass to a size greater than half the distance between point A and A'. With the compass at A, draw an arc above and below the approximate midpoint of $\overline{AA'}$.

4. Do the same from point A'. Label points P and Q at the points where the arcs intersect.

5. Draw $\overline{PQ}$. To check your work, do the same from points B and B'.

9-2 Practice

Form G

Reflections

Find the coordinates of each image.

1. $R_{x\text{-axis}}(A)$

2. $R_{y\text{-axis}}(B)$

3. $R_{y=1}(C)$

4. $R_{x=-1}(D)$

5. $R_{y=-1}(E)$

6. $R_{x=2}(F)$

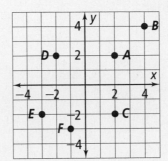

Coordinate Geometry Given points $M(3, 3)$, $N(5, 2)$, and $O(4, 4)$, graph $\triangle MNO$ and its reflection image as indicated.

7. $R_{y\text{-axis}}$

8. $R_{x\text{-axis}}$

9. $R_{x=1}$

10. $R_{y=-2}$

Copy each figure and line ℓ. Draw each figure's reflection image across line ℓ.

11.

12.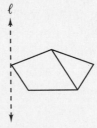

13.

14.

231

9-2

Practice (continued)
Reflections

Form G

Copy each pair of figures. Then draw the line of reflection you can use to map one figure onto the other.

15.

16.

Find the image of $Z(1, 1)$ after two reflections, first across line ℓ_1, and then across line ℓ_2.

17. $\ell_1 : x = 2, \ell_2 : y$-axis

18. $\ell_1 : x = -2, \ell_2 : x$-axis

19. $\ell_1 : y = 2, \ell_2 : x$-axis

20. $\ell_1 : y = -3, \ell_2 : y$-axis

21. $\ell_1 : x = 3, \ell_2 : y = 2$

22. $\ell_1 : x = -1, \ell_2 : y = -3$

Use the graph at the right for Exercises 23 and 24.

23. Berit lives 3 mi east of Rt. 147 and 1 mi north of Rt. 9. Jane lives 3 mi east of Rt. 147 and 5 mi north of Rt. 9. The girls want to start at Berit's house, hike to Rt. 147, then on to Jane's house. They want to hike the shortest distance possible. To which point on Rt. 147 should they walk? (*Hint*: First find the line of reflection if Berit's house is reflected onto Jane's house.)

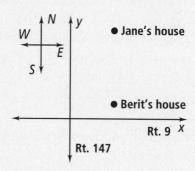

24. Instead of ending the hike at Jane's house, the girls want to hike to an inn 2 mi north of Jane's house. They want to hike the shortest possible total distance, starting from Berit's house, walking to Rt. 147, and then to the inn. To which point on Rt. 147 should they walk? (*Hint*: First find the line of reflection if Berit's house is reflected onto the inn.)

25. Point A on a coordinate grid is at $(3, 4)$. What are the coordinates of $R_{y=x}(A)$?

26. Point Z on a coordinate grid is at $(-1, 3)$. What are the coordinates of $R_{y=-x}(Z)$?

27. Give an example of a place you may see a geometric reflection in everyday life. Explain.

9-2 Standardized Test Prep

Reflections

Multiple Choice

For Exercises 1–5, choose the correct letter.

1. In the graph at the right, what are the coordinates of $R_{y\text{-axis}}(D)$?

   Ⓐ (3, −1)   Ⓒ (−3, −1)

   Ⓑ (3, 1)   Ⓓ (−3, 1)

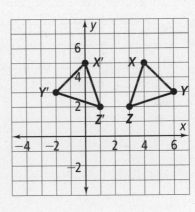

2. The coordinates of the vertices of $\triangle CDE$ are $C(1, 4)$, $D(3, 6)$, and $E(7, 4)$. What are the coordinates of $R_{y=3}(D)$?

   Ⓕ (3, −6)   Ⓖ (3, −3)

   Ⓗ (3, 0)   Ⓘ (3, 9)

3. What is true for an image and a preimage in a reflection?

   Ⓐ The image is larger than the preimage.

   Ⓑ The image is smaller than the preimage.

   Ⓒ The image and the preimage have the same orientation.

   Ⓓ The image and the preimage have different orientations.

4. In the graph at the right, what is the line of reflection for $\triangle XYZ$ and $\triangle X'Y'Z'$?

   Ⓕ the x-axis

   Ⓖ the y-axis

   Ⓗ $x = 2$

   Ⓘ $y = 2$

5. What is the image of $A(3, -1)$ after a reflection, first across the line $y = 3$, and then across the line $x = -1$?

   Ⓐ (−5, 7)   Ⓒ (−5, −1)

   Ⓑ (3, −1)   Ⓓ (1, −5)

Extended Response

6. The coordinates of the vertices of parallelogram $RSTU$ are $R(0, 0)$, $S(2, 3)$, $T(6, 3)$, and $U(4, 0)$. What are the coordinates of the vertices of $R_{y\,=\,x}(RSTU)$?

9-3 Think About a Plan

Rotations

Coordinate Geometry Graph $A(5, 2)$. Graph B, the image of A for a 90°
rotation about the origin O. Graph C, the image of A for a 180° rotation about O.
Graph D, the image of A for a 270° rotation about O. What type of quadrilateral
is $ABCD$? Explain.

1. To find the coordinates of B, you can use the rule for rotating a point 90° about
   the origin O in a coordinate plane. What are the coordinates of $B = r_{(90°, O)}(A)$?

   _____

2. To find the coordinates of C, you can use the rule for rotating a point 180°
   about the origin O in a coordinate plane. What are the coordinates of
   $C = r_{(180°, O)}(A)$?

   _____

3. To find the coordinates of D, you can use the rule for rotating a point 270°
   about the origin O in a coordinate plane. What are the coordinates of
   $D = r_{(270°, O)}(A)$?

   _____

4. Graph A, B, C, and D.

5. Draw $\overline{AB}$, $\overline{BC}$, $\overline{CD}$, and $\overline{DA}$.

6. The figure appears to be a square. How can you
   show that the figure is a square?

   _____

   _____

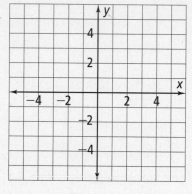

7. Using the Distance Formula, what are AB, BC, CD, and DA?

   _____

   _____

8. What are the slopes of $\overline{AB}$, $\overline{BC}$, $\overline{CD}$, and $\overline{DA}$?

   _____

   _____

9. What can you conclude about $\angle A$, $\angle B$, $\angle C$, and $\angle D$? Explain.

   _____

   _____

9-3 **Practice**   Form G

Rotations

Copy each figure and point *P*. Draw the image of each figure for the given rotation about *P*. Use prime notation to label the vertices of the image.

1. 60°

• *P*

2. 90°

• *P*

3. 120°

• *P*

4. 180°

Copy each figure and point *P*. Then draw the image of $\overline{JK}$ for a 180° rotation about *P*. Use prime notation to label the vertices of the image.

5.
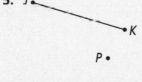
P •

6.
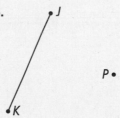
P •

Point *O* is the center of regular hexagon *BCDEFG*. Find the image of the given point or segment for the given rotation.

7. $r_{(120°, O)}(F)$

8. $r_{(180°, O)}(B)$

9. $r_{(300°, O)}(\overline{BG})$

10. $r_{(360°, O)}(\overline{CD})$

11. $r_{(60°, O)}(E)$

12. $r_{(240°, O)}(\overline{FE})$

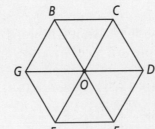

9-3 Practice (continued)   Form G
Rotations

For Exercises 13–15, △ABC has vertices A(2, 2), B(3, −2), and C(−1, 3).

13. Graph $r_{(90°, O)}(△ABC)$.   **14.** Graph $r_{(180°, O)}(△ABC)$.   **15.** Graph $r_{(270°, O)}(△ABC)$.

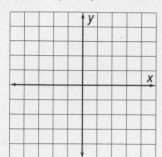 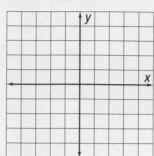 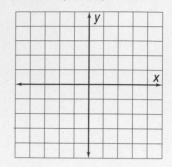

16. The vertices of *PQRS* have coordinates P(−1, 5), Q(3, 4), R(2, −4), and S(−3, −2). What are the coordinates of the vertices of $r_{(270°, O)}(PQRS)$?

17. The vertices of $r_{(90°, O)}(KLMN)$ have coordinates K′(−3, 2), L′(2, 3), M′(4, −2), and N′(−2, −4). What are the coordinates of the vertices of *KLMN*?

18. Reasoning The vertices of quadrilateral *ABCD* have coordinates A(4, 3), B(−3, 4), C(−4, −3), and D(3, −4). Explain how the transformation $r_{(90°, O)}(ABCD) = BCDA$ can be used to show that the quadrilateral is square.

Find the angle of rotation about *D* that maps the solid-line figure to the dashed-line figure.

19.

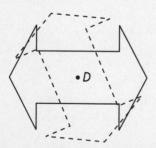

20.

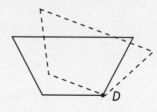

21. A pie is cut into 12 equal slices. What is the angle of rotation about the center that will map a piece of pie to a piece that is two slices away from it?

22. △*RST* has vertices at R(0, 3), S(4, 0), and T(0, 0). What are the coordinates of the vertices of $r_{(−90°, T)}(△RST)$?

23. △*FGH* has vertices F(−1, 2), G(0, 0), and H(3, −1). What are the coordinates of the vertices of $r_{(−90°, G)}(△FGH)$?

9-3 Standardized Test Prep
Rotations

Multiple Choice

In Exercises 1–5, choose the correct letter.

1. Square $ABCD$ has vertices $A(3, 3)$, $B(-3, 3)$, $C(-3, -3)$, and $D(3, -3)$.
   Which of the following images is A?

   Ⓐ $r_{(90°, O)}(C)$ Ⓑ $r_{(180°, O)}(D)$ Ⓒ $r_{(270°, O)}(B)$ Ⓓ $r_{(270°, O)}(C)$

2. $r_{(90°, O)}(PQRS)$ has vertices $P'(1, 5), Q'(3, -2), R'(-3, -2)$, and $S'(-5, 1)$.
   What are the coordinates of Q?

   Ⓐ $(-2, -3)$ Ⓑ $(-3, 2)$ Ⓒ $(2, 3)$ Ⓓ $(-3, -2)$

3. Point A is the center of regular hexagon $GHIJKL$.
   What is $r_{(300°, A)}(I)$?

   Ⓐ J Ⓒ L

   Ⓑ K Ⓓ M

4. A Ferris wheel has 16 cars spaced equal distances apart. The cars are
   numbered 1–16 clockwise. What is the measure of the angle of rotation
   that will map the position of car 16 onto the position of car 13?

   Ⓕ $22.5°$ Ⓖ $45°$ Ⓗ $67.5°$ Ⓘ $90°$

5. Given $P(2, -5)$, what are the coordinates of $r_{(90°, O)}(P)$?

   Ⓐ $(5, 2)$ Ⓑ $(-5, 2)$ Ⓒ $(5, -2)$ Ⓓ $(-2, -5)$

Short Response

6. $\triangle ABC$ has coordinates $A(3, 3)$, $B(0, 0)$, and $C(3, 0)$. What are the coordinates
   of $r_{(180°, B)}(A)$ and $r_{(180°, B)}(C)$?

9-4 Think About a Plan

Compositions of Isometries

Identify the mapping $\triangle EDC \rightarrow \triangle PQM$ as a translation, reflection, rotation, or glide reflection. Write the rule for each translation, reflection, rotation, or glide reflection. For glide reflections, write the rule as a composition of a translation and reflection.

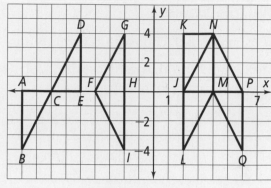

Know

1. What strategy could you use to isolate the figures with which you are working?

_____

2. What kind of mapping appears to have happened here? Explain.

_____

_____

Need

3. What more do we need to know to have a complete answer?

_____

Plan

4. Write a translation rule that maps $\triangle EDC$ onto $\triangle PQM$.

_____

5. Write a reflection rule that maps $\triangle EDC$ onto $\triangle PQM$.

_____

6. Write a rule that maps $\triangle EDC$ onto $\triangle PQM$.

_____

9-4

Practice

Form G

Compositions of Isometries

Find the image of each letter after the transformation $R_m \circ R_\ell$. Is the resulting transformation a translation or a rotation? For a translation, describe the distance and direction. For a rotation, tell the center of rotation and the angle of rotation.

1.

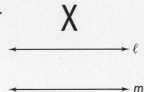

2.

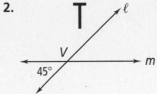

Graph $\triangle DML$ and its glide reflection image.

3. $(R_{y\text{-axis}} \circ T_{<0, -2>})(\triangle DML)$

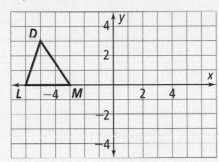

4. $(R_{y=1} \circ T_{<-1, 0>})(\triangle DML)$

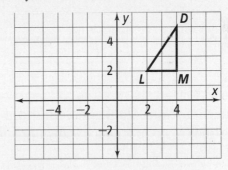

5. $(R_{x=2} \circ T_{<0, 1>})(\triangle DML)$

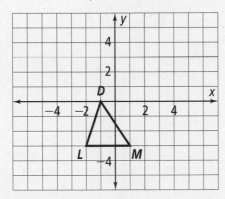

6. $(R_{y=x} \circ T_{<3, 3>})(\triangle DML)$

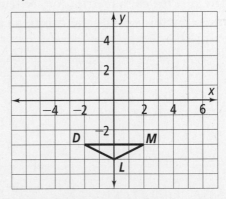

7. Lines ℓ and m intersect at point P and are perpendicular. If a point Q is reflected across ℓ and then across m, what transformation rule describes this composition?

8. A triangle is reflected across line ℓ and then across line m. If this composition of reflections is a translation, what is true about m and ℓ?

Name _____ Class _____ Date _____

9-4 Practice (continued) Form G
Compositions of Isometries

Graph $\overline{AB}$ and its image $\overline{A'B'}$ after a reflection first across ℓ_1 and then across ℓ_2. Is the resulting transformation a translation or a rotation? For a translation, describe the direction and distance. For a rotation, tell the center of rotation and the angle of rotation.

9. $A(-3, 4)$, $B(-1, 0)$;
$\ell_1 : x = 1$;
$\ell_2 : y = -1$

10. $A(-5, 2)$, $B(-3, 6)$;
$\ell_1 : x = -2$;
$\ell_2 : x = 3$

11. Open-Ended Draw a quadrilateral on a coordinate grid. Describe a reflection, translation, rotation, and glide reflection. Then draw the image of the quadrilateral for each transformation.

Identify each mapping as a translation, reflection, rotation, or glide reflection. Write the rule for each translation, reflection, rotation, or glide reflection. For glide reflections, write the rule as a composition of a translation and a reflection.

12. $\triangle ABC \rightarrow \triangle DEF$

13. $\triangle DEF \rightarrow \triangle GHF$

14. $\triangle DEF \rightarrow \triangle IJK$

15. $\triangle GHF \rightarrow \triangle IJK$

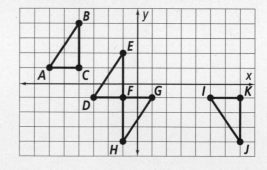

P maps to $P'(2, 3)$ by the given glide reflection. What are the coordinates of P?

16. $(R_{x\text{-axis}} \circ T_{<2, 0>})(P)$

17. $(R_{y=x} \circ T_{<3, 3>})(P)$

9-4

Standardized Test Prep

Compositions of Isometries

Multiple Choice

For Exercises 1–5, choose the correct letter.

1. Which transformation is the same as the composition $R_{x\,=\,-1} \circ R_{x\,=\,2}$?

    (A) $r_{(180°,\,(-1,\,2))}$ (B) $r_{(180°,\,(2,\,-1))}$ (C) $T_{<3,\,0>}$ (D) $T_{<6,\,0>}$

2. What type of transformation maps $\triangle ABC$ onto $\triangle DEF$?

    (F) translation

    (G) rotation

    (H) reflection

    (I) glide reflection

    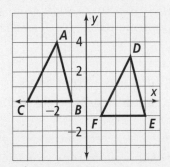

3. A triangle is reflected across line ℓ and then across line m. If the lines intersect, what type of isometry is this composition of reflections?

    (A) translation   (B) rotation   (C) reflection   (D) glide reflection

4. What type of isometry is shown at the right?

    (F) translation   (H) reflection

    (G) rotation   (I) glide reflection

    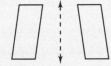

5. If $(R_{y\,=\,-1} \circ T_{<0,3>})(X) = X'(3,\,-2)$, what are the coordinates of X?

    (A) $(-5,\,-2)$ (B) $(-2,\,-2)$ (C) $(-2,\,-5)$ (D) $(3,\,-3)$

Short Response

6. What type of transformation is shown? Give the translation rule, reflection rule, rotation rule, or composition rule of the glide reflection.

    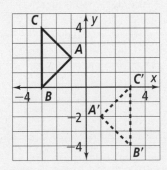

9-5 Think About a Plan

Congruence Transformations

Use congruence transformations to prove the Isosceles Triangle Theorem.

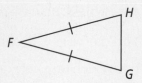

Given: $\overline{FG} \cong \overline{FH}$

Prove: $\angle G \cong \angle H$

1. Since you want to show that $\angle G \cong \angle H$, you want to find a congruence transformation that will map $\angle G$ to $\angle H$. If the preimage of this transformation is $\triangle FGH$, what is the image?

   _____

2. Identify the congruence transformation as a translation, reflection, rotation, or a composition of rigid motions.

   _____

3. For each rigid motion used in the transformation, describe the translation rule, the line of reflection, or the center and angle of rotation.

   _____

   _____

4. Explain why this transformation maps $\triangle FGH$ to $\triangle FHG$.

   _____

   _____

   _____

5. Since this transformation maps point F to point F, point G to point H, and point H to point G, you know that it maps $\angle G$ to $\angle H$. Why does it show that $\angle G \cong \angle H$?

   _____

   _____

   _____

9-5

Practice

Form G

Congruence Transformations

For each coordinate grid, identify a pair of congruent figures. Then determine a congruence transformation that maps the preimage to the congruent image.

1.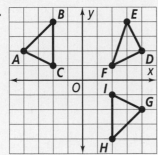

2.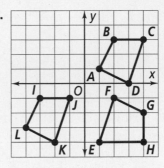

3.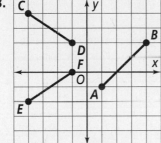

4.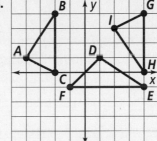

Find a congruence transformation that maps $\triangle ABC$ to $\triangle DEF$.

5.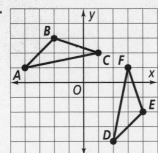

6.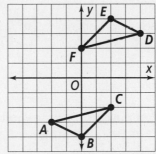

9-5 Practice   Form G
Congruence Transformations

7. Verify the ASA Postulate for triangle congruence by using congruence transformations.

Given: $\angle A \cong \angle K$, $\angle B \cong \angle L$, $\overline{AB} \cong \overline{KL}$
Prove: $\triangle ABC \cong \triangle KLM$

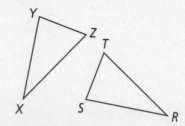

8. Verify the SSS Postulate for triangle congruence by using congruence transformations.

Given: $\overline{XY} \cong \overline{RS}$, $\overline{YZ} \cong \overline{ST}$, $\overline{ZX} \cong \overline{TR}$
Prove: $\triangle XYZ \cong \triangle RST$

Determine whether the figures are congruent. If so, describe a congruence transformation that maps one to the other. If not, explain.

9.

10.

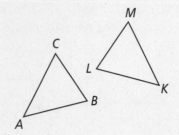

11. Error Analysis For the figure at the right, a student says that $\triangle ABC \cong \triangle DEF$ because $R_{y\text{-axis}}(\triangle ABC) = \triangle DEF$. What is the student's error?

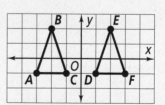

12. Reasoning Suppose one congruence transformation maps $\triangle LMN$ onto $\triangle PQR$ and another congruence transformation maps $\triangle LMN$ onto $\triangle PRQ$. How would you classify the two triangles? Explain.

9-5 Standardized Test Prep

Congruence Transformations

Multiple Choice

For Exercises 1–3, choose the correct letter.

1. Which congruence transformation maps $\triangle ABC$ to $\triangle DEF$?

   Ⓐ $T_{<5, -5>}$　　　Ⓒ $R_{x\text{-axis}} \circ T_{<5, 0>}$

   Ⓑ $r_{(180°, O)}$　　Ⓓ $R_{y\text{-axis}} \circ r_{(90°, O)}$

   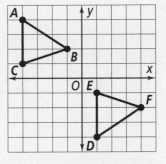

2. Which congruence transformation does *not* map $\triangle ABC$ to $\triangle DEF$?

   Ⓕ $r_{(180°, O)}$　　Ⓗ $R_{x\text{-axis}} \circ R_{y\text{-axis}}$

   Ⓖ $T_{<0, 6>} \circ R_{y\text{-axis}}$　Ⓘ $R_{y\text{-axis}} \circ R_{x\text{-axis}}$

   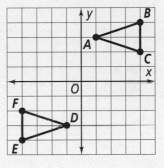

3. Which of the following best describes a congruence transformation that maps $\triangle FGH$ to $\triangle LMN$?

   Ⓐ a reflection only

   Ⓑ a translation only

   Ⓒ a translation followed by a reflection

   Ⓓ a translation followed by a rotation

   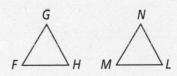

Short Response

4. What is a congruence transformation that maps $ABCD$ to $RSTU$?

   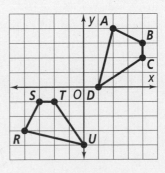

9-6

Think About a Plan

Dilations

Reasoning You are given $\overline{AB}$ and its dilation image $\overline{A'B'}$ with A, B, A', and B' noncollinear. Explain how to find the center of dilation and scale factor.

Know

1. What do you know about the relationship of A, A', and C, the center of dilation?

   _____

2. Is this true also of B, B', and C?

3. What relationship exists between the lengths of the segments $\overline{A'B'}$ and $\overline{AB}$?

   _____

Need

4. Is it possible to answer this question using a specific point C and a specific scale factor? Explain.

   _____

   _____

Plan

5. How do you find the center of dilation?

   _____

   _____

6. How do you find the scale factor?

   _____

9-6

Practice

Form G

Dilations

The solid-line figure is a dilation of the dashed-line figure. The labeled point is the center of dilation. Tell whether the dilation is an enlargement or a reduction. Then find the scale factor of the dilation.

1.

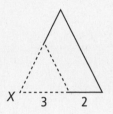

X   3   2

2.

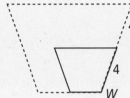

4

4

W

3.

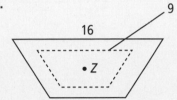

16

9

•Z

4.

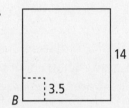

14

3.5

B

5.

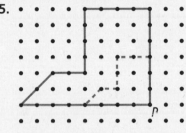

P

6.

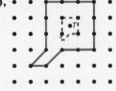

7.

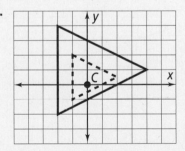

C

8.

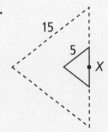

15

5

X

You look at each object described in Exercises 9–11 under a magnifying glass. Find the actual dimension of each object.

9. The image of a ribbon is 10 times the ribbon's actual size and has a width of 1 cm.

10. The image of a caterpillar is three times the caterpillar's actual size and has a width of 4 in.

11. The image of a beetle is five times the beetle's actual size and has a length of 1.75 cm.

12. $\triangle P'Q'R'$ is a dilation image of $\triangle PQR$. The scale factor for the dilation is 0.12. Is the dilation an enlargement or a reduction?

9-6 Practice (continued)

Form G

Dilations

A dilation has center (0, 0). Find the image of each point for the given scale factor.

13. $X(3, 4); D_7(X)$

14. $P(-3, 5); D_{1.2}(P)$

15. $Q(0, 4); D_{3.4}(Q)$

16. $T(-2, -1); D_4(T)$

17. $S(5, -6); D_{\frac{5}{3}}(S)$

18. $M(2, 2); D_5(M)$

19. A square has 16-cm sides. Describe its image for a dilation with center at one of the vertices and scale factor 0.8.

20. Graph pentagon $ABCDE$ and its image $A'B'C'D'E'$ for a dilation with center (0, 0) and a scale factor of 1.5. The vertices of $ABCDE$ are: $A(0, 3)$, $B(3, 3)$, $C(3, 0)$, $D(0, -3)$, $E(-1, 0)$.

Copy $\triangle BCD$ **and point** X **for each of Exercises 21–23. Draw the dilation image** $\triangle B'C'D'$.

21. $D_{(1.5, X)}(\triangle BCD)$

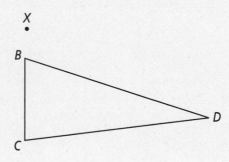

22. $D_{(1.5, B)}(\triangle BCD)$

23. $D_{(0.8, C)}(\triangle BCD)$

9-6 Standardized Test Prep

Dilations

Gridded Response

The solid-line figure is a dilation of the dashed-line figure. The labeled point is the center of dilation. Find the scale factor for each dilation. Use whole numbers or decimals. Enter your responses on the grid provided.

1.

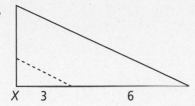

X   3   6

2.

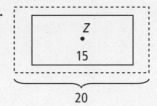

Z
15

20

Solve the problem and enter your response on the grid provided.

3. The image of an eraser in a magnifying glass is three times the eraser's actual size and has a width of 14.4 cm. What is the actual width in cm?

4. A square on a transparency is 1.7 in. long. The square's image on the screen is 11.05 in. long. What is the scale factor of the dilation?

5. A dilation maps $\triangle LMN$ to $\triangle L'M'N'$. $MN = 14$ in. and $M'N' = 9.8$ in. If $LN = 13$ in., what is $L'N'$?

Answers

1.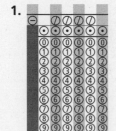
2.
3.
4.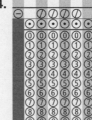
5.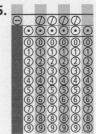

9-7 Think About a Plan

Similarity Transformations

A printing company enlarges a banner for a graduation party by a scale factor of 8.

  a. What are the dimensions of the larger banner?

  b. How can the printing company be sure that the enlarged banner is similar to the original? Explain.

  1. What is the scale factor for this problem?

_____

  2. What can you do with the scale factor to find the dimensions of the large banner?

_____

  3. What is the width of the larger banner?

_____

  4. What is the height of the larger banner?

_____

  5. What kind of transformation did the printing company apply to the original banner in order to produce the larger banner?

_____

  6. Explain how the printing company can be sure that the enlarged banner is similar to the original.

_____

_____

_____

9-7 Practice   Form G

Similarity Transformations

$\triangle ABC$ has vertices $A(-2, 2)$, $B(2, 0)$, and $C(1, -2)$. For each similarity transformation, draw the image.

1. $D_2 \circ R_{y\text{-axis}}$

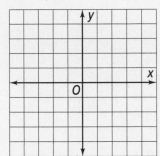

2. $r_{90°} \circ D_{1.5}$

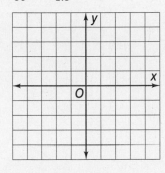

3. $D_{0.5} \circ T_{<2, -2>}$

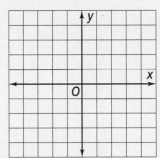

4. $r_{270°} \circ D_2 \circ R_{x\text{-axis}}$

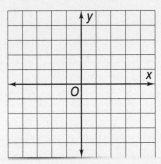

For each graph, describe the composition of transformations that maps $\triangle DEF$ to $\triangle LMN$.

5.

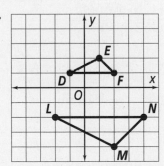

6.

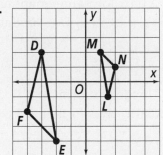

9-7 Practice   Form G
Similarity Transformations

For each pair of figures, determine if there is a similarity transformation that maps one figure onto the other. If so, identify the similarity transformation and write a similarity statement. If not, explain.

7.

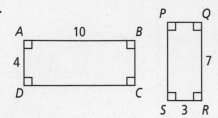

8.

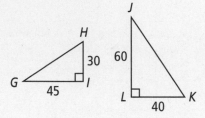

Determine whether or not each pair of figures below are similar. Explain your reasoning.

9.

10.

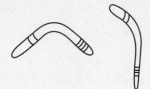

11. **Reasoning** A transformation maps each point (x, y) of $\triangle ABC$ to the point $(-4x + 3, -4y + 2)$. Is $\triangle ABC$ similar to the image of $\triangle ABC$? Explain.

12. **Reasoning** Do the compositions $T_{<4, -2>} \circ D_2$ and $D_2 \circ T_{<2, -1>}$ describe the same similarity transformation? Explain.

9-7

Standardized Test Prep
Similarity Transformations

Multiple Choice

For Exercises 1–3, choose the correct letter.

1. Which similarity transformation maps $\triangle ABC$ to $\triangle DEF$?

   Ⓐ $R_{x\text{-axis}} \circ D_{0.5}$ Ⓒ $R_{x\text{-axis}} \circ D_2$

   Ⓑ $r_{(270°,\, O)} \circ D_{0.5}$ Ⓓ $r_{(90°,\, O)} \circ D_2$

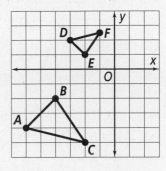

2. Which similarity transformation does not map $\triangle PQR$ to $\triangle STU$?

   Ⓕ $r_{(180°,\, O)} \circ D_2$ Ⓗ $D_2 \circ R_{x\text{-axis}} \circ R_{y\text{-axis}}$

   Ⓖ $D_2 \circ r_{(180°,\, O)}$ Ⓘ $D_2 \circ R_{x\text{-axis}} \circ r_{(90°,\, O)}$

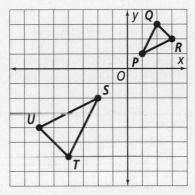

3. Which of the following best describes a similarity transformation that maps $\triangle JKP$ to $\triangle LMP$?

   Ⓐ a dilation only

   Ⓑ a rotation followed by a dilation

   Ⓒ a reflection followed by a dilation

   Ⓓ a translation followed by a dilation

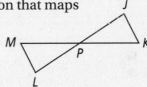

Short Response

4. $\triangle ABC$ has vertices $A(1, 0)$, $B(2, 4)$, and $C(3, 2)$. $\triangle RST$ has vertices $R(0, 3)$, $S(-12, 6)$, and $T(-6, 9)$. What is a similarity transformation that maps $\triangle ABC$ to $\triangle RST$?

10-1 Think About a Plan

Areas of Parallelograms and Triangles

Coordinate Geometry Find the area of a polygon with the given vertices.

$A(3, 9)$, $B(8, 9)$, $C(2, -3)$, $D(-3, -3)$

Understanding the Problem

1. What is the first thing you need to know about the polygon to find its area?

_____

2. What is the simplest way to determine this?

_____

Planning the Solution

3. Plot the points on the coordinate grid.
   What type of polygon is it? How can you tell?

_____

_____

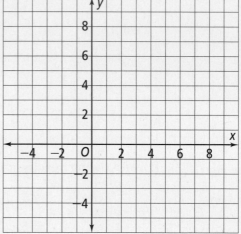

4. What is the formula for finding the area of this type of polygon?

5. Which segment will you use as the base?

_____

6. How can you add to the figure to find the height?

_____

_____

7. How can you find the measure of the base and height? What are the base and the height?

_____

Getting an Answer

8. Substitute the values for the base and height into the formula and solve.

9. What unit should you use for your answer? What is the area?

_____

10-1 Practice

Form G

Areas of Parallelograms and Triangles

Find the area of each parallelogram.

1.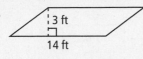
3 ft
14 ft

2.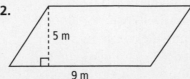
5 m
9 m

3.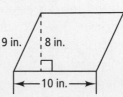
9 in. 8 in.
←—— 10 in. ——→

4.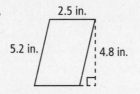
12 mm
8 mm
10 mm

5.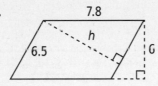
2.5 in.
5.2 in.
4.8 in.

6.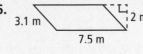
3.1 m
7.5 m
2 m

Find the value of *h* for each parallelogram.

7.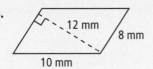
h
8
3
4

8.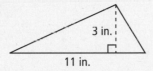
7.8
h
6.5
G

9.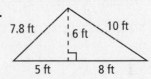
4
9.5
h
3.8

Find the area of each triangle.

10.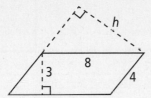
3 in.
11 in.

11.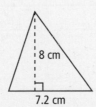
8 cm
7.2 cm

12.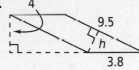
7.8 ft
6 ft
10 ft
5 ft
8 ft

13.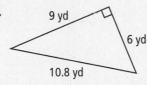
9 yd
6 yd
10.8 yd

14.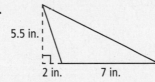
5.5 in.
2 in.   7 in.

15.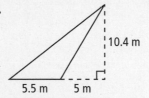
10.4 m
5.5 m   5 m

16. **Algebra** In a parallelogram, a base, *b*, and its corresponding height, *h*, are in the ratio of 5 : 3. The area is 135 mm². Find *b* and *h*.

17. **Reasoning** A triangle has an area of 18 ft². List all the possible positive integers that could represent its base and height.

10-1

Practice (continued)   Form G

Areas of Parallelograms and Triangles

18. A company wants to paint its logo on the side of a building. The entire area needs to be covered with a primer. The two triangular areas will be painted red, the rectangle containing the company's name will be white, and the rest of the parallelogram will be yellow.

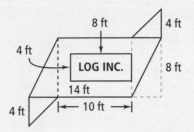

a. Find the area for each different color.

b. Find the area that must be painted with primer.

19. A scale drawing of the side view of a house is shown at the right. Find the total area (in square inches) of the side of the house in the drawing.

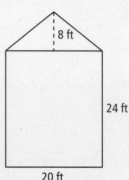

20. Open-Ended Using graph paper, draw a figure with area 42 units² made up of a parallelogram and a triangle.

Coordinate Geometry Find the area of a polygon with the given vertices.

21. $A(2, 2), B(5, 2), C(3, -1), D(0, -1)$

22. $A(1, 4), B(-2, -2), C(-7, -2), D(-4, 4)$

23. $A(5, -3), B(-1, -3), C(-1, 2), D(5, 6)$

24. $A(5, 0), B(5, 8), C(-1, 7), D(-1, -6)$

20 ft
Scale: 1 in. : 20 ft

Find the area of each figure.

25.

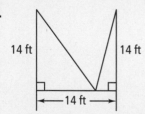

26.

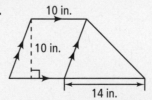

27.

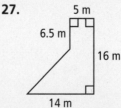

28. Reasoning A parallelogram has a height of 6 units and a corresponding base of 7 units. What is the area of each triangle formed when one diagonal of the parallelogram is drawn? What is the area of each small triangle formed when two diagonals are drawn?

29. A parallelogram has sides 24 m and 5 m. The height corresponding to a 24-m base is 4 m. What it the height corresponding to a 5-m base?

10-1 Standardized Test Prep

Areas of Parallelograms and Triangles

Multiple Choice

For Exercises 1–6, choose the correct letter.

1. What is the area of the parallelogram at the right?

   Ⓐ 18 in.^{2} Ⓒ 36 in.^{2}

   Ⓑ 30 in.^{2} Ⓓ 60 in.^{2}

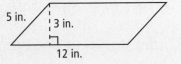

2. What is the area of the parallelogram at the right?

   Ⓕ 31.5 m^2 Ⓗ 84 m^2

   Ⓖ 63 m^2 Ⓘ 126 m^2

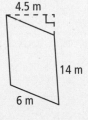

3. What is the value of h for the parallelogram at the right?

   Ⓐ 9.6 units   Ⓒ 48 units

   Ⓑ 26.7 units   Ⓓ 96 units

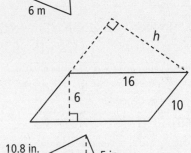

4. What is the area of the figure at the right?

   Ⓕ 26 in.^{2} Ⓗ 52 in.^{2}

   Ⓖ 27 in.^{2} Ⓘ 54 in.^{2}

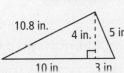

5. A parallelogram has sides 8 ft and 6 ft and an area of 54 ft^2. What is the length of the altitude to the 8-ft base?

   Ⓐ 6.75 ft   Ⓑ 9 ft   Ⓒ 24 ft   Ⓓ 27 ft

6. What is the area of the figure at the right?

   Ⓕ 36 m^2 Ⓗ 72 m^2

   Ⓖ 60 m^2 Ⓘ 96 m^2

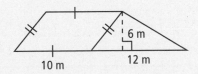

Short Response

7. In a triangle, a base and a corresponding height are in the ratio 5 : 2. The area is 80 ft^2. What is the base and the corresponding height? Show your work.

10-2 Think About a Plan

Areas of Trapezoids, Rhombuses, and Kites

a. **Coordinate Geometry** Graph the lines $x = 0$, $x = 6$, $y = 0$, and $y = x + 4$.

b. What type of quadrilateral do the lines form?

c. Find the area of the quadrilateral.

Understanding the Problem

1. What type of line does $x = 0$ and $x = 6$ represent? What type of line does $y = 0$ represent?

_____

2. What can you tell about the relationships among the lines $x = 0$, $x = 6$, and $y = 0$?

_____

3. How do you graph a line in the form $y = mx + b$?

_____

_____

Planning the Solution

4. Graph the lines on the coordinate grid. What type of quadrilateral is formed? How can you tell?

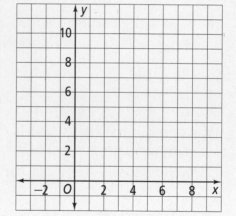

_____

_____

5. What is the formula for finding the area of this type of quadrilateral?

6. Which lines contain the bases? Explain.

_____

7. How can you find the lengths of the bases?

_____

8. Which line contains the height? How can you find the length of the height?

_____

Getting an Answer

9. Substitute the values for the bases and height into the formula and solve for the area.

10-2 Practice

Areas of Trapezoids, Rhombuses, and Kites

Form G

Find the area of each trapezoid.

1.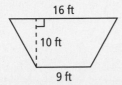
16 ft
10 ft
9 ft

2.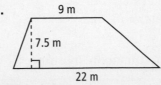
9 m
7.5 m
22 m

3.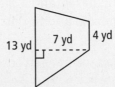
13 yd
7 yd
4 yd

4. Find the area of a trapezoid with bases 20 cm and 14 cm and height 5 cm.

5. Find the area of a trapezoid with bases 8 in. and 7 in. and height 5.2 in.

Find the area of each trapezoid. If your answer is not an integer, leave it in simplest radical form.

6.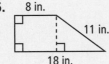
8 in.
11 in.
18 in.

7.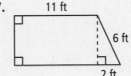
11 ft
6 ft
2 ft

8.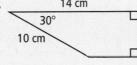
14 cm
30°
10 cm

Find the area of each kite.

9.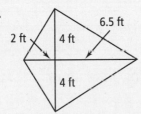
2 ft
4 ft
6.5 ft
4 ft

10.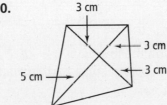
3 cm
3 cm
3 cm
5 cm

11.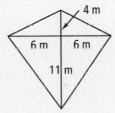
4 m
6 m
6 m
11 m

12. Find the area of a kite with diagonals 12 ft and 3 ft.

13. Find the area of a kite with diagonals 16 m and 14 m.

Find the area of each rhombus.

14.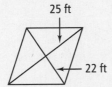
25 ft
22 ft

15.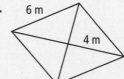
6 m
4 m

16.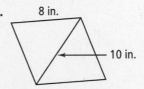
8 in.
10 in.

17. Find the area of a rhombus with diagonals 9 yd and 6 yd.

18. Find the area of a rhombus with diagonals 4.5 in. and 5.2 in.

19. Open-Ended Draw a rhombus. Measure the lengths of its diagonals. Find its area.

10-2 Practice (continued)   Form G
Areas of Trapezoids, Rhombuses, and Kites

20. A trapezoid has two right angles, 16 in. and
20 in. bases, and 5 in. height. Sketch the
trapezoid and find its perimeter and area.

Find the area of each trapezoid to the nearest tenth.

21.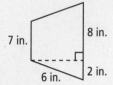
7 in.   8 in.   2 in.   6 in.

22.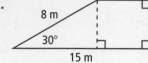
8 m   30°   15 m

23.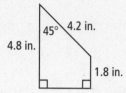
45°   4.2 in.   4.8 in.   1.8 in.

Coordinate Geometry Find the area of quadrilateral *QRST*.

24.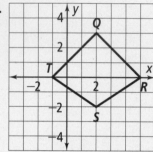

25.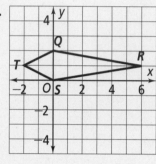

26.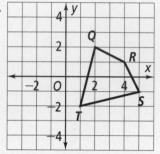

27. **Coordinate Geometry** Graph the lines $y = x - 2$, $y = -x + 2$,
$y = 2x - 10$, and $y = -2x - 2$. What type of quadrilateral do the lines form?
Find the area of the quadrilateral.

28. **Algebra** One diagonal of a rhombus is 5 less than twice the other diagonal.
The area is 75 cm². Find the length of each diagonal.

Find the area of each rhombus. Leave your answer in simplest radical form.

29.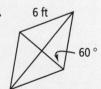
6 ft   60°

30.
45°   4 m

31.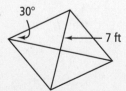
30°   7 ft

32. Trapezoid *QRST* has two right angles. A 5 in. altitude can be drawn dividing
QRST into a rectangle and an isosceles right triangle. The longer side of the
rectangle measures 9 in. What is the area of the trapezoid?

33. In isosceles trapezoid *EFGH*, $\overline{FG} \parallel \overline{EH}$, $FG = 10$, $GH = 12$, and $m\angle E = 60$.
Find the area of *EFGH*.

10-2 Standardized Test Prep

Areas of Trapezoids, Rhombuses, and Kites

Multiple Choice

For Exercises 1–6, choose the correct letter.

1. What is the area of a trapezoid with height 5 m and bases 8 m and 1 m?

    Ⓐ 6.5 m^2 Ⓑ 22.5 m^2 Ⓒ 24 m^2 Ⓓ 45 m^2

2. What is the area of the figure at the right?

    Ⓕ 45 in.^2 Ⓗ 135 in.^2

    Ⓖ 90 in.^2 Ⓘ 180 in.^2

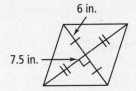

3. What is the area of the kite at the right?

    Ⓐ 30 ft^2 Ⓒ 96 ft^2

    Ⓑ 60 ft^2 Ⓓ 120 ft^2

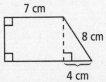

4. What is the area of the trapezoid at the right?

    Ⓕ $36\sqrt{3} \text{ cm}^2$ Ⓗ 65 cm^2

    Ⓖ $44\sqrt{3} \text{ cm}^2$ Ⓘ 88 cm^2

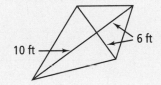

5. What is the area of the figure at the right?

    Ⓐ 7.5 m^2 Ⓒ 21.25 m^2

    Ⓑ 15 m^2 Ⓓ 42.5 m^2

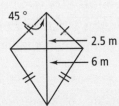

6. A trapezoid has an area of 166.5 in.^2, height 9 in., and one base 15 in. What is the length of the other base?

    Ⓕ 3.5 in.   Ⓗ 18.5 in.

    Ⓖ 7 in.   Ⓘ 22 in.

Extended Response

7. A trapezoid has two right angles and bases that measure 16 m and 8 m. The right triangle formed by an altitude has a hypotenuse of $4\sqrt{5}$ m. Sketch the trapezoid. What are its perimeter and area? Show your work.

10-3 Think About a Plan

Areas of Regular Polygons

A regular hexagon has perimeter 120 m. Find its area.

Understanding the Problem

1. What is the formula for the area of a regular polygon?

2. What information is given? What information do you need?

   _____

Planning the Solution

3. Divide the hexagon into six congruent triangles. What type
   of triangle are these? Explain how you know.

   _____

   _____

   _____

   _____

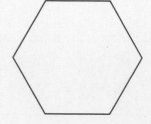

4. What is the length of the radius? Explain.

   _____

   _____

5. Draw an apothem. What type of triangle is formed by one radius, half of one
   side, and the apothem? What are the angles in this polygon?

   _____

6. What relationships exist among the sides of this type of triangle?

   _____

   _____

7. How can you find the length of the apothem? Find its length.

   _____

Getting an Answer

8. Substitute the values for the apothem and the perimeter into the
   formula and solve.

10-3 Practice   Form G
Areas of Regular Polygons

Each regular polygon has radii and apothem as shown. Find the measure of each numbered angle.

1.
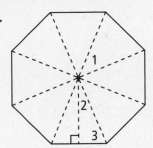

2.
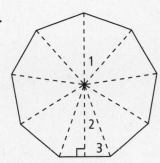

3.
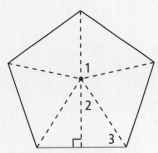

Find the area of each regular polygon with the given apothem a and side length s.

4. pentagon, $a = 4.9$ in., $s = 7.1$ in.

5. hexagon, $a = 12.1$ ft, $s = 14$ ft

6. octagon, $a = 20.8$ m, $s = 17.2$ m

7. nonagon, $a = 50.9$ m, $s = 37$ m

8. decagon, $a = 31$ in., $s = 20.1$ in.

9. dodecagon, $a = 40.6$ m, $s = 21.7$ m

Find the area of each regular polygon. Round your answer to the nearest tenth.

10.

12 in.

11.
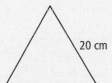
20 cm

12.

8.6 ft

13. Your math teacher draws a regular hexagon with a circle circumscribed around it. The radius of the circle is 5 m. To the nearest tenth, what is the area of the hexagon?

Find the measures of the angles formed by (a) two consecutive radii and (b) a radius and a side of the given regular polygon.

14. hexagon

15. square

16. octagon

17. pentagon

18. 15-gon

19. 20-gon

10-3 Practice (continued) Form G

Areas of Regular Polygons

Find the area of each regular polygon with the given radius or apothem. If your answer is not an integer, leave it in simplest radical form.

20.

8 mm

21.
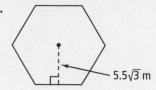
5.5√3 m

22.
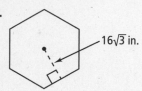
16√3 in.

23.
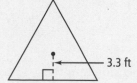
3.3 ft

24.
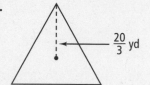
20/3 yd

25.

20 mm

26. A soccer ball's outer covering is made by stitching together 12 regular pentagons and 20 regular hexagons. Both polygons have a side length of 3 cm. The pentagons have an apothem of 2.06 cm. To the nearest whole number, what is the total surface area of the soccer ball?

27. A stop sign is a regular octagon. Each side of the sign is 12.6 in. long. The area of the stop sign is 770 in.^{2}. What is the length of the apothem to the nearest whole number?

28. A quilter is cutting fabric for her quilt. She has several pieces of fabric from an old project that are in the shape of regular octagons. She wants to cut the octagons into right triangles. If she divides each octagon into 16 triangles, what is the measure of the non-right angles of each triangle?

29. An equilateral triangle has a perimeter of 36 cm. Find its area to the nearest tenth.

30. The logo for a school is an equilateral triangle inscribed inside a circle. The seniors are painting the logo on an outside wall of the school. The radius of the circle will be 6 feet. Find the area of the triangle.

31. **Algebra** Find the length of one side of each of the regular polygons named below if its area is 64 ft^2. Round your answer to the nearest tenth.

   a. triangle

   b. hexagon

10-3 Standardized Test Prep
Areas of Regular Polygons

Multiple Choice

For Exercises 1–6, choose the correct letter.

For Exercises 1 and 2, use the diagram at the right.

1. The figure at the right is a regular octagon with radii and an apothem drawn. What is $m\angle 1$?

    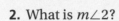

    Ⓐ 22.5

    Ⓒ 60

    Ⓑ 45

    Ⓓ 67.5

2. What is $m\angle 2$?

    Ⓕ 22.5   Ⓖ 45   Ⓗ 60   Ⓘ 67.5

3. A regular pentagon has an apothem of 3.2 m and an area of 37.2 m². What is the length of one side of the pentagon?

    Ⓐ 3.96 m   Ⓑ 4.65 m   Ⓒ 11.875 m   Ⓓ 23.75 m

4. What is the area of the square at the right?

    Ⓕ 16.97 cm²

    Ⓗ 144 cm²

    Ⓖ 72 cm²

    Ⓘ 288 cm²

    12 cm

5. A regular hexagon has perimeter 60 in. What is the hexagon's area?

    Ⓐ $75\sqrt{3}$ in.²   Ⓑ $150\sqrt{3}$ in.²   Ⓒ $300\sqrt{3}$ in.²   Ⓓ $600\sqrt{3}$ in.²

6. For which regular polygon can you *not* use special triangles to find the apothem?

    Ⓕ pentagon   Ⓖ triangle   Ⓗ square   Ⓘ hexagon

Short Response

7. The area of an equilateral triangle is $108\sqrt{3}$ ft². What is the length of a side and the apothem in simplest radical form? Draw a diagram and show your work.

10-4 Think About a Plan

Perimeters and Areas of Similar Figures

The shorter sides of a parallelogram are 5 m. The shorter sides of a similar parallelogram are 15 m. The area of the smaller parallelogram is 28 m². What is the area of the larger parallelogram?

Understanding the Problem

1. How are the lengths of corresponding sides of similar figures related?

   _____

2. How can you represent this relationship mathematically?

   _____

3. How can you use this relationship to find the scale factor of the figures?

   _____

4. How are the areas of two similar figures related to the scale factor?

   _____

Planning the Solution

5. Write the mathematical relationship that relates the lengths of corresponding sides in the two parallelograms.

6. Use this relationship to find the scale factor for the parallelograms.

7. Use the scale factor to find the relationship between the areas of the parallelograms.

Getting an Answer

8. Substitute the known quantities in the relationship you wrote in Step 7. Then solve.

9. What is the larger parallelogram's area? Be sure to use correct units.

10-4 Practice

Perimeters and Areas of Similar Figures

Form G

The figures in each pair are similar. Compare the first figure to the second.
Give the ratio of the perimeters and the ratio of the areas.

1.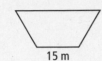

8 mm   6 mm

2.

3 in.   6 in.

3.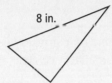

10 m   15 m

4.

20 ft   8 ft

The figures in each pair are similar. The area of one figure is given. Find the area
of the other figure to the nearest whole number.

5. 4 in.   8 in.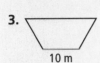

area of smaller triangle = 12 in.^{2}

6.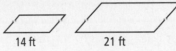

14 ft   21 ft

area of smaller parallelogram = 72 ft^2

7.

24 cm   8 cm

area of larger pentagon = 135 cm^2

8.

6 m   15 m

area of smaller rhombus = 60 m^2

9. It took James 5 h to paint an 8 ft by 24 ft wall. At this rate, how long would it
take him to paint a 12 ft by 36 ft wall?

Find the scale factor and the ratio of perimeters for each pair of similar figures.

10. two regular pentagons with areas 144 in.^{2} and 36 in.^{2}

11. two rectangles with areas 72 m^2 and 50 m^2

12. two regular pentagons with areas 147 ft^2 and 12 ft^2

13. two equilateral triangles with areas $121\sqrt{3}$ cm^2 and $16\sqrt{3}$ cm^2

14. two circles with areas 12π in.^{2} and 27π in.^{2}

10-4 Practice (continued)

Perimeters and Areas of Similar Figures

Form G

The scale factor of two similar polygons is given. Find the ratio of their perimeters and the ratio of their areas.

15. $5 : 1$

16. $2 : 7$

17. $\frac{3}{4}$

18. $\frac{10}{7}$

19. $10 : 3$

20. $\frac{5}{9}$

Algebra Find the values of x and y when the smaller similar rectangle shown here has the area given.

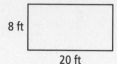

21. 10 ft^2

22. 20 ft^2

23. 22.5 ft^2

24. 40 ft^2

25. 44.1 ft^2

26. 50 ft^2

27. The area of a regular octagon is 45 ft^2. What is the area of a regular octagon with sides $\frac{1}{3}$ the length of sides of the larger octagon?

28. The longer base of a right trapezoid is 12 ft. The longer base of a similar right trapezoid is 30 ft. The area of the smaller right trapezoid is 20 ft^2. What is the area of the larger right trapezoid?

29. A postcard costs $0.95. Leslie wants to buy a poster that is a similar shape with a scale factor for the poster to the postcard of $5 : 1$. How much should she expect to pay for the poster?

30. Two similar parallelograms have areas 125 m^2 and 80 m^2. The height of the larger parallelogram is 10 m. What are the lengths of the bases of both parallelograms?

31. A team is excavating an archeological site. The original plan was to excavate a rectangular area 35 ft long by 20 ft wide. Instead, the team decided to excavate a similar rectangle that is 50 ft wide. Find the length and the area of the new rectangle.

The pair of figures is similar. Compare the larger figure to the smaller figure. Find the ratio of their perimeters and the ratio of their areas.

32.
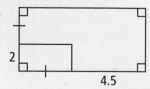

33.
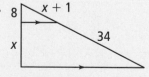

34.
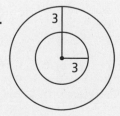

10-4 Standardized Test Prep

Perimeters and Areas of Similar Figures

Gridded Response

Solve each exercise and enter your answer on the grid provided.

For Exercises 1 and 2, use the diagram at the right.

1. The triangles at the right are similar. What is the ratio (larger to smaller) of the perimeters?

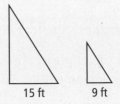

15 ft   9 ft

2. The triangles at the right are similar. What is the ratio (larger to smaller) of the areas?

3. The pentagons at the right are similar. The area of the smaller pentagon is 30 m². What is the area of the larger pentagon in m²?

4 m   10 m

4. It costs $350 to carpet an 8 ft by 10 ft room. At this rate, how many dollars would it cost to put the same carpeting in a 24 ft by 30 ft room?

5. The areas of two similar octagons are 112 in.² and 63 in.². What is the ratio (larger to smaller) of their perimeters?

Answers

1. 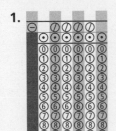   2. 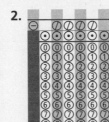   3. 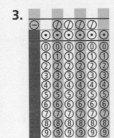   4. 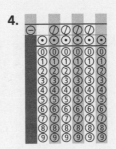   5.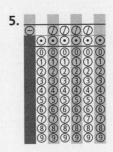

Name _____ Class _____ Date _____

10-5 Think About a Plan

Trigonometry and Area

Architecture The Pentagon in Arlington, Virginia, is one of the world's largest office buildings. It is a regular pentagon, and the length of each of its sides is 921 ft. What is the area of land the Pentagon covers to the nearest thousand square feet?

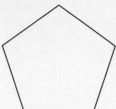

Understanding the Problem

1. The figure at the right is a regular pentagon. Label the side length with the information given in the problem.

2. The formula for the area of a regular polygon is $A = \frac{1}{2}ap$. Which measures do you need to solve the problem?

_____

Planning the Solution

3. How can you find the perimeter?

_____

4. Draw an apothem and radius on the figure. Label the center A, and draw right $\triangle ABC$ formed by the apothem and radius, where $\overline{AB}$ is the hypotenuse.

5. How can you find $m\angle ABC$? Write this measure on the diagram.

_____

_____

6. Which trigonometric ratio can you use to find the apothem? Explain.

_____

_____

Getting an Answer

7. Complete the equation below. Then solve for a, the apothem.

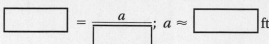

$$\boxed{} = \frac{a}{\boxed{}}; \ a \approx \boxed{} \text{ft}$$

8. Use the formula for the area of a regular polygon to find the area.

10-5 Practice

Form G

Trigonometry and Area

Find the area of each regular polygon. Round your answers to the nearest tenth.

1.
8 m

2.
6 ft

3.
14 cm

Find the area of each regular polygon. Round your answers to the nearest tenth.

4. hexagon with side length 4 m

5. pentagon with side length 10 in.

6. nonagon with radius 6 ft

7. decagon with radius 5 mm

8. octagon with radius 9 cm

9. 20-gon with radius 3 in.

10. 15-gon with perimeter 120 ft

11. 18-gon with perimeter 54 m

Find the area of each triangle. Round your answers to the nearest tenth.

12.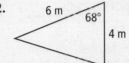
6 m
68°
4 m

13.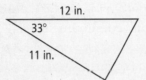
12 in.
33°
11 in.

14.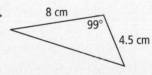
8 cm
99°
4.5 cm

15.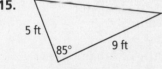
5 ft
85°
9 ft

16.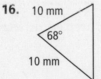
10 mm
68°
10 mm

17.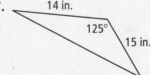
14 in.
125°
15 in.

18. *ABCDEFGH* is a regular octagon with center *X* and radius 6 cm. Find each measure. If necessary, round your answers to the nearest tenth.

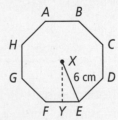

a. $m\angle FXE$

b. $m\angle YXE$

c. XY

d. FE

e. perimeter of *ABCDEFGH*

f. area of *ABCDEFGH*

19. Octagonal houses were popular in the 19th century. One reason was that an octagon with the same perimeter as a square encloses a greater area than the square. To the nearest square ft, find the areas of an octagon and a square with perimeters of 80 ft.

10-5

Practice (continued)

Trigonometry and Area

Form G

20. The Tribeca neighborhood in New York City gets its name from its shape and location (a triangle below Canal Street). The triangular part of the neighborhood is formed by the intersection of Canal Street, Hudson Street, and West Broadway. This section of Hudson Street is about 3000 ft long, this section of West Broadway is about 2500 ft long, and the angle enclosed by the two streets is approximately 25°. What is the area of this part of Tribeca? Round your answer to the nearest thousand square feet.

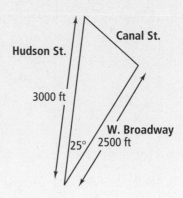

Find the perimeter and area of each regular polygon to the nearest tenth.

21.

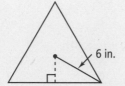

22.

23.

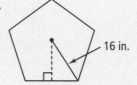

24. The central angle of a regular polygon is 18°. The perimeter of the polygon is 144 ft. What is the area of the polygon to the nearest tenth?

25. The cost for refinishing a floor is $2.50/ft². What is the cost of refinishing a hexagonal floor that has a radius of 5.5 ft?

The polygons are regular polygons. Find the area of the shaded region.

26.

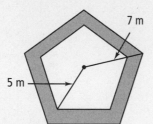

27.

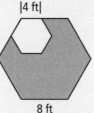

28.

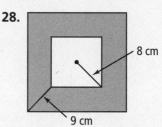

29. **Reasoning** Which has the greater area, a regular octagon or a regular nonagon, if both have the same length sides? Explain.

30. **Reasoning** Which has the greater perimeter, a regular pentagon, or a regular hexagon, if they have the same area? Explain.

10-5 Standardized Test Prep

Trigonometry and Area

Multiple Choice

For Exercises 1–6, choose the correct letter.

1. What is the area of the regular pentagon at the right?

   Ⓐ 688.2 ft^2 Ⓒ 951.1 ft^2

   Ⓑ 850.7 ft^2 Ⓓ 1376.4 ft^2

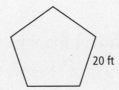

20 ft

2. What is the area of the regular octagon at the right?

   Ⓕ 114.5 m^2 Ⓗ 391.1 m^2

   Ⓖ 229.1 m^2 Ⓘ 458.2 m^2

9 m

3. What is the area of a regular hexagon with sides 8 cm?

   Ⓐ 110.1 cm^2 Ⓑ 166.3 cm^2 Ⓒ 309.0 cm^2 Ⓓ 332.6 cm^2

4. What is the area of a regular nonagon with a radius of 14 in.?

   Ⓕ 70.9 in.^{2} Ⓖ 141.7 in.^{2} Ⓗ 566.9 in.^{2} Ⓘ 1211.6 in.^{2}

5. What is the area of a 15-gon with a perimeter of 90 m?

   Ⓐ 528.2 m^2 Ⓑ 635.1 m^2 Ⓒ 1270.3 m^2 Ⓓ 142,903.1 m^2

6. What is the area of the triangle at the right?

   Ⓕ 6.0 ft^2 Ⓗ 15.0 ft^2

   Ⓖ 8.6 ft^2 Ⓘ 17.2 ft^2

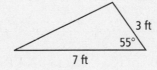

3 ft

55°

7 ft

Short Response

7. What is the area of the triangle shown at the right?
   Show your work and explain how you got your answer.

5 in.

31°   31°

10-6

Think About a Plan

Circles and Arcs

Time Hands of a clock suggest an angle whose measure is continually changing. How many degrees does a minute hand move through during each time interval?

  a. 1 min   **b.** 5 min   **c.** 20 min

Understanding the Problem

1. Draw the minute hand pointing to 12. Then draw the minute hand where it would be 5 min later.

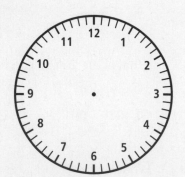

2. What type of angle is formed by the hand in these two positions?

   _____

3. How many degrees are in a complete circle? How many minutes are in an hour?

Planning the Solution

4. How can you show the relationship between the number of minutes in an hour and the total number of degrees in a circle? _____

5. Use words to write a proportion that can be used to find the number of degrees represented by any time interval.

   _____

   _____

6. Which part of this proportion will be represented by a variable?

   _____

7. What is the ratio of the minutes in one hour to the degrees in a circle in simplest form?

Getting an Answer

8. Write and solve a proportion to find the number of degrees the minute hand moves through in a 1-min interval.

9. Write and solve proportions to find the number of degrees the minute hand moves through in 5-min and 20-min intervals.

10-6 Practice

Form G

Circles and Arcs

Name the following in ⊙G.

1. the minor arcs

2. the major arcs

3. the semicircles

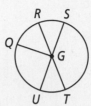

Find the measure of each arc in ⊙B.

4. $\overparen{GJ}$

5. $\overparen{HI}$

6. $\overparen{HIJ}$

7. $\overparen{GJI}$

8. $\overparen{GHJ}$

9. $\overparen{GJH}$

10. $\overparen{HGJ}$

11. $\overparen{GH}$

12. $\overparen{GHI}$

13. $\overparen{HJI}$

14. $\overparen{JHI}$

15. $\overparen{JIG}$

Find the circumference of each circle. Leave your answers in terms of π.

16.

16 in.

17.

22 m

18.

6.8 m

19. A dartboard consists of five concentric circles. The radius of the smallest circle is about 1 in. The radius of the second circle is about 3 in. longer. The radius of the third circle is about 1 in. longer than the previous circle. The radius of the fourth circle is about 2 in. longer than the previous circle. The radius of the largest circle is about 0.75 in. greater than the previous circle. What is the difference between the circumferences of the largest and the smallest circle? Round your answer to the nearest tenth of an inch.

20. The wheels on Reggie's bike each have a 20-in. diameter. His sister's mountain bike has wheels that each have a 26-in. diameter. To the nearest inch, how much farther does Reggie's sister's bike travel in one revolution than Reggie's bike?

21. A Ferris wheel has a 50-m radius. How many kilometers will a passenger travel during a ride if the wheel makes 10 revolutions? Round your answer to the nearest tenth of a kilometer.

22. The marching band has ordered a banner with its logo. The logo is a circle with a 45° central angle. If the diameter of the circle is 3 ft, what is the length of the major arc to the nearest tenth?

10-6

Practice (continued)

Form G

Circles and Arcs

Find the length of each darkened arc. Leave your answer in terms of π.

23.

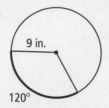

9 in.

120°

24.

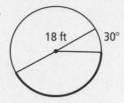

18 ft   30°

25.

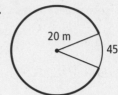

20 m   45°

26.

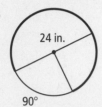

24 in.

90°

27.

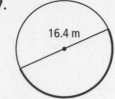

16.4 m

28.

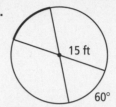

15 ft   60°

Find each indicated measure for $\odot Y$.

29. $m\angle EYD$

30. $m\widehat{EAB}$

31. $m\widehat{DB}$

32. $m\angle DYC$

33. $m\widehat{AEC}$

34. $m\widehat{BDA}$

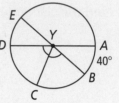

35. Kiley's in-line skate wheels have a 43-mm diameter. How many meters will Kiley travel after 5000 revolutions of the wheels on her in-line skates? Round your answer to the nearest tenth of a meter.

36. It is 5:00. What is the measure of the minor arc formed by the hands of an analog clock?

37. In $\odot B$, the length of $\widehat{ST}$ is 3π in. and $m\widehat{ST}$ is 120. What is the radius of $\odot B$?

Algebra Find the value of each variable.

38.

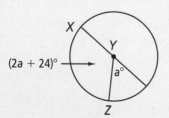

X
Y
(2a + 24)°
a°
Z

39.

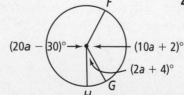

F
(20a − 30)°   (10a + 2)°
(2a + 4)°
G
H

40.

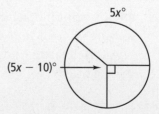

5x°
(5x − 10)°

41. A 45° arc of $\odot D$ has the same length as a 30° arc of $\odot E$. What is the ratio of the radius of $\odot D$ to the radius of $\odot E$?

10-6

Standardized Test Prep

Circles and Arcs

Multiple Choice

For Exercises 1–6, choose the correct letter.

For Exercises 1–3, use the figure at the right.

1. Which is a minor arc in $\odot L$?

   (A) $\overset{\frown}{AB}$ (C) $\overset{\frown}{ABD}$

   (B) $\overset{\frown}{DB}$ (D) $\overset{\frown}{CBD}$

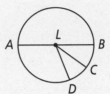

2. Which is a major arc in $\odot L$?

   (F) $\overset{\frown}{ADB}$ (G) $\overset{\frown}{DBA}$ (H) $\overset{\frown}{AD}$ (I) $\overset{\frown}{CA}$

3. Which is a semicircle in $\odot L$?

   (A) $\overset{\frown}{ADB}$ (B) $\overset{\frown}{BCD}$ (C) $\overset{\frown}{BC}$ (D) $\overset{\frown}{ADC}$

4. What is the degree measure of $\overset{\frown}{TUR}$?

   (F) 32   (H) 238

   (G) 122   (I) 248

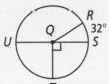

5. Which shows the circumference of $\odot Z$?

   (A) 6π (C) 24π

   (B) 12π (D) 144π

6. Which shows the length of the darkened arc?

   (F) 1.5π (H) 7.5π

   (G) 3π (I) 15π

Short Response

7. The wheel of one car has a diameter of 20 in. The wheel of another car has a diameter of 24 in. About how many more revolutions must the smaller wheel make than the larger wheel to travel 100 ft?

10-7 Think About a Plan

Areas of Circles and Sectors

Industrial Design Refer to the diagram of the regular hexagonal nut. What is the area of the hexagonal face to the nearest millimeter?

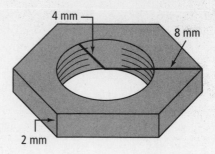

Understanding the Problem

1. On the diagram at the right, what is the area that you need to find?

   _____

2. How does this area differ from that of a regular hexagon?

   _____

3. What two areas must you find to solve this problem?

   _____

Planning the Solution

4. What is the formula for the area of a circle?

5. What is the formula for the area of a regular polygon?

6. What information do you have about the hexagon? What information do you need?

   _____

7. What special triangle relationship can you use to find the information you need?

   _____

Getting an Answer

8. Use this relationship to find the length of the shorter leg, the perimeter, and the apothem.

9. Use the formula to calculate the area of the hexagon.

10. Use the formula to calculate the area of the circle.

11. What is the area of the hexagonal face?

10-7 **Practice**

Areas of Circles and Sectors

Form G

Find the area of each of the following. Leave your answer in terms of π.

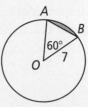

1. $\odot O$

2. $\triangle AOB$

3. sector AOB

4. the shaded segment

Find the area of each of the following. Leave your answer in terms of π.

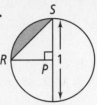

5. $\odot P$

6. $\triangle RPS$

7. sector RPS

8. the shaded segment

Find the area of each shaded sector of a circle. Leave your answer in terms of π.

9.

10.

11.

12.

13.

14.
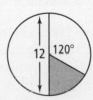

15.

16.

17.

Find the area of each shaded segment. Round your answer to the nearest tenth.

18.
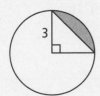

19.
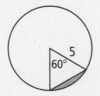

20.

21. The table in the figure at the right is 24 in. across. The shaded regions are made of mahogany. What is the area of the mahogany? Round your answer to the nearest tenth.

├── 24 in. ──┤

10-7 Practice (continued)
Areas of Circles and Sectors

Find the area of sector *RST* in ⊙*S* using the given information. Leave your answer in terms of π.

22. $r = 3$ in., $m\widehat{RT} = 30$

23. $r = 8$ mm, $m\widehat{RT} = 90$

24. $d = 10$ ft, $m\widehat{TR} = 180$

25. $d = 13$ m, $m\widehat{TR} = 120$

Find the area of the shaded region. Leave your answer in terms of π and in simplest radical form.

26.
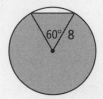

27.
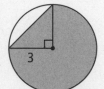

28.
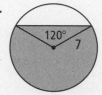

Find the area of each shaded segment. Round your answer to the nearest tenth.

29.
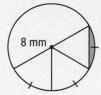

30.

31.

32. Draw a Diagram Draw a circle and a sector so that the area of the sector is three-tenths of the area of the circle. Give the radius of the circle, the measure of the arc, and area of the sector.

33. Reasoning If $\widehat{AC} \cong \widehat{DF}$ and Area of sector $ABC =$ Area of sector DEF, is $\odot B \cong \odot E$? Explain.

34. In a circle, a 60° sector has area 25π ft². What is the circumference of the circle? Leave your answer in terms of π and in simplest radical form.

10-7 Standardized Test Prep
Areas of Circles and Sectors

Multiple Choice

For Exercises 1–4, choose the correct letter.

1. What is the area of a circle with a diameter of 8?

   A 4π B 8π C 16π D 64π

2. Which sector below has the greatest area?

   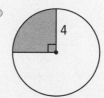

3. If $\odot B$ has a radius of 4 and $m\widehat{AC} = 36$, what is the area of sector ABC?

   A $\frac{5}{8}\pi$ B $\frac{4}{5}\pi$ C $\frac{5}{4}\pi$ D $\frac{8}{5}\pi$

4. Which of the following is equal to the area of the sector ABC in the figure at the right?

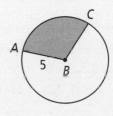

   F $\frac{m\widehat{AC}}{360} \cdot 10\pi$ H $\frac{m\widehat{AC}}{360} \cdot 25\pi$

   G $\frac{360}{m\widehat{AC}} \cdot 5\pi$ I $\frac{360}{m\widehat{AC}} \cdot 25\pi$

Short Response

5. What is the area of the shaded segment in the figure at the right? Use at least three steps. Show your work. Leave your answer in terms of π and in simplest radical form.

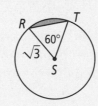

10-8

Think About a Plan

Geometric Probability

Games To win a prize at a carnival game, you must toss a quarter so that it lands entirely within a 1-in. circle as shown at the right. Assume that the center of a tossed quarter is equally likely to land at any point within the 8-in. square.

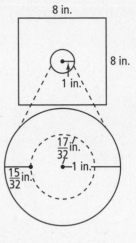

   a. What is the probability that the quarter lands entirely in the circle in one toss?

   b. Reasoning On average, how many coins must you toss to win a prize? Explain.

1. In this problem, what represents the favorable outcome? Be specific.

_____

2. In this problem, what represents all the possible outcomes?

_____

3. If a section of the quarter is in the circle, does this count as a favorable outcome?

_____

4. How can you determine a smaller circle within which the center of the quarter must land for the quarter to be entirely within the 1-in. circle? What is the radius of this circle? The radius of a quarter is $\frac{15}{32}$ in.

_____

_____

_____

5. Use words to write a probability ratio. Then rewrite the ratio using the appropriate formulas. Substitute the appropriate measures and find the probability.

_____

_____

6. Based on this, what is the average number of coins you must toss before you can expect to win a prize? Explain.

_____

_____

10-8 Practice   Form G
Geometric Probability

Find the probability that a point chosen at random from $\overline{AK}$ is on the given segment.

A B C D E F G H I J K
0 2 4 6 8 10 12 14 16 18 20

1. $\overline{CF}$ **2.** $\overline{BI}$ **3.** $\overline{GK}$

4. $\overline{FG}$ **5.** $\overline{AK}$ **6.** $\overline{AC}$

7. Roberto's trolley runs every 45 minutes. It he arrives at the trolley stop at a random time, what is the probability that he will *not* have to wait more than 10 minutes? Draw a geometric model to solve the problem.

8. The state of Connecticut is approximated by a rectangle 100 mi by 50 mi. Hartford is approximately at the center of Connecticut. If a meteor hit the earth within 200 mi of Hartford, find the probability that the meteor landed in Connecticut.

9. A stoplight at an intersection stays red for 60 second, changes to green for 45 seconds, and then turns yellow for 15 seconds. If Jamal arrives at the intersection at a random time, what is the probability that he will have to wait at a red light for more than 15 seconds?

A point between A and B on each number line is chosen at random. What is the probability that the point is between C and D?

10.
A C D B
−2 0 2 4

11.
A C   D B
−10 0 10 20

12.
A C D B
−2 0 2 4

13.
A C D B
−3 0 3 6

Use the dartboard at the right for Exercises 14–16. Assume that a dart you throw will land on the dartboard and is equally likely to land at any point on the board.

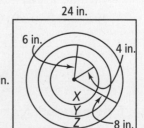

24 in.

6 in.

4 in.

24 in.

X
Y
Z

8 in.

14. What is the probability of hitting region X?

15. What is the probability of hitting region Y?

16. What is the probability of hitting region Z?

10-8

Practice (continued)   *Form G*

Geometric Probability

A point in the figure is chosen at random. Find the probability that the point lies in the shaded region.

17.

18.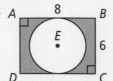

19.

20.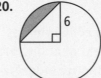

21. See the figure at the right. The wind comes out of one of the directions at random. What is the probability that the wind comes out of the southwest (SW)?

22. Reasoning Point *P* is chosen at random from the perimeter of rectangle *ABCD*.

   a. What is the probability that *P* lies on $\overline{DC}$?

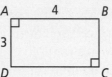

   b. Now *P* is chosen at random from the perimeter or the diagonals. Does this increase or decrease the probability that *P* lies on $\overline{DC}$? Explain. Find the new probability to support your conclusion.

23. You and your friend are playing a target game based on the board at the right (not drawn to scale). You must hit the border to win a point. Your friend must hit the circle in the center.

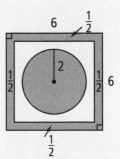

   a. Is the game fair? That is, do you or your friend have an equal probability of hitting your target zones? Explain. If the game is not fair, find the radius of the circle that would make it fair.

   b. Find the probability that you do not score a point.

24. Open-Ended Make a game board using polygons and circles. Switch games with a partner and use geometric probability to find the likelihood of choosing each particular region of the game board.

10-8 Standardized Test Prep

Multiple Choice

For Exercises 1–4, choose the correct letter.

1. Point X on $\overline{QT}$ is chosen at random. What is the probability that X is on $\overline{ST}$?

   (A) $\dfrac{QT}{ST}$　　　　(B) $\dfrac{ST}{QT}$　　　　(C) $\dfrac{QS}{ST}$　　　　(D) $\dfrac{ST}{QS}$

2. Point P on $\overline{AD}$ is chosen at random. For which of the figures below is the probability that P is on $\overline{BC}$ 25%? Note: Diagrams not drawn to scale.

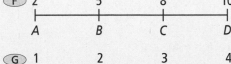

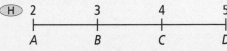

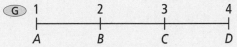

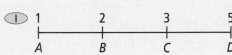

3. Point P is chosen at random in a circle. If a square is inscribed in the circle, what is the probability that P lies outside the square?

   (A) $1 - \dfrac{1}{2\pi}$　　　　(B) $1 - \dfrac{2}{\pi}$　　　　(C) $1 - \dfrac{\pi}{2}$　　　　(D) $1 - \dfrac{1}{4\pi}$

4. You have a 7-cm straw and a 10-cm straw. You want to cut the 10-cm straw into two pieces so that the three pieces make a triangle. If you cut the straw at a random point, what is the probability that you can make a triangle?

   (F) 30%　　　　(G) 40%　　　　(H) 60%　　　　(I) 70%

Short Response

5. Point P is chosen at random in $\odot S$. What is the probability that P lies in the shaded segment shown in the diagram at the right? Show your work.

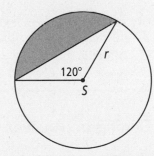

11-1 Think About a Plan

Space Figures and Cross Sections

Visualization Draw and describe a cross section formed by a plane intersecting the cube as follows.

The plane is tilted and intersects the front and back faces of the cube perpendicular to the left and right faces.

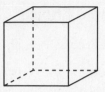

Understanding the Problem

1. What is a cube? Draw a typical view of a cube and describe a cube.

_____

2. What is a plane? Draw a typical view of a plane and describe a plane.

_____

3. What is a cross section? Draw a plane passing through your cube that is parallel to the top and bottom faces of your cube. Explain why the cross section is a square. _____

_____

_____

_____

Planning the Solution

4. How can you use your understanding of cubes, planes, and cross sections to draw a plane that is tilted and intersects the front and back faces of the cube perpendicular to the left and right faces?

_____

5. You showed that if a plane is not tilted, the cross section is a square. How can you use this knowledge to predict what the cross section will look like if the plane is tilted? _____

_____

Getting an Answer

6. Prepare to draw a plane that is tilted and intersects the front and back faces of the cube perpendicular to the left and right faces by studying your drawing of a plane parallel to the top and bottom faces. Imagine the thin slice created when this tilted plane passes through the cube. Describe this cross section.

_____

_____

11-1 Practice

Form G

Space Figures and Cross Sections

For each polyhedron, how many vertices, edges, and faces are there? List them.

1.

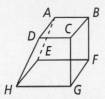

2.

For each polyhedron, use Euler's Formula to find the missing number.

3. Faces: ☐   Edges: 12   Vertices: 8

4. Faces: 9   Edges: ☐   Vertices: 14

5. Faces: 10   Edges: 18   Vertices: ☐

6. Faces: ☐   Edges: 24   Vertices: 16

7. Faces: 8   Edges: ☐   Vertices: 6

Verify Euler's Formula for each polyhedron. Then draw a net for the figure and verify Euler's Formula for the two-dimensional figure.

8.

9.

Describe each cross section.

10.

11.

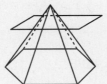

12.

11-1 Practice (continued) Form G
Space Figures and Cross Sections

13. Open-Ended Sketch a polyhedron with more than four faces whose faces are all triangles. Label the lengths of its edges. Use graph paper to draw a net of the polyhedron.

Use Euler's Formula to find the number of vertices in each polyhedron.

14. 6 faces that are all parallelograms

15. 2 faces that are heptagons, 7 rectangular faces

16. 6 triangular faces

Reasoning Can you find a cross section of a square pyramid that forms the figure? Draw the cross section if the cross section exists. If not, explain.

17. square

18. isosceles triangle

19. rectangle that is not a square

20. equilateral triangle

21. scalene triangle

22. trapezoid

23. What is the cross section formed by a plane containing a vertical line of symmetry for the figure at the right?

24. What is the cross section formed by a plane that is parallel to the base of the figure at the right?

25. Reasoning Can a polyhedron have 19 faces, 34 edges, and 18 vertices? Explain.

26. Reasoning Is a cone a polyhedron? Explain.

27. Visualization What is the cross section formed by a plane that intersects the front, right, top, and bottom faces of a cube?

Prentice Hall Gold Geometry • Practice and Problem Solving Workbook
288

11-1 Standardized Test Prep

Space Figures and Cross Sections

Multiple Choice

For Exercises 1–5, choose the correct letter.

1. A polyhedron has 6 vertices and 9 edges. How many faces does it have?

   Ⓐ 3　　　　　　Ⓑ 5　　　　　　Ⓒ 7　　　　　　Ⓓ 9

2. A polyhedron has 25 faces and 36 edges. How many vertices does it have?

   Ⓕ 11　　　　　Ⓖ 12　　　　　Ⓗ 13　　　　　Ⓘ 14

3. Which of the following shows a net for a solid that has 8 faces, 12 vertices, and 18 edges?

   Ⓐ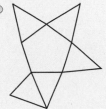

   Ⓒ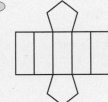

   Ⓑ

   Ⓓ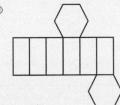

4. What is the cross section formed by a plane that contains a vertical line of symmetry for a tetrahedron?

   Ⓕ triangle　　　　Ⓖ square　　　　Ⓗ rectangle　　　　Ⓘ pentagon

5. What is the cross section formed by a plane that intersects three faces of a cube?

   Ⓐ triangle　　　　Ⓑ square　　　　Ⓒ rectangle　　　　Ⓓ pentagon

Short Response

6. How many edges and vertices are there for an octahedron, a polyhedron with eight congruent triangular faces?

11-2 Think About a Plan

Surface Areas of Prisms and Cylinders

Reasoning Suppose you double the radius of a right cylinder.
   a. How does that affect the lateral area?
   b. How does that affect the surface area?
   c. Use the formula for surface area of a right cylinder to explain why the surface area in part (b) was not doubled.

Understanding the Problem

1. What is the formula for the lateral area of a right cylinder?

2. What is the formula for the surface area of a right cylinder?

Planning the Solution

3. How does doubling the radius affect the formulas for the lateral and surface areas? In the formula for the surface area, where do you need to be most careful?

   _____

   _____

4. How do you compare the new formulas you get after doubling the radius in the original formulas?

   _____

Getting an Answer

5. Write the formula for the new lateral area after the radius has been doubled. Compare this to the original formula for the lateral area. What effect does doubling the radius have?

   _____

   _____

   _____

6. Write the formula for the new surface area after the radius has been doubled. Compare this to the original formula for the surface area. What effect does doubling the radius have?

   _____

   _____

   _____

11-2 Practice

Form G

Surface Areas of Prisms and Cylinders

Use a net to find the surface area of each prism. Round your answer to the nearest whole number.

1.

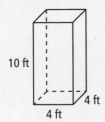

10 ft
4 ft
4 ft

2.

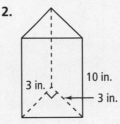

10 in.
3 in.
3 in.

3. a. Classify the prism at the right.

   b. The bases are regular pentagons. Find the lateral area of the prism.

   c. The area of each is 43 cm². Find the sum of their areas.

   d. Find the surface area of the prism.

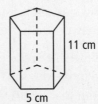

11 cm
5 cm

Use formulas to find the lateral area and surface area of each prism. Round your answer to the nearest whole number.

4.

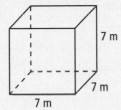

7 m
7 m
7 m

5.

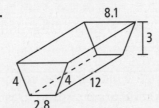

8.1
3
4
4
12
2.8

6.

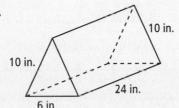

10 in.
10 in.
24 in.
6 in.

Find the lateral area of each cylinder to the nearest whole number.

7.

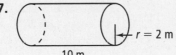

r = 2 m
10 m

8.

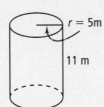

r = 5m
11 m

9.

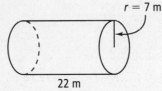

r = 7 m
22 m

10. A box of cereal measures 8 in. wide, 11 in. high, and 2 in. deep. If all surfaces are made of cardboard and the total amount of overlapping cardboard in the box is 7 in.², how much cardboard is used to make the cereal box?

11. Judging by appearances, what is the surface area of the solid shown at the right? Show your answer to the nearest whole number.

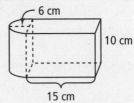

6 cm
10 cm
15 cm

11-2 Practice (continued) Form G
Surface Areas of Prisms and Cylinders

Find the surface area of each cylinder in terms of π.

12.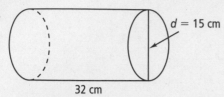

13.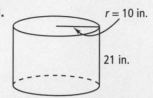

14. **a.** A cylindrical container of paint with radius 6 in. is 15 in. tall. If all of the surfaces except the top are made of metal, how much metal is used to make the container? Assume the thickness of the metal is negligible. Show your answer to the nearest square inch.

   b. If the top of the paint container is made of plastic, how much plastic is used to make the top? Assume the thickness of the plastic is negligible. Show your answer to the nearest square inch.

15. **a. Reasoning** Suppose that a cylinder has a radius of r units and a height of $2r$ units. The lateral area of the cylinder is 64π square units. What is the value of r?

   b. What is the surface area of the cylinder? Round your answer to the nearest square unit.

Visualization **Suppose you revolve the plane region completely about the given line to sweep out a solid of revolution. Describe the solid and find its surface area in terms of π.**

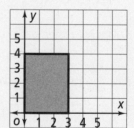

16. the x-axis

17. the y-axis

18. the line $x = 3$

19. the line $y = 2$

20. An artist creates a right prism whose bases are regular decagons. He wants to paint the surface of the prism. One can of paint can cover 32 square feet. How many cans of paint must he buy if the height of the prism is 11 ft and the length of each side of the decagon is 2.4 ft? The area of a base is approximately 89 ft^2.

21. **Open-Ended** Draw a cylinder with a surface area of 136π cm^2.

11-2 Standardized Test Prep

Surface Areas of Prisms and Cylinders

Multiple Choice

For Exercises 1–8, choose the correct letter.

1. What is the lateral surface area of a cube with side length 9 cm?

   Ⓐ 72 cm^2 Ⓑ 324 cm^2 Ⓒ 405 cm^2 Ⓓ 486 cm^2

2. What is the surface area of a prism whose bases each have area 16 m^2 and whose lateral surface area is 64 m^2?

   Ⓕ 80 m^2 Ⓖ 96 m^2 Ⓗ 144 m^2 Ⓘ 160 m^2

3. A cylindrical container with radius 12 cm and height 7 cm is covered in paper. What is the area of the paper? Round to the nearest whole number.

   Ⓐ 528 cm^2 Ⓑ 835 cm^2 Ⓒ 1055 cm^2 Ⓓ 1432 cm^2

For Exercises 4 and 5, use the prism at the right.

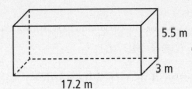

4. What is the surface area of the prism?

   Ⓕ 283.8 m^2 Ⓗ 325.4 m^2

   Ⓖ 292.4 m^2 Ⓘ 407 m^2

5. What is the lateral surface area of the prism?

   Ⓐ 283.8 m^2 Ⓑ 292.4 m^2 Ⓒ 325.4 m^2 Ⓓ 407 m^2

For Exercises 6 and 7, use the cylinder at the right.

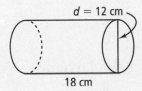

6. What is the lateral surface area of the cylinder?

   Ⓕ 12π cm^2 Ⓗ 216π cm^2

   Ⓖ 18π cm^2 Ⓘ 288π cm^2

7. What is the surface area of the cylinder?

   Ⓐ 12π cm^2 Ⓑ 18π cm^2 Ⓒ 216π cm^2 Ⓓ 288π cm^2

8. The height of a cylinder is three times the diameter of the base. The surface area of the cylinder is 126π ft^2. What is the radius of the base?

   Ⓕ 3 ft   Ⓖ 6 ft   Ⓗ 9 ft   Ⓘ 18 ft

Short Response

9. What are the lateral area and the surface area of the prism?

11-3 Think About a Plan

Surface Areas of Pyramids and Cones

Find the lateral area of the cone to the nearest whole number.

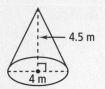

Understanding the Problem

1. What is the formula for the lateral area of a cone?

2. How are the two variables in this formula defined?

_____

_____

3. What two pieces of information are given in the figure of the cone?

_____

Planning the Solution

4. How can you use the given information to find the radius?

_____

5. How can you use the given information and the radius to find the slant height?

_____

Getting an Answer

6. What is the radius?

7. What is the slant height of the cone?

8. What is the lateral area of the cone?

11-3 Practice

Surface Areas of Pyramids and Cones

Form G

Find the lateral area of each pyramid to the nearest whole number.

1.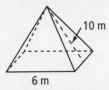
10 m
6 m

2.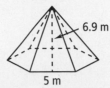
6.9 m
5 m

Find the surface area of each pyramid to the nearest whole number.

3.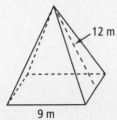
12 m
9 m

4.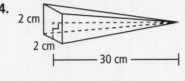
2 cm
2 cm
|— 30 cm —|

5.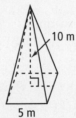
10 m
5 m

Find the lateral area of each cone to the nearest whole number.

6.
6 cm
4 cm

7.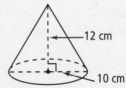
10 cm
13 cm

Find the surface area of each cone in terms of π.

8.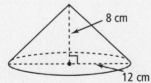
8 cm
12 cm

9.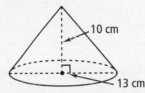
16 cm
12 cm

10.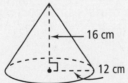
12 cm
10 cm

11. The surface area of a cone is 16.8π in.^{2}. The radius is 3 in. What is the slant height?

12. The lateral area of a cone is 155.25π m^2. The slant height is 13.5 m. What is the radius?

13. The roof of a clock tower is a pentagonal pyramid. Each side of the base is 7 ft long. The slant height is 9 ft. What is the area of the roof?

14. Write a formula to show the relationship between lateral area and the length of a side of the base (s) and slant height in a square pyramid.

11-3 Practice (continued)   Form G
Surface Areas of Pyramids and Cones

Find the surface area to the nearest whole number.

15.
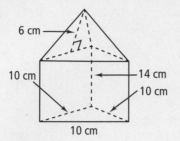
6 cm

10 cm · · · · 14 cm
· · · · · · 10 cm

10 cm

16.
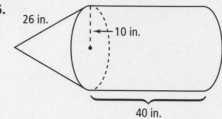
26 in.   10 in.

40 in.

17. Write a formula to show the relationship between surface area and the length of a side of the base (s) and slant height in a square pyramid.

The length of a side (s) of the base, slant height (ℓ), height (h), lateral area (L.A.), and surface area (S.A.) are measurements of a square pyramid. Given two of the measurements, find the other three to the nearest tenth.

18. $s = 9$ cm, $\ell = 14.5$ cm

19. L.A. $= 1542.4$ m^2, S.A. $= 2566.4$ m^2

20. $h = 9$ cm, $\ell = 11.4$ cm

Visualization Suppose you revolve the plane region completely about the given line to sweep out a solid of revolution. Describe the solid. Then find its surface area in terms of π. Round to the nearest tenth.

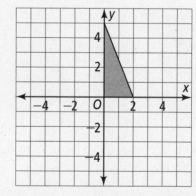

21. about the y-axis

22. about the x-axis

23. about the line $x = 2$

24. about the line $y = 5$

25. Open-Ended Draw a cone with a lateral area of 28π cm^2. Label its dimensions. Then find its surface area.

11-3 Standardized Test Prep

Surface Areas of Pyramids and Cones

Multiple Choice

For Exercises 1–5, choose the correct letter.

1. What is the lateral surface area of a square pyramid with side length 11.2 cm and slant height 20 cm?

   Ⓐ 224 cm²   Ⓑ 448 cm²   Ⓒ 896 cm²   Ⓓ 2508.8 cm²

2. What is the lateral surface area of a cone with radius 19 cm and slant height 11 cm?

   Ⓕ 19π cm²   Ⓖ 30π cm²   Ⓗ 200π cm²   Ⓘ 209π cm²

3. What is the lateral area of the square pyramid, to the nearest whole number?

   Ⓐ 165 m²   Ⓒ 330 m²

   Ⓑ 176 m²   Ⓓ 351 m²

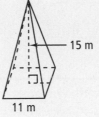

4. What is the surface area of the cone, to the nearest whole number?

   Ⓕ 221 cm²   Ⓗ 304 cm²

   Ⓖ 240 cm²   Ⓘ 620 cm²

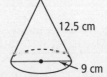

5. What is the surface area of a cone with diameter 28 cm and height 22 cm in terms of π?

   Ⓐ 196π cm²   Ⓑ 365π cm²   Ⓒ 561.1π cm²   Ⓓ 2202.8π cm²

Extended Response

6. What are the perimeter of the base, slant height, lateral area, and surface area for the square pyramid, to the nearest tenth of a meter or square meter?

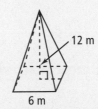

11-4   Think About a Plan

Volumes of Prisms and Cylinders

Swimming Pool The approximate dimensions of an Olympic-size swimming pool are 164 ft by 82 ft by 6.6 ft.

    a. Find the volume of the pool to the nearest cubic foot.

    b. If 1 ft^3 ≈ 7.48 gallons, about how many gallons does the pool hold?

Understanding the Problem

  1. What are the dimensions of the pool?

    _____

  2. How long is the pool? How wide is the pool? How deep is the pool?

    _____

  3. What are the dimensions of the base of the pool?

    _____

  4. How do you convert cubic feet to gallons?

    _____

Planning the Solution

  5. How would you use the dimensions of the pool to find its volume?

    _____

    _____

    _____

  6. How would you use the volume of the pool to find the number of gallons the pool holds?

    _____

Getting an Answer

  7. What is the area of the base of the pool?

  8. What is the volume of the pool?

  9. About how many gallons of water does the pool hold?

    _____

11-4 Practice

Form G

Volumes of Prisms and Cylinders

Find the volume of each rectangular prism.

1.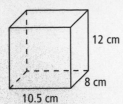
12 cm
8 cm
10.5 cm

2.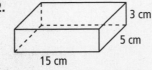
3 cm
5 cm
15 cm

3.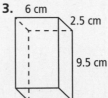
6 cm
2.5 cm
9.5 cm

4.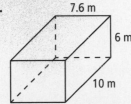
7.6 m
6 m
10 m

5.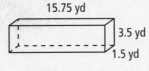
15.75 yd
3.5 yd
1.5 yd

6.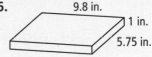
9.8 in.
1 in.
5.75 in.

7. The base is a square, 4.5 cm on a side. The height is 5 cm.

8. The base is a rectangle with length 3.2 cm and width 4 cm. The height is 10 cm.

Find the volume of each triangular prism to the nearest tenth.

9.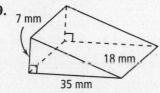
7 mm
18 mm
35 mm

10.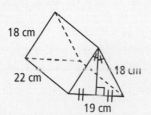
18 cm
22 cm
18 cm
19 cm

11.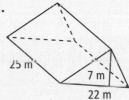
25 m
7 m
22 m

12. The base is a right triangle with a leg of 12 in. and hypotenuse of 15 in. The height of the prism is 10 in.

13. The base is a 30°-60°-90° triangle with a hypotenuse of 10 m. The height of the prism is 15 m. Find the volume to the nearest tenth.

Find the volume of each cylinder in terms of π and to the nearest tenth.

14.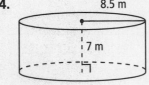
8.5 m
7 m

15.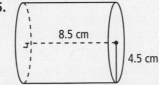
8.5 cm
4.5 cm

16.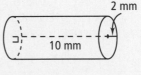
2 mm
10 mm

17. a right cylinder with a radius of 3.2 cm and a height of 10.5 cm

18. a right cylinder with a diameter of 8 ft and a height of 15 ft

11-4 Practice (continued)   Form G

Volumes of Prisms and Cylinders

Find the volume of each composite figure to the nearest whole number.

19.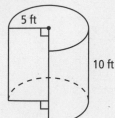

20.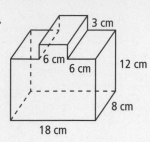

21.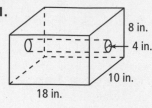

Find the value of x to the nearest tenth.

22. Volume: 576 cm³

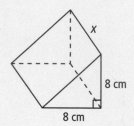

23. Volume: 980 mm³

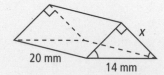

24. Volume: 602.88 cm³

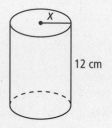

25. A cylindrical weather satellite has a diameter of 6 ft and a height of 10 ft. What is the volume available for carrying instruments and computer equipment, to the nearest tenth of a cubic foot?

26. A No. 10 can has a diameter of 15.5 cm and a height of 17.5 cm. A No. 2.5 can has a diameter of 9.8 cm and a height of 11 cm. What is the difference in volume of the two can types, to the nearest cubic centimeter?

27. The NCAA recommends that a competition diving pool intended for use with two 1-m springboards and two 3-m springboards, in addition to diving platforms set at 5 m, 7.5 m, and 10 m above the water, have a width of 75 ft 1 in., a length of 60 ft, and a minimum water depth of 14 ft 10 in. What is the minimum volume of water such a pool would hold in cubic yards, to the nearest whole number?

28. What is the volume of the solid figure formed by the net?

11-4 Standardized Test Prep

Volumes of Prisms and Cylinders

Gridded Response

Solve each exercise and enter your answer on the grid provided.

1. What is the volume in cubic inches of the prism?

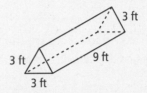

5 in.   3 in.   8 in.

2. What is the volume in cubic feet of the prism, rounded to the nearest cubic foot?

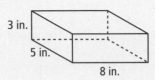

3 ft   3 ft   9 ft   3 ft   3 ft

3. What is the volume in cubic inches of the cylinder, rounded to the nearest cubic inch?

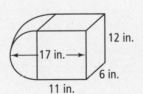

9 in.   7 in.

4. What is x, if the volume of the cylinder is 768π cm^3?

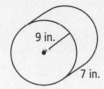

x cm   8 cm

5. What is the volume in cubic inches of the solid figure, rounded to the nearest cubic inch?

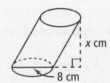

12 in.   17 in.   6 in.   11 in.

Answers

1. **2.** **3.** **4.** **5.**

11-5 Think About a Plan

Volumes of Pyramids and Cones

Writing The two cylinders pictured at the right are congruent. How does the volume of the larger cone compare to the total volume of the two smaller cones? Explain.

Understanding the Problem

1. You are told that the two cylinders are congruent. What does that tell you about the cones?

   _____

2. You are asked to compare the volumes of the cones. Can you find the exact volumes of the cones? In what other way can you compare their volumes?

   _____

   _____

Planning the Solution

3. What are the variables in the formula for the volume of a cone? What do they represent?

   _____

4. Let r represent the radius of the larger cone. What is the radius of the smaller cones in terms of r? Let h represent the height of the larger cone. What is the height of the smaller cones in terms of h? Explain.

   _____

   _____

Getting an Answer

5. What is the formula for the volume of the larger cone? What is the formula for the volume of the smaller cones?

   _____

6. How does the volume of the larger cone compare to the total volume of the smaller cones?

   _____

   _____

Prentice Hall Geometry • Practice and Problem Solving Workbook

302

11-5 Practice

Volumes of Pyramids and Cones

Form G

Find the volume of each square pyramid. Round to the nearest tenth if necessary.

1.
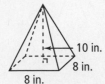
10 in.
8 in.
8 in.

2.
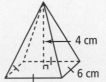
4 cm
6 cm

3.
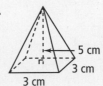
5 cm
3 cm
3 cm

Find the volume of each square pyramid, given its slant height. Round to the nearest tenth.

4.
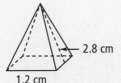
2.8 cm
1.2 cm

5.
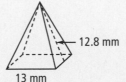
12.8 mm
13 mm

6.
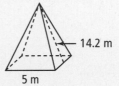
14.2 m
5 m

7. The base of a pyramid is a square, 4.5 cm on a side. The height is 5 cm. Find the volume.

8. The base of a pyramid is a square, 3.2 cm on a side. The height is 10 cm. Find the volume to the nearest tenth.

Find the volume of each cone in terms of π and also rounded as indicated.

9. nearest cubic foot
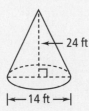
24 ft
|←— 14 ft —→|

10. nearest cubic meter
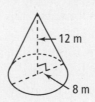
12 m
8 m

11. nearest cubic inch
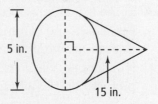
5 in.
15 in.

12. The base has a radius of 16 cm and a height of 12 cm. Round to the nearest cubic centimeter.

13. The base has a diameter of 24 m and a height of 15.3 m. Round to the nearest cubic meter.

Find the volume to the nearest whole number.

14.
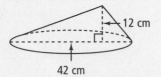
12 cm
42 cm

15.

15 cm
36 cm

16.

|←— 28 m —→|
25 m

Name _____ Class _____ Date _____

11-5 **Practice** (continued)   Form G
Volumes of Pyramids and Cones

Find the volume of each figure to the nearest whole number.

17.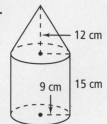

18.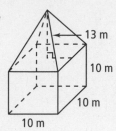

19.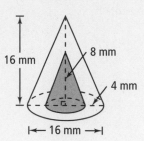

Algebra Find the value of *x* in each figure. Leave answers in simplest radical form. The diagrams are not to scale.

20.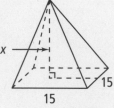
15
Volume = 1500

21.
Volume = 8π

22.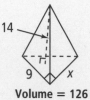
Volume = 126

23. One right circular cone is set inside a larger right circular cone. The cones share the same axis, the same vertex, and the same height. Find the volume of the space between the cones if the diameter of the inside cone is 6 in., the diameter of the outside cone is 9 in., and the height of both is 5 in. Round to the nearest tenth.

24. Some Native Americans still use tepees for special occasions and ceremonial purposes. Each group attending a family reunion, for example, might bring a small tepee, while using a larger tepee like the one pictured at the right for gathering together. The many poles form a rough cone with a circular base. What is the approximate volume of air in the tepee at the right, to the nearest cubic foot?

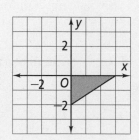

Visualization Suppose you revolve the plane region completely about the given line to sweep out a solid of revolution. Describe the solid. Then find its volume in terms of *π*.

25. the *x*-axis

26. the *y*-axis

27. the line $x = 3$

28. the line $y = -2$

11-5 Standardized Test Prep

Volumes of Pyramids and Cones

Multiple Choice

For Exercises 1–5, choose the correct letter.

1. What is the volume of the pyramid?

   (A) 56 ft³   (C) 196 ft³

   (B) 130 ⅔ ft³   (D) 392 ft³

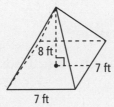

2. What is the volume of the cone, rounded to the nearest cubic inch?

   (F) 72 in.³   (H) 905 in.³

   (G) 226 in.³   (I) 2714 in.³

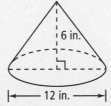

3. What is the volume of the figure?

   (A) 15 cm³   (C) 45 cm³

   (B) 33 cm³   (D) 54 cm³

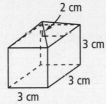

4. What is the value of x, if the volume of the cone is 12π m³?

   (F) 4 m   (H) 6 m

   (G) 5 m   (I) 10 m

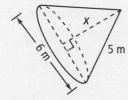

5. What is the diameter of a cone with height 8 m and volume 150π m³?

   (A) 7.5 m   (B) 5√3 m   (C) 7.5√3 m   (D) 15 m

Short Response

6. **Error Analysis** A student calculates the volume of the given cone as approximately 2094 cm³. Explain the error in the student's reasoning and find the actual volume of the cone rounded to the nearest whole number.

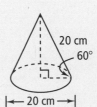

11-6

Think About a Plan

Surface Areas and Volumes of Spheres

Meteorology On September 3, 1970, a hailstone with diameter 5.6 in. fell at Coffeyville, Kansas. It weighed about 0.018 lb/in.^{3} compared to the normal 0.033 lb/in.^{3} for ice. About how heavy was this Kansas hailstone?

Understanding the Problem

1. What is the situation described in the problem?

_____

2. What key piece of information is unstated or implicit?

_____

3. What question do you have to answer?

_____

4. Is there any unnecessary information? Explain.

_____

Planning the Solution

5. What formula can you use to find the volume of the hailstone?

_____

6. How can you use the volume of the hailstone to find its weight?

_____

Getting an Answer

7. What is the volume of the hailstone? Show your work.

_____

8. How do you find the weight of the hailstone?

_____

11-6 Practice

Form G

Surface Areas and Volumes of Spheres

Find the surface area of the sphere with the given diameter or radius. Leave your answer in terms of π.

1. $d = 8$ ft

2. $r = 10$ cm

3. $d = 14$ in.

4. $r = 3$ yd

Find the surface area of each sphere. Leave each answer in terms of π.

5.  5 cm

6.  4 yd

7. 6 ft

8.  9 in.

9.  20 mm

10.  9 m

Use the given circumference to find the surface area of each spherical object. Round your answer to the nearest whole number.

11. an asteroid with $C = 83.92$ m

12. a meteorite with $C = 26.062$ yd

13. a rock with $C = 16.328$ ft

14. an orange with $C = 50.24$ mm

Find the volume of each sphere. Give each answer in terms of π and rounded to the nearest cubic unit.

15.  18 mm

16.  5 yd

17. 3 m

18. 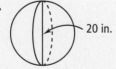 20 in.

19.

S.A. $= 16\pi$ cm^2

20.

S.A. $= 64\pi$ cm^2

A sphere has the volume given. Find its surface area to the nearest whole number.

21. $V = 1200$ ft^3

22. $V = 750$ m^3

23. $V = 4500$ cm^3

11-6

Practice (continued)   *Form G*

Surface Areas and Volumes of Spheres

Find the volume in terms of π of each sphere with the given surface area.

24. 900π in.^{2} **25.** 81π in.^{2} **26.** 6084π m^2

27. The difference between drizzle and rain has to do with the size of the drops, not how much water is actually falling from the sky. If rain consists of drops larger than 0.02 in. in diameter, and drizzle consists of drops less than 0.02 in. in diameter, what can you say about the surface area and volume of rain and drizzle?

28. A spherical scoop of ice cream with a diameter of 4 cm rests on top of a sugar cone that is 10 cm deep and has a diameter of 4 cm. If all of the ice cream melts into the cone, what percent of the cone will be filled?

29. Point A is the center of the sphere. Point C is on the surface of the sphere. Point B is the center of the circle that lies in plane P and includes point C. The radius of the circle is 12 mm. $AB = 5$ mm. What is the volume of the sphere to the nearest cubic mm?

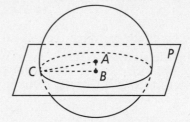

30. Writing What are the formulas for the volumes of a sphere, a cone with a height equal to its radius, and a cylinder with its height equal to its radius? How are these formulas related?

31. Candlepin bowling balls have no holes in them and are smaller than the bowling balls used in tenpin bowling. The regulation size is 4.5 in. in diameter, and their density is 0.05 lb/in.^{3}. What is the regulation weight of a candlepin bowling ball? Round your answer to the nearest tenth of a pound.

32. Find the radius of a sphere such that the ratio of the surface area in square inches to the volume in cubic inches is $4 : 1$.

33. Find the radius of a sphere such that the ratio of the surface area in square feet to the volume in cubic feet is $2 : 5$.

11-6 Standardized Test Prep

Surface Areas and Volumes of Spheres

Multiple Choice

For Exercises 1–5, choose the correct letter.

1. What is the approximate volume of the sphere?
   - Ⓐ 524 m³
   - Ⓒ 1256 m³
   - Ⓑ 1000 m³
   - Ⓓ 1570 m³

2. What is the approximate surface area of the sphere?
   - Ⓕ 225 yd²
   - Ⓗ 1767 yd²
   - Ⓖ 707 yd²
   - Ⓘ 5301 yd²

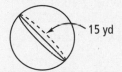

3. What is the approximate volume of the sphere if the surface area is 482.8 mm²?
   - Ⓐ 998 mm³
   - Ⓑ 1126 mm³
   - Ⓒ 2042 mm³
   - Ⓓ 2993 mm³

4. What is the approximate surface area of the sphere?
   - Ⓕ 342.3 km²
   - Ⓗ 903.4 km²
   - Ⓖ 451.9 km²
   - Ⓘ 2713 km²

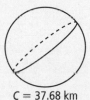

5. What is the approximate radius of a sphere whose volume is 1349 cm³?
   - Ⓐ 5.7 cm
   - Ⓑ 6.9 cm
   - Ⓒ 11 cm
   - Ⓓ 14.7 cm

Short Response

6. Suppose a wealthy entrepreneur commissions the design of a spherical spaceship to house a small group for a week in orbit around the Earth. The designer allocates 1000 ft³ for each person, plus an additional 4073.5 ft³ for various necessary machines. As in a recreational vehicle, the personal space is largely occupied by items such as beds, shower and toilet facilities, and a kitchenette. The diameter of the ship is 26.8 ft. What is the volume of the spaceship, and for approximately how many people is the ship designed?

11-7 Think About a Plan

Areas and Volumes of Similar Solids

Reasoning A carpenter is making a blanket chest based on an antique chest. Both chests have the shape of a rectangular prism. The length, width, and height of the new chest will all be 4 in. greater than the respective dimensions of the antique. Will the chests be similar? Explain.

Understanding the Problem

1. How much longer will the blanket chest be than the antique chest? How much wider will it be? How much taller will it be? Draw a diagram of the blanket chest showing the increase in each dimension.

   _____

2. If two solids are similar, what must be true about their corresponding dimensions?

   _____

Planning the Solution

3. Practice explaining your reasoning. Imagine a chest has dimensions 3 ft-by-3 ft-by-3 ft. Add 4 in. to each dimension. Is the new chest similar to the old chest? Explain.

   _____

4. Practice explaining your reasoning. Suppose a chest has dimensions 4 ft-by-3 ft-by-3 ft. Add 4 in. to each dimension. Is the new chest similar to the old chest? Explain.

   _____

   _____

Getting an Answer

5. How can you generalize the dimensions of the old chest?

   _____

6. Using the dimensions of the chest, determine whether the new chest and the old chest will be similar.

   _____

   _____

11-7 Practice
Areas and Volumes of Similar Solids

Form G

Are the two figures similar? If so, give the scale factor of the first figure to the second figure.

1.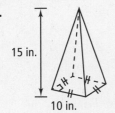

2.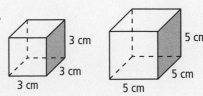

3.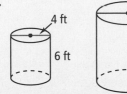

4.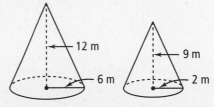

5. two cubes, one with 5-in. edges, the other with 6-in. edges

6. a cylinder and a cone, each with 6-m radii and 4-m heights

Each pair of figures is similar. Use the given information to find the scale factor of the smaller figure to the larger figure.

7.
$V = 64\pi$ in.^{3} $V = 125\pi$ in.^{3}

8.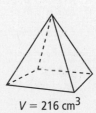
$V = 125$ cm^3 $V = 216$ cm^3

9.
S.A. = 150 m^2 S.A. = 294 m^2

10.
S.A. = 36π ft^2 S.A. = 121π ft^2

The surface areas of two similar figures are given. The volume of the larger figure is given. Find the volume of the smaller figure.

11. S.A. = 36 m^2
S.A. = 225 m^2
$V = 750$ m^3

12. S.A. = 108 in.^{2}
S.A. = 192 in.^{2}
$V = 1408$ in.^{3}

13. S.A. = 49 m^2
S.A. = 441 m^2
$V = 432$ m^3

14. A shipping box holds 350 golf balls. A larger shipping box has dimensions triple the size of the other box. How many golf balls does the larger box hold?

11-7 Practice (continued) Form G

Areas and Volumes of Similar Solids

The volumes of two similar figures are given. The surface area of the smaller figure is given. Find the surface area of the larger figure.

15. $V = 8\ m^3$
$V = 27\ m^3$
S.A. $36 = m^2$

16. $V = 125\ in.^3$
$V = 216\ in.^3$
S.A. $= 200\ in.^2$

17. $V = 3\ ft^3$
$V = 375\ ft^3$
S.A. $= 4\ ft^2$

18. A cylindrical thermos has a radius of 2 in. and is 5 in. high. It holds 10 fl oz. To the nearest ounce, how many ounces will a similar thermos with a radius of 3 in. hold?

19. Compare and Contrast You have a set of three similar nesting gift boxes. Each box is a regular hexagonal prism. The large box has 10-cm base edges. The medium box has 6-cm base edges. The small box has 3-cm base edges. How does the volume of each box compare to every other box?

20. Two similar pyramids have heights 6 m and 9 m.

  a. What is their scale factor?

  b. What is the ratio of their surface areas?

  c. What is the ratio of their volumes?

21. A small, spherical hamster ball has a diameter of 8 in. and a volume of about $268\ in.^3$. A larger ball has a diameter of 14 in. Estimate the volume of the larger hamster ball.

22. Error Analysis A classmate says that a rectangular prism that is 6 cm long, 8 cm wide, and 15 cm high is similar to a rectangular prism that is 12 cm long, 14 cm wide, and 21 cm high. Explain your classmate's error.

23. The lateral area of two similar cylinders is $64\ m^2$ and $144\ m^2$. The volume of the larger cylinder is $216\ m^3$. What is the volume of the smaller cylinder?

24. The volumes of two similar prisms are $135\ ft^3$ and $5000\ ft^3$.

  a. Find the ratio of their heights.

  b. Find the ratio of the area of their bases.

11-7 Standardized Test Prep
Areas and Volumes of Similar Solids

Multiple Choice

For Exercises 1–5, choose the correct letter.

1. Which of the figures shown below are similar?

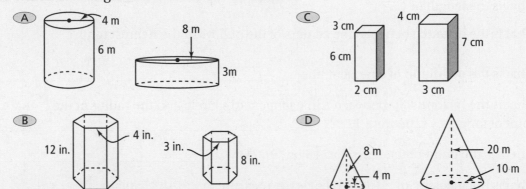

2. The measure of the side of a cube is 6 ft. The measure of the side of a second cube is 18 ft. What is the scale factor of the cubes?

    Ⓕ 1 : 2   Ⓖ 1 : 3   Ⓗ 1 : 9   Ⓘ 1 : 27

3. What is the ratio of the surface areas of the similar square pyramids at the right?

    Ⓐ 4 : 5   Ⓒ 16 : 25

    Ⓑ 8 : 10   Ⓓ 64 : 125

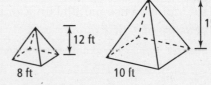

4. What is the ratio of the volumes of the similar square pyramids above?

    Ⓕ 4 : 5   Ⓖ 8 : 10   Ⓗ 16 : 25   Ⓘ 64 : 125

5. The surface areas of two similar triangular prisms are 132 m^2 and 297 m^2. The volume of the smaller prism is 264 m^3. What is the volume of the larger prism?

    Ⓐ 594 m^3 Ⓑ 891 m^3 Ⓒ 1336.5 m^3 Ⓓ 3007.125 m^3

Short Response

6. A medium-sized box can hold 55 T-shirts. If the dimensions of a jumbo box are three times that of the medium box, how many T-shirts can the jumbo box hold? Explain.

12-1

Think About a Plan

Tangent Lines

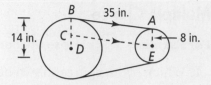

a. A belt fits snugly around the two circular pulleys.
$\overline{CE}$ is an auxiliary line from E to $\overline{BD}$. $\overline{CE} \parallel \overline{AB}$.
What type of quadrilateral is *ABCE*? Explain.

b. What is the length of $\overline{CE}$?

c. What is the distance between the centers of the pulleys to the nearest tenth?

1. What is the definition of a tangent line? _____

2. What is the relationship between a line tangent to a circle and the radius at the
   point of tangency (Theorem 12-1)? _____

3. Where is the point of tangency for $\overline{AB}$ on $\odot D$? On $\odot E$? _____

4. What is the measure of $\angle CBA$? What is the measure of $\angle BAE$? Explain.

   _____

5. How can you use parallel lines to find the measure of $\angle CEA$?

   _____

6. How can you use parallel lines or the Polygon Angle-Sum Theorem to find the
   measure of $\angle BCE$?

   _____

   _____

   _____

7. What type of quadrilateral has four right angles? _____

8. What is the length of $\overline{BA}$?

9. What is the length of $\overline{CE}$?

10. What are the center points of the pulleys?

11. How can you use the Segment Addition Postulate to find $\overline{CD}$?

    _____

12. What is the measure of $\overline{CD}$?

13. How can you use the Pythagorean Theorem to find the length of $\overline{DE}$?

    _____

12-1 | Practice

Tangent Lines

Form G

Algebra Assume that lines that appear to be tangent are tangent. *O* is the center of each circle. What is the value of *x*?

1.

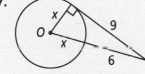

2.

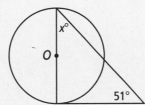

3.

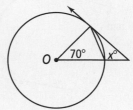

The circle at the right represents Earth. The radius of the Earth is about 6400 km. Find the distance *d* that a person can see on a clear day from each of the following heights *h* above Earth. Round your answer to the nearest tenth of a kilometer.

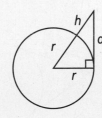

4. 12 km

5. 20 km

6. 1300 km

In each circle, what is the value of *x* to the nearest tenth?

7.

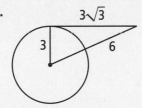

8.

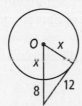

9.

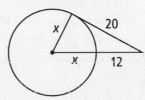

Determine whether a tangent line is shown in each diagram. Explain.

10.

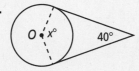

11.

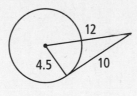

12.

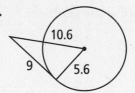

13. $\overline{TY}$ and $\overline{ZW}$ are diameters of $\odot S$. $\overline{TU}$ and $\overline{UX}$ are tangents of $\odot S$. What is $m\angle SYZ$?

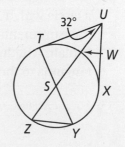

12-1

Practice (continued)

Tangent Lines

Form G

Each polygon circumscribes a circle. What is the perimeter of each polygon?

14.

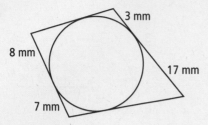

3 mm

8 mm

17 mm

7 mm

15.

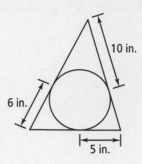

10 in.

6 in.

5 in.

16.

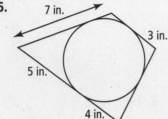

7 in.

3 in.

5 in.

4 in.

17.

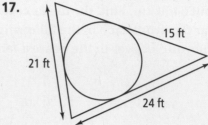

15 ft

21 ft

24 ft

18. Error Analysis A classmate states that $\overline{BC}$ is tangent to ⊙A. Explain how to show that your classmate is wrong.

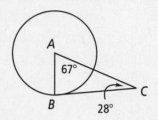

A

67°

B

28°

C

19. The peak of Mt. Everest is about 8850 m above sea level. About how many kilometers is it from the peak of Mt. Everest to the horizon if the Earth's radius is about 6400 km? Draw a diagram to help you solve the problem.

20. The design of the banner at the right includes a circle with a 12-in. diameter. Using the measurements given in the diagram, explain whether the lines shown are tangents to the circle.

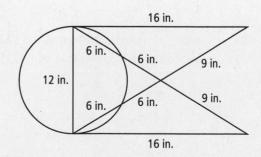

16 in.

6 in.

6 in.

9 in.

12 in.

6 in.

6 in.

9 in.

16 in.

12-1 Standardized Test Prep
Tangent Lines

Multiple Choice

For Exercises 1–5, choose the correct letter.

1. $\overline{AB}$ and $\overline{BC}$ are tangents to $\odot P$. What is the value of x?

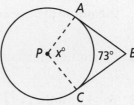

   (A) 73   (C) 117

   (B) 107   (D) 146

2. Earth's radius is about 4000 mi. To the nearest mile, what is the distance a person can see on a clear day from an airplane 5 mi above Earth?

   (F) 63 mi   (G) 200 mi   (H) 4000 mi   (I) 5660 mi

3. $\overline{YZ}$ is a tangent to $\odot X$, and X is the center of the circle. What is the length of the radius of the circle?

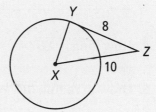

   (A) 4   (C) 12

   (B) 6   (D) 12.8

4. The radius of $\odot G$ is 4 cm. Which is a tangent of $\odot G$?

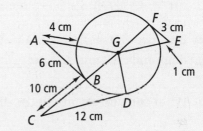

   (F) $\overline{AB}$ (H) $\overline{BF}$

   (G) $\overline{CD}$ (I) $\overline{FE}$

5. $\odot A$ is inscribed in a quadrilateral. What is the perimeter of the quadrilateral?

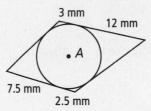

   (A) 25 mm   (C) 60 mm

   (B) 50 mm   (D) 150 mm

Short Response

6. **Given:** $\overline{GI}$ is a tangent to $\odot J$.

   Prove: $\triangle FGH \cong \triangle FIH$

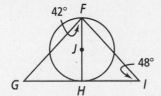

12-2 Think About a Plan

Chords and Arcs

⊙A and ⊙B are congruent. $\overline{CD}$ is a chord of both circles.
If $AB = 8$ in. and $CD = 6$ in., how long is a radius?

1. Draw the radius of each circle that includes point C. What is the name of each of the two line segments drawn?

2. Label the intersection of $\overline{CD}$ and $\overline{AB}$ point X.

3. You know that $\overline{CD} \cong \overline{CD}$. How can you use the converse of Theorem 12-7 to show that $AX = XB$?

_____

_____

4. How long is $\overline{XB}$?

5. Draw in radius $\overline{BD}$. What is true about BC and BD? Explain.

_____

6. Because $AD = AC = BD = BC$, $ACBD$ is a _____ and its
   diagonals $\overline{AB}$ and $\overline{CD}$ are _____.

7. What can you say about the diagram using Theorem 12-8? _____

8. How long is $\overline{CX}$?

9. How can you use the Pythagorean Theorem to find BC?

_____

10. How long is the radius of each circle?

12-2 Practice

Chords and Arcs

Form G

In Exercises 1 and 2, the $\odot X \cong \odot E$. What can you conclude?

1.

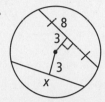

2.

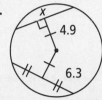

Find the value of x.

3.

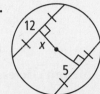

4.

5.

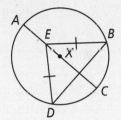

6. In $\odot X$, $\overline{AC}$ is a diameter and $\overline{ED} \cong \overline{EB}$. What can you conclude about $\overset{\frown}{DC}$ and $\overset{\frown}{CB}$? Explain.

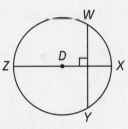

7. In $\odot D$, $\overline{ZX}$ is the diameter of the circle and $\overline{ZX} \perp \overline{WY}$. What conclusions can you make? Justify your answer.

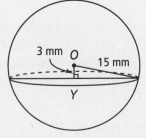

Find the value of x to the nearest tenth.

8.

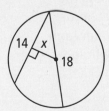

9.

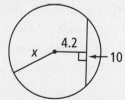

10.

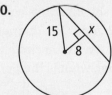

11. In the figure at the right, sphere O with radius 15 mm is intersected by a plane 3 mm from the center. To the nearest tenth, find the radius of the cross section $\odot Y$.

12-2 Practice (continued) Form G
Chords and Arcs

12. Given: $\odot J$ with diameter $\overline{HK}$; $\overset{\frown}{KL} \cong \overset{\frown}{LM} \cong \overset{\frown}{MK}$
   Prove: $\triangle KIL \cong \triangle KIM$

13. Given: $\overline{AC}$ and $\overline{DB}$ are diameters of $\odot E$.
   Prove: $\triangle EAD \cong \triangle ECB$

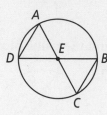

$\odot N$ and $\odot O$ **are congruent.** $\overline{PQ}$ **is a chord of both circles.**

14. If $NO = 12$ in. and $\overline{PQ} = 8$ in., how long is the radius to the
   nearest tenth of an inch?

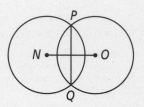

15. If $NO = 30$ mm and radius $= 16$ mm, how long is $\overline{PQ}$ to the
   nearest tenth of a millimeter?

16. If radius $= 12$ m and $\overline{PQ} = 9$ m, how long is $\overline{NO}$ to the nearest tenth?

17. Draw a Diagram A student draws $\odot X$ with a diameter of 12 cm. Inside the
   circle she inscribes equilateral $\triangle ABC$ so that $\overline{AB}$, $\overline{BC}$, and $\overline{CA}$ are all chords
   of the circle. The diameter of $\odot X$ bisects $\overline{AB}$. The section of the diameter from
   the center of the circle to where it bisects $\overline{AB}$ is 3 cm. To the nearest whole
   number, what is the perimeter of the equilateral triangle inscribed in $\odot X$?

18. Two concentric circles have radii of 6 mm and 12 mm. A segment tangent
   to the smaller circle is a chord of the larger circle. What is the length of the
   segment to the nearest tenth.

12-2 Standardized Test Prep

Chords and Arcs

Multiple Choice

For Exercises 1–5, choose the correct letter.

1. The circles at the right are congruent. Which conclusion can you draw?

   Ⓐ $\overline{CD} \cong \overline{ST}$ Ⓒ $\angle AEB \cong \angle QUR$

   Ⓑ $\angle CED \cong \angle SUT$ Ⓓ $\overset{\frown}{BD} \cong \overset{\frown}{RT}$

2. $\overline{JG}$ is the diameter of $\odot M$. Which conclusion *cannot* be drawn from the diagram?

   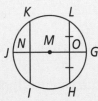

   Ⓕ $\overline{KN} \cong \overline{NI}$ Ⓗ $\overline{JG} \perp \overline{HL}$

   Ⓖ $\overset{\frown}{LG} \cong \overset{\frown}{GH}$ Ⓘ $\overline{GH} \cong \overline{GL}$

For Exercises 3 and 4, what is the value of x to the nearest tenth?

3.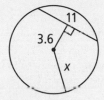

4.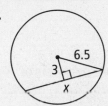

   Ⓐ 4.2   Ⓒ 10.4   Ⓕ 3.6   Ⓗ 11.5

   Ⓑ 6.6   Ⓓ 11.6   Ⓖ 5.8   Ⓘ 14.3

5. If $\angle AFB \cong \angle DFE$, what must be true?

   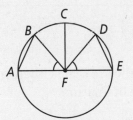

   Ⓐ $\overset{\frown}{AB} \cong \overset{\frown}{DE}$ Ⓒ $\overline{CF} \perp \overline{AE}$

   Ⓑ $\overset{\frown}{BC} \cong \overset{\frown}{DE}$ Ⓓ $\angle BFC \cong \angle DFC$

Short Response

6. **Given:** $\odot A \cong \odot C, \overset{\frown}{DB} \cong \overset{\frown}{EB}$

   Prove: $\triangle ADB \cong \triangle CEB$

   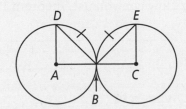

12-3

Think About a Plan

Inscribed Angles

Find the value of each variable. The dot represents the center of the circle.

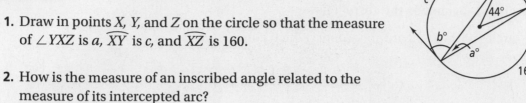

1. Draw in points *X*, *Y*, and *Z* on the circle so that the measure of ∠*YXZ* is *a*, $\overarc{XY}$ is *c*, and $\overarc{XZ}$ is 160.

2. How is the measure of an inscribed angle related to the measure of its intercepted arc?

_____

_____

3. What is the measure of $\overarc{YZ}$, by the definition of an arc?

4. How can you use Theorem 12-11 to find *a*?

_____

_____

5. What is *a*?

6. What is the sum of the measures of $\overarc{XY}$, $\overarc{YZ}$, and $\overarc{XZ}$?

7. How can you use the sum of the measures of all these non-overlapping arcs of a circle to find *c*?

_____

_____

8. What is *c*?

9. What is the arc that is intercepted by the angle measuring *b*? What is the measure of this arc?

10. How can you use Theorem 12-12 to find *b*?

_____

_____

11. What is *b*?

12-3 Practice   Form G
Inscribed Angles

Find the value of each variable. For each circle, the dot represents the center.

1.
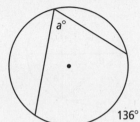
136°

2.
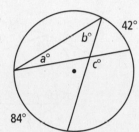
a°
17°

3.
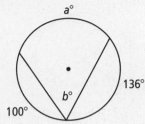
a°
b°
136°
100°

4.
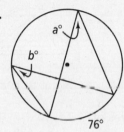
42°
b°
a°
c°
84°

5.
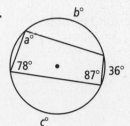
b°
a°
78°
87° 36°
c°

6.
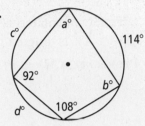
a°
c°
114°
92°
b°
d°
108°

7.
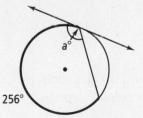
a°
b°
76°

8.
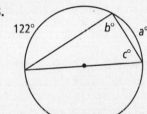
122°
b°
a°
c°

9.
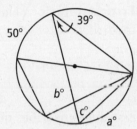
39°
50°
b°
c°
a°

Find the value of each variable. Lines that appear to be tangent are tangent.

10.
a°
256°

11.
224°
b°
a°

12.
b°
a°
144°

Find each indicated measure for ⊙M.

13. a. $m\angle B$ **b.** $m\angle C$
     c. $m\widehat{BC}$ **d.** $m\widehat{AC}$

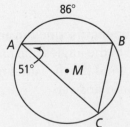
86°
A   B
51° •M
C

12-3

Practice (continued)   Form G

Inscribed Angles

Find the value of each variable. For each circle, the dot represents the center.

14.
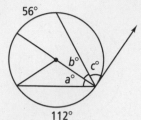
56°
b°
c°
a°
112°

15.
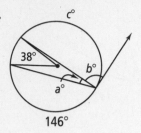
c°
38°
b°
a°
146°

16.
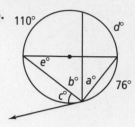
110°
d°
e°
b° a°
c°
76°

17. **Given:** Quadrilateral *ABCD* is inscribed in ⊙*Z*.
    $\overleftrightarrow{XY}$ is tangent to ⊙*Z*.

    Prove: $m\angle XAD + m\angle YAB = m\angle C$

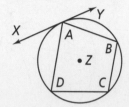

18. **Error Analysis** A classmate says that $m\angle E = 90$. Explain why this is incorrect.

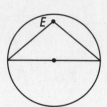

19. A student inscribes quadrilateral *ABCD* inside a circle. The measures of angles *A*, *B*, and *C* are given below. Find the measure of each angle of quadrilateral *ABCD*.

    $m\angle A = 8x - 4 \quad m\angle B = 5x + 4 \quad m\angle C = 7x + 4$

20. **Reasoning** Quadrilateral *WXYZ* is inscribed in a circle. If $\angle W$ and $\angle Y$ are each inscribed in a semicircle, does this mean the quadrilateral is a rectangle? Explain.

21. **Writing** A student inscribes an angle inside a semicircle to form a triangle. The measures of the angles that are not the vertex of the inscribed angle are x and $2x - 9$. Find the measures of all three angles of the triangle. Explain how you got your answer.

12-3 Standardized Test Prep

Inscribed Angles

Multiple Choice

For Exercises 1–6, choose the correct letter.

1. What is the value of x?

   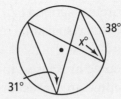

   Ⓐ 19   Ⓒ 38

   Ⓑ 31   Ⓓ 62

For Exercises 2–3, use the diagram at the right.

2. What is the value of a?

   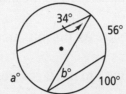

   Ⓕ 34   Ⓗ 68

   Ⓖ 56   Ⓘ 146

3. What is the value of b?

   Ⓐ 28   Ⓒ 56

   Ⓑ 34   Ⓓ 112

4. What is the value of s?

   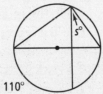

   Ⓕ 35   Ⓗ 70

   Ⓖ 55   Ⓘ 90

5. What is the value of y if the segment outside the circle is tangent to the circle?

   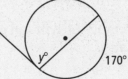

   Ⓐ 85   Ⓒ 190

   Ⓑ 95   Ⓓ cannot determine

6. What is the value of z?

   Ⓕ 77   Ⓗ 126

   Ⓖ 95   Ⓘ 154

Extended Response

7. A student inscribes quadrilateral QRST in ⊙D so that $m\widehat{QR} = 86$ and $m\angle R = 93$. What is the measure of $\widehat{RS}$? Draw a diagram and explain the steps you took to find the answer.

12-4 Think About a Plan

Angle Measures and Segment Lengths

A circle is inscribed in a quadrilateral whose four angles have measures 85, 76, 94, and 105. Find the measures of the four arcs between consecutive points of tangency.

1. Draw a diagram of a circle inscribed in a quadrilateral. The diagram does not have to be exact; it is just a visual aid.

2. Label as $a°$ the intercepted arc closest to the angle measuring 85. Label as $b°$ the intercepted arc closest to the angle measuring 76. Label as $c°$ the intercepted arc closest to the angle measuring 94. Finally, label as $d°$ the intercepted arc closest to the angle measuring 105.

3. What is the sum of the measures of the four arcs $(a + b + c + d)$?

4. Write an equation that relates a to the measures of the other arcs.

5. Repeat Step 4 to write three more equations that relate the measure of each arc to the measures of the other arcs.

6. How is the measure of each angle in the quadrilateral related to the measures of the intercepted arcs? (*Hint:* Use Theorem 12–14.)

_____

7. Write expressions for the measures of the two arcs intercepted by the 85° angle.

8. Using Theorem 12-14, write an equation that relates 85 to the measures of the intercepted arcs.

9. Multiply each side of this equation by 2.

10. Look at your equation from Step 4. What is the value of $b + c + d$?

11. How can you use the equations from Steps 9 and 10 to find a?

_____

_____

12. What is the value of a?

13. Repeat this process to find b, c, and d. What are their values?

12-4 Practice

Angle Measures and Segment Lengths

Form G

Find the value of x.

1.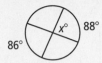
88°
86°
x°

2.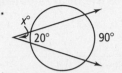
x°
20°
90°

3.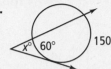
x° 60°
150°

4.
60° *x*°

5.
140°
x°
38°

6.
x°
6°

7. There is a circular cabinet in the dining room. Looking in from another room at point *A*, you estimate that you can see an arc of the cabinet of about 100°. What is the measure of ∠*A* formed by the tangents to the cabinet?

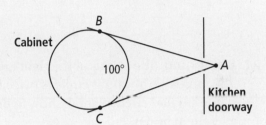
Cabinet
B
100°
A
C
Kitchen doorway

Algebra Find the value of each variable using the given chord, secant, and tangent lengths. If the answer is not a whole number, round to the nearest tenth.

8.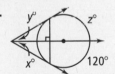
y°
z°
x°
120°

9.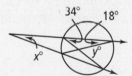
34° 18°
x°
y°

10.
42° *x*°
z°
y°

11.
9
2
y

12.
8 12
x 10

13.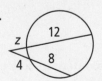
z 12
4 8

Algebra $\overline{CA}$ and $\overline{CB}$ are tangents to ⊙*O*. Write an expression for each arc or angle in terms of the given variable.

14. $m\widehat{AB}$ using *x*

15. $m\widehat{AB}$ using *y*

16. $m\angle C$ using *x*

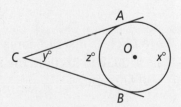
A
O
x°
C *y*° *z*°
B

12-4 Practice (continued) Form G

Angle Measures and Segment Lengths

Find the diameter of ⊙O. A line that appears to be tangent is tangent. If your answer is not a whole number, round to the nearest tenth.

17.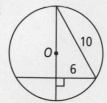

18.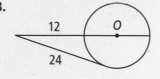

19.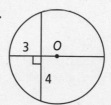

20. The distance from your ship to a lighthouse is *d*, and the distance to the buoy is *b*. Express the distance to the shore in terms of *d* and *b*.

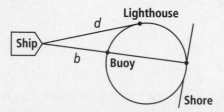

21. **Reasoning** The circles at the right are concentric. The radius of the larger circle is twice the radius, *r*, of the smaller circle. Explain how to find the ratio *x* : *r*, then find it.

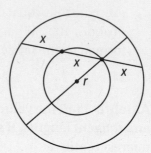

22. A circle is inscribed in a parallelogram. One angle of the parallelogram measures 60. What are the measures of the four arcs between consecutive points of tangency? Explain.

23. An isosceles triangle with height 10 and base 6 is inscribed in a circle. Create a plan to find the diameter of the circle. Find the diameter.

24. If three tangents to a circle form an equilateral triangle, prove that the tangent points form an equilateral triangle inscribed in the circle.

25. A circle is inscribed in a quadrilateral whose four angles have measures 86, 78, 99, and 97. Find the measures of the four arcs between consecutive points of tangency.

12-4

Standardized Test Prep

Angle Measures and Segment Lengths

Multiple Choice

For Exercises 1–6, choose the correct letter.

1. Which of the following statements is false?
   - Ⓐ Every chord is part of a secant.
   - Ⓑ Every diameter is part of a secant.
   - Ⓒ Every chord is a diameter.
   - Ⓓ Every diameter is a chord.

2. In the figure at the right, what is $m\angle C$?
   - Ⓕ 15
   - Ⓖ 35
   - Ⓗ 50
   - Ⓘ 65

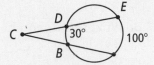

3. In the figure at the right, what is the value of x?
   - Ⓐ 45
   - Ⓑ 60
   - Ⓒ 75
   - Ⓓ 90

4. In the figure at the right, what is the value of z?
   - Ⓕ 2.9
   - Ⓖ 5.6
   - Ⓗ 6
   - Ⓘ 8.75

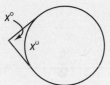

5. An equilateral triangle with sides of length 6 is inscribed in a circle. What is the diameter of the circle?
   - Ⓐ 5.2
   - Ⓑ 6
   - Ⓒ 6.9
   - Ⓓ 7.5

6. In the figure at the right, what is $m\ \overset{\frown}{ABC}$ in terms of x?
   - Ⓕ $180 + x$
   - Ⓖ $180 - x$
   - Ⓗ $2(180 + x)$
   - Ⓘ $360 - x$

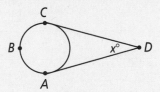

Short Response

7. Use $\odot O$ to prove that $\triangle AED \sim \triangle BEC$.

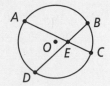

12-5 Think About a Plan

Circles in the Coordinate Plane

What are the x- and y-intercepts of the line tangent to the circle $(x - 2)^2 + (y - 2)^2 = 5^2$ at the point $(5, 6)$?

1. What is the relationship between the line tangent to the circle at the point $(5, 6)$ and the radius of the circle containing the point $(5, 6)$?

   _____

2. What is the product of the slopes of two perpendicular lines or line segments?

3. What is the center of the circle?

4. How can you use the slope formula to find the slope of the radius of the circle containing the point $(5, 6)$? What is this slope?

   _____

5. What is the slope of the line tangent to the circle at point $(5, 6)$?

6. What is the slope-intercept equation for a line?

7. How can you use the slope-intercept equation to find the y-intercept for the line tangent to the circle at point $(5, 6)$?

   _____

   _____

8. How can you use this equation to find the x-intercept for the line tangent to the circle at point $(5, 6)$?

   _____

   _____

9. What are the x- and y-intercepts for the line tangent to the circle at point $(5, 6)$?

12-5 Practice

Form G

Circles in the Coordinate Plane

Find the center and radius of each circle.

1. $x^2 + y^2 = 36$

2. $(x - 2)^2 + (y - 7)^2 = 49$

3. $(x + 1)^2 + (y + 6)^2 = 16$

4. $(x + 3)^2 + (y - 11)^2 = 12$

Write the standard equation of each circle.

5. center $(0, 0)$; $r = 7$

6. center $(4, 3)$; $r = 8$

7. center $(5, 3)$; $r = 2$

8. center $(-5, 4)$; $r = \frac{1}{2}$

9. center $(-2, -5)$; $r = \sqrt{2}$

10. center $(-1, 6)$; $r = \sqrt{5}$

Write the standard equation of each circle.

11.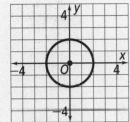

12.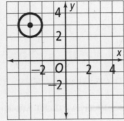

13.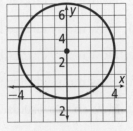

14.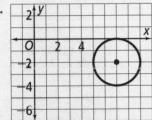

15.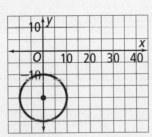

16.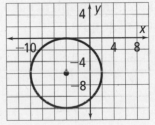

Find the center and radius of each circle. Then graph the circle.

17. $x^2 + y^2 = 25$

18. $(x - 3)^2 + (y - 5)^2 = 9$

19. $(x + 2)^2 + (y + 4)^2 = 16$

20. $(x + 1)^2 + (y - 1)^2 = 36$

Write the standard equation of the circle with the given center that passes through the given point.

21. center $(0, 0)$; point $(3, 4)$

22. center $(5, 9)$; point $(2, 9)$

23. center $(-4, -3)$; point $(2, 2)$

24. center $(7, -2)$; point $(-1, -6)$

Write the standard equation of each circle in the diagram at the right.

25. $\odot B$

26. $\odot F$

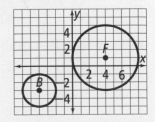

12-5 Practice (continued)   Form G
Circles in the Coordinate Plane

Write an equation of a circle with diameter $\overline{AB}$.

27. $A(0, 0)$, $B(-6, 8)$ **28.** $A(0, -1)$, $B(2, 1)$ **29.** $A(7, 5)$, $B(-1, -1)$

30. Reasoning Circles in the coordinate plane that have the same center and congruent radii are identical. Circles with congruent radii are congruent. In (a) through (g), circles lie in the coordinate plane.

   a. Two circles have equal areas. Are the circles congruent?

   b. Two circles have circumferences that are equal in length. Are the circles congruent?

   c. How many circles have an area of 36π m^2?

   d. How many circles have a center of $(4, 7)$?

   e. How many circles have an area of 36π m^2 and center $(4, 7)$?

   f. How many circles have a circumference of 6π in. and center $(4, 7)$?

   g. How many circles have a diameter with endpoints $A(0, 0)$ and $B(-6, 8)$?

Sketch the graph of each equation. Find all points of intersection of each pair of graphs.

31. $x^2 + y^2 = 65$ **32.** $x^2 + y^2 = 10$ **33.** $(x + 2)^2 + (y - 2)^2 = 16$

   $y = x - 3$ $y = 3$ $y = -x + 4$

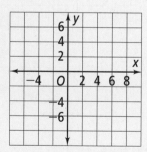   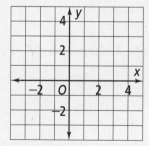   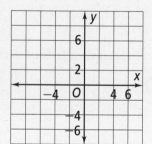

34. Writing Two circles in the coordinate plane with congruent radii intersect in exactly two points. Why is it not possible for these circles to be concentric?

35. Find the circumference and area of the circle whose equation is $(x - 5)^2 + (y + 4)^2 = 49$. Leave your answer in terms of π.

36. What are the x- and y-intercepts of the line tangent to the circle $(x + 6)^2 + (y - 2)^2 = 100$ at the point $(2, -4)$?

12-5 Standardized Test Prep

Circles in the Coordinate Plane

Multiple Choice

For Exercises 1–4, choose the correct letter.

1. Which is the equation of a circle with center $(-2, 3)$ and radius $r = 5$?

   Ⓐ $(x + 2)^2 + (y - 3)^2 = 10$ Ⓒ $(x - 2)^2 + (y + 3)^2 = 10$

   Ⓑ $(x + 2)^2 + (y - 3)^2 = 25$ Ⓓ $(x - 2)^2 + (y + 3)^2 = 25$

2. A circle with center $(-1, 2)$ passes through point $(2, -2)$. Which is true?

   Ⓕ The radius is $\sqrt{5}$.   Ⓗ The equation is $(x + 1)^2 + (y - 2)^2 = 10$.

   Ⓖ The diameter is 10.   Ⓘ The circumference is 25π.

3. Which of the following is the graph of $(x - 2)^2 + (y + 1)^2 = 9$?

  Ⓐ 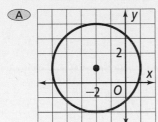   Ⓒ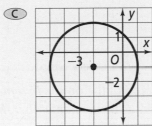

  Ⓑ 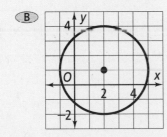   Ⓓ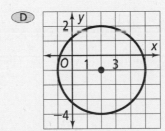

4. Which is the equation of a circle with diameter $\overline{AB}$ with $A(5, 4)$ and $B(-1, -4)$?

   Ⓕ $(x - 5)^2 + (y - 4)^2 = 10$ Ⓗ $(x - 2)^2 + y^2 = 25$

   Ⓖ $(x + 5)^2 + (y + 4)^2 = 100$ Ⓘ $(x + 2)^2 + y^2 = 5$

Short Response

5. Write the standard equation of a circle with a circumference of 14π and center $(4, -1)$. (*Hint:* Use the formula for circumference.)

12-6 Think About A Plan

Locus: A Set of Points

Describe the locus of points in a plane 3 cm from the points on a circle with radius 8 cm.

Know

1. What is a locus of points in a plane? _____

_____

Need

2. Make a sketch of a circle with radius 8 cm.

Plan

3. How can you create a sketch of the points *in a plane* that are 3 cm from the points on a circle with radius 8 cm? *Remember these points can be outside or inside the circle.*

_____

_____

4. Make a sketch like the one you described in Step 3.

5. Describe the points you have drawn.

_____

_____

12-6 Practice
Locus: A Set of Points

Sketch and describe each locus of points in a plane.

1. points 1.5 cm from point T

2. points 1 in. from $\overline{PQ}$

3. points that are equidistant from two concentric circles whose radii are
   8 in. and 12 in.

4. points equidistant from the endpoints of $\overline{AB}$

5. points that belong to a given angle or its interior and are equidistant from the
   sides of the given angle

Describe each locus of points in space.

6. the set of points in space a given distance from a point

7. all points in space 2 cm from a segment

8. all points 5 ft from a given plane P

Sketch the locus of points in a plane that satisfy the given conditions.

9. points equidistant from two perpendicular lines ℓ and m

10. all points equidistant from the centers of two given
    intersecting circles of the same radius

11. all points equidistant from the vertices of a given
    regular hexagon

12. all points that are equidistant from two concentric circles
    with larger radius r and smaller radius s

12-6 Practice (continued)   Form G
Locus: A Set of Points

For Exercises 13–18, describe each locus.

13. What locus contains all the houses that are 1 mi from the library?

14. What locus contains all the bushes that can be placed 20 ft outside of a circular path with a radius of 80 ft?

15. Identify the locus of points equidistant from two opposite vertices of a cube.

16. Identify the locus of points equidistant from two concentric circles of radii a and b in a plane.

17. Identify the locus of points a units from a circle of radius r in a plane.

18. Identify the locus of points a units from a given line ℓ in a plane.

For Exercises 19 and 20, sketch and describe each locus in a plane.

19. all points within n units of point Z

20. Given $\angle LMN$ with bisector $\overline{MO}$ in plane P, describe the locus of the centers of circles that are tangent to $\overline{MO}$ and the outside ray of the angle.

Describe the locus that each thick line represents.

21.

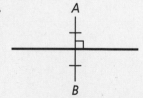

22.

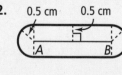

23. Describe the locus of points in a plane 4 cm from the points on a circle with radius 7 cm.

12-6 Standardized Test Prep

Locus: A Set of Points

Multiple Choice

For Exercises 1 and 2 choose the correct letter.

1. Which sketch represents the locus of points in a plane 5 cm from a point *M*?

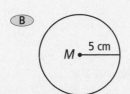

Ⓐ P $\xrightarrow{\text{5 cm}}$ M

Ⓑ

Ⓒ

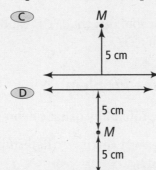

Ⓓ

2. Which description best represents the locus of points in a plane equidistant from parallel lines $\overleftrightarrow{AB}$ and $\overleftrightarrow{CD}$?

Ⓕ a circle with radius *a*

Ⓖ a plane equidistant from $\overleftrightarrow{AB}$ and $\overleftrightarrow{CD}$

Ⓗ a sphere with chords $\overleftrightarrow{AB}$ and $\overleftrightarrow{CD}$

Ⓘ a line equidistant from and between $\overleftrightarrow{AB}$ and $\overleftrightarrow{CD}$

Extended Response

3. The town's emergency response planning committee wants to place four emergency response centers at the four corners of town. Each would serve the people who live within 3 mi of the response center. Sketch the loci of points for the areas served. What are the problems with this idea? What is one potential solution?

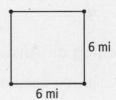

6 mi

6 mi

13-1

Think About a Plan

Experimental and Theoretical Probability

Music A music collection includes 10 rock CDs, 8 country CDs, 5 classical CDs, and 7 hip hop CDs.

    a. What is the probability that a CD randomly selected from the collection is a classical CD?

    b. What is the probability that a CD randomly selected from the collection is not a classical CD?

Understanding the Problem

    1. In what form is probability usually expressed?

    2. What operation must you use to determine the number of outcomes for the events described?

Planning the Solution

    3. How can you express a probability as a fraction?

    _____

    _____

    4. How can you find the number of possible outcomes in this scenario?

    _____

    5. Describe how to find the number of favorable outcomes.

    _____

Getting an Answer

    6. Find the number of possible outcomes. Show your work.

    7. How many CDs in the collection are classical?

    8. What is the probability that a CD randomly selected from the collection is a classical CD? Write your answer as a fraction in simplest form and as a decimal.

    9. Use the probability that a CD randomly selected from the collection is a classical CD to find the probability that a CD randomly selected from the collection is *not* a classical CD.

13-1

Practice

Form G

Experimental and Theoretical Probability

You roll a standard number cube 10 times. The results are shown below.

6, 4, 6, 1, 5, 2, 4, 2, 4, 3

Find the experimental probability of each outcome.

1. P(rolling a 5)

2. P(rolling a 6)

3. P(rolling an even number)

4. P(rolling a 1)

5. What is the experimental probability of rolling an odd number on a standard number cube? For 50 rolls of the number cube, predict the number of rolls that will result in an odd number.

Find the theoretical probability of each outcome.

6. P(rolling a 5)

7. P(rolling a 6)

8. P(rolling an even number)

9. P(rolling a 1)

10. P(rolling an odd number)

11. P(rolling a multiple of 3)

A bag contains 2 red ping-pong balls, 3 green ping-pong balls, 3 blue ping-pong balls, and 1 yellow ping-pong ball. Find the probability of randomly selecting each outcome.

12. P(not red)

13. P(not green)

14. P(not blue)

15. P(not yellow)

13-1

Practice (continued)   Form G

Experimental and Theoretical Probability

16. A game is played where students throw beanbags at the target
shown to the right. Each region of the target is the same size and
every beanbag hits the target. For one game, section A was hit
6 times, section B 3 times, section C 8 times, and section D 5 times.

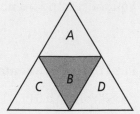

a. What is the experimental probability of hitting section D?

b. What is the theoretical probability of hitting section D?

17. **Reasoning** How are the probability of an event and the probability of its
complement related mathematically?

Two standard number cubes are rolled. Find each probability.

18. P(a sum equal to 2)   19. P(sum not equal to 2)

20. P(a product equal to 15)   21. P(a sum greater than 6)

22. P(a product less than or equal to 2)   23. P(a sum equal to 12)

24. **Open-Ended** Is it possible for an event to have a probability of 1? Explain
your answer.

25. **Error Analysis** Out of 20 coin flips, your classmate gets heads 14 times.
She determines that the experimental probability of getting heads is $\frac{1}{2}$.
What error did your classmate make? What is the correct value for
experimental probability? Explain.

13-1

Standardized Test Prep

Experimental and Theoretical Probability

Multiple Choice

For Exercises 1–4, choose the correct letter.

1. What is the probability of rolling a number greater than 2 on a number cube?

   Ⓐ $\frac{1}{6}$ Ⓑ $\frac{1}{3}$ Ⓒ $\frac{1}{2}$ Ⓓ $\frac{2}{3}$

2. A coin is tossed 30 times and lands on heads 17 times. What is the experimental probability of the coin landing on *tails*?

   Ⓕ $\frac{17}{30}$ Ⓖ $\frac{1}{2}$ Ⓗ $\frac{13}{30}$ Ⓘ $\frac{8}{15}$

3. What is the theoretical probability of randomly choosing a science book from a shelf that holds 3 mystery books, 5 science books, and 4 nature books?

   Ⓐ $\frac{1}{4}$ Ⓑ $\frac{1}{3}$ Ⓒ $\frac{5}{12}$ Ⓓ $\frac{7}{12}$

4. What is the complement of rolling a 2 or 5 on a number cube?

   Ⓕ {5, 2}   Ⓖ {1, 3, 4, 6}   Ⓗ {1, 3, 4, 5}   Ⓘ {7}

Short Response

5. A spinner has four equal sections labeled 2, 4, 6 and 8. Suppose you spin the spinner twice. What is the theoretical probability that the sum of the outcomes is 10? Show the favorable outcomes.

13-2 Think About a Plan

Probability Distributions and Frequency Tables

Survey The results of a survey of 80 households in Westville are shown at the right.

a. What is the probability distribution of the number of computers in Westville households?

b. If Westville has 15,200 households, predict the number of households that will have exactly 3 computers.

c. How many households will have either two or three computers?

Computer Survey

Number of Computers	Frequency
0	12
1	29
2	31
3	6
More than 3	2

Understanding the Problem

1. How can you find the number of households in parts (b) and (c) if the survey did not poll all of the households in Westville?

Planning the Solution

2. How can a probability distribution for the surveyed households assist in calculating the answers?

_____

_____

_____

Getting an Answer

3. Complete the probability distribution based on the given information.

Number of Computers	0	1	2	3	>3
Frequency	12			6	
Probability					

4. Predict the number of households in Westville that will have exactly 3 computers. Show your work.

5. Use your answer to Step 4 to find the number of households that will have two or three computers. Show your work.

13-2 Practice

Form G

Probability Distributions and Frequency Tables

A camp counselor records the number of camp attendees who participate in the daily activities. The results are shown in the table below.

Camp Activities

Activity	Number of People
Waterskiing	12
Hiking	18
Canoeing	13

Find the relative frequency of each activity.

1. Waterskiing
2. Hiking
3. Canoeing

A spinner has 3 equal sections colored red, blue, and green. A student conducts an experiment where she spins the spinner twice and records the results. The results are shown in the frequency table below.

Colors	RR	RB	RG	BB	BR	BG	GG	GR	GB
Frequency	3	5	2	1	4	2	3	2	1

4. What is the probability of spinning red *exactly* once on the next two spins?

5. What is the probability of spinning blue twice on the next two spins?

At a mini-golf course, 20 friends each take 5 shots to try and get a hole-in-one. The results are shown in the probability distribution below. Complete the table.

Number of Holes-in-one	0	1	2	3	4	5
Frequency	2	6	5	4	2	1
Probability	6.	7.	8.	9.	10.	11.

13-2 **Practice** (continued)

Form G

Probability Distributions and Frequency Tables

12. A student records the favorite season for 50 students.
The results are shown in the table at the right.
   a. What is the relative frequency of spring?

   b. What is the relative frequency of winter?

   c. If the table included the number of responses for
   only three of the seasons, could you determine the
   relative frequency of the remaining season? Explain.

Favorite Season

Season	Number of Responses
Winter	7
Spring	13
Summer	19
Fall	11

13. **Reasoning** How are the relative frequencies in a frequency table
mathematically related?

14. A student randomly chooses songs on her MP3 player. Out of 30 different
choices, she chooses 8 hip-hops songs, 4 country songs, 11 rock songs,
and 7 classical songs. What is the probability that the student chooses a
country song?

15. **Writing** A certain probability distribution includes simplified fractions for
some of the probabilities. Will the sum of the numerators be equal to the total
frequency? Explain.

16. **Error Analysis** A cross-country coach makes the probability distribution
below for the number of wins for some of the team members.

Number of Wins	0	1	2	3	4
Frequency	7	4	6	5	3
Probability	$\frac{7}{10}$	$\frac{4}{10}$	$\frac{6}{10}$	$\frac{5}{10}$	$\frac{3}{10}$

Explain the error the coach made when making the table.

13-2 Standardized Test Prep

Probability Distributions and Frequency Tables

Multiple Choice

Use the table below for Exercises 1–4. Choose the correct letter.

The table below shows the results of a soccer team's scores for games played this season.

Goals	0	1	2	3
Frequency	4	7	5	3

1. How many games did the team play?

   (A) 3   (B) 6   (C) 19   (D) 25

2. What is the relative frequency of games with 1 goal scored?

   (F) $\frac{3}{19}$ (G) $\frac{7}{25}$ (H) $\frac{7}{19}$ (I) $\frac{8}{15}$

3. What is the probability that the team scored 2 or more goals?

   (A) $\frac{5}{19}$ (B) $\frac{8}{19}$ (C) $\frac{5}{8}$ (D) $\frac{8}{11}$

4. Which expression can be used to determine the probability of scoring fewer than 3 goals?

   (F) $1 - \frac{3}{19}$ (G) $\frac{3}{19} - 1$ (H) $1 - \frac{16}{19}$ (I) $1 + \frac{3}{19}$

Short Response

5. The relative frequencies of two of three possible outcomes are $\frac{1}{2}$ and $\frac{1}{3}$. What is the relative frequency of the third outcome?

13-3

Think About a Plan

Permutations and Combinations

A 4-digit code is needed to unlock a bicycle lock. The digits 0 through 9 can be used only once in the code.

    a. What is the probability that all of the digits are even? (Hint: 0 is not considered an even number.)

    b. Writing These types of locks are usually called combination locks. What name might a mathematician prefer? Why?

Understanding the Problem

  1. There are ☐ possible numbers that can appear in a code.

  2. Of those, a total of ☐ digit(s) are even.

Planning the Solution

  3. To solve the problem, I need to find _____
_____.

  4. Use the probability formula: $P\left(\text{choosing} \boxed{}\right)$ equals the number of possible ways to choose _____ divided by the total number of ways to choose ____ numbers.

Getting an Answer

  5. Find the number of possible ways to choose 2, 4, 6, and 8.
There are ____ way(s) to pick the first digit, ____ way(s) to pick the second digit, ____ way(s) to pick the third digit, and ____ way(s) to pick the fourth digit, so there are ____ × ____ × ____ × ____ = ____ ways.

  6. Because choosing the code 2-4-6-8 is not the same as choosing the code 8-6-4-2, the order does matter. Use the _____ formula to find the total number of ways to choose ____ numbers from ____ numbers.

  7. Find probability that all of the digits are even by finding the quotient of the answers to Step 7 and Step 8. Write your answer in simplest form.

  8. These types of locks are usually called combination locks. What name might a mathematician prefer? Why?

13-3 Practice

Form G

Permutations and Combinations

1. A band sells t-shirts in 3 sizes and 2 different colors. How many different t-shirts are there to choose from?

2. Each player on the baseball team can order a baseball bat using the table to the right. How many choices does each player have?

Finish	Length	Wood Type
Natural	32"	Ash
Black	33"	Maple
	34"	

3. In how many different orders can 5 runners finish a race?

4. Evaluate 7!.

5. What is the value of $\frac{25!}{24!}$?

6. How many possible combinations of 3 items from a group of 5 are possible?

7. Evaluate $_6P_3$.

8. A basketball coach will choose 5 players from a group of 8 players to start the next game. How many different groups of starting players are possible?

9. What is the value of $_nC_r$ when $n = 7$ and $r = 4$?

10. What is the probability of randomly choosing a penny and a nickel from a cup of coins that contains a penny, a nickel, a dime, and a quarter?

11. Three playing cards are randomly chosen from a set numbered from 1 to 7. What is the probability that the chosen cards are numbered 1, 2 and 3?

13-3

Practice (continued)

Permutations and Combinations

Form G

12. Recreation When renting a bike from a local bike shop, you can choose from the types, sizes, and colors in the table shown below?

Type	Size	Color
Mountain	Small	Green
Cruising	Medium	Red
Road	Large	Blue

How many different choices do you have?

13. Open-Ended Use an example to explain why you can use $n!$ to find the number of possible orders for n objects.

14. Reasoning A hiker has 2 pairs of hiking shoes, 3 different shirts, and 2 different pairs of shorts to choose from. How does the number of combinations of shoes, shirts, and shorts change as the hiker adds shirts to his collection? Explain.

15. Business For each weekly meeting of a group of business leaders, members take turns being the note-taker, the facilitator, and the speaker. In how many different ways can these positions be chosen from the 9 members?

16. Writing Explain how the Fundamental Counting Principle is related to a tree diagram.

17. A game at the fair involves ping-pong balls numbered 1 to 18. You can win a prize if you correctly choose the 5 numbers that are randomly drawn. What are your chances of winning?

13-3 Standardized Test Prep
Permutations and Combinations

Gridded response

Solve each exercise and enter your answer on the grid provided.

1. In how many different ways can 6 books be arranged on a bookshelf?

2. The options for a college's science classes are shown in the table.

Title	Grade Types	Times
Science 101	Pass/Fail	9:00 am
Science 105	Letter Grade	10:30 am

   How many combinations of class, type, and times are available?

3. How many combinations of 4 fish can you choose from a tank containing 8 fish?

4. A bag contains 7 marbles: one each of red, orange, yellow, green, blue, violet, and white. A child randomly pulls 4 marbles from the bag. What is the probability that the marbles chosen are green, blue, red, and yellow? Round your answer to the nearest hundredth.

5. A teacher wants to choose one student to take attendance, one student to hand out papers, and one student to collect homework. If there are 16 students in the class, in how many different ways can the students be chosen?

Answers

1.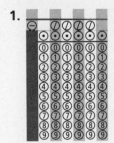
2.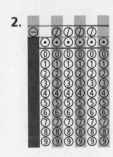
3.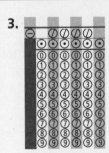
4.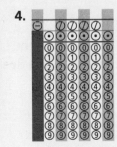
5.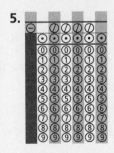

13-4 Think About a Plan

Compound Probability

Pets In a litter of 8 kittens, there are 2 brown females, 1 brown male, 3 spotted females, and 2 spotted males. If a kitten is selected at random, what is the probability that the kitten will be female or brown?

Understanding the Problem

1. Can a kitten be both female and brown?

2. Can a kitten be both female and male?

Planning the Solution

3. What are the characteristics of the selected kitten?

4. How many brown kittens are there?

5. How many female kittens are there?

6. How many kittens are brown and female?

Getting an Answer

7. Determine the probabilities for choosing a brown kitten, choosing a female kitten, and choosing a brown female kitten.

8. Since this is an overlapping probability, use your values in the following formula:

$P(\text{female or brown}) = P(\text{female}) + P(\text{brown}) - P(\text{female and brown})$

9. What is the probability that the kitten will be female or brown? Write your answer as a fraction and as a decimal.

13-4 Practice

Form G

Compound Probability

For Exercises 1–3, determine whether the events are *independent* or *dependent*.

1. You roll a 2 on a number cube and spin a 3 on a spinner.

2. You choose a King from a deck of cards and get heads in a coin toss.

3. You roll a number cube and get a 6, and roll again if the first roll is a 6.

4. What is $P(A$ and $B)$ if $P(A) = \frac{1}{2}$ and $P(B) = \frac{2}{7}$, where A and B are independent events?

5. What is the probability of rolling a 4 on a fair number cube and getting "tails" when tossing a coin?

6. What is $P(A$ or $B)$ if $P(A) = 32\%$ and $P(B) = 17\%$, where A and B are mutually exclusive events?

7. At a local high school, 34% of the students take a bus to school and 56% of the students walk to school. What is the probability of randomly selecting a student that takes a bus or walks to school?

8. What is $P(A$ or $B)$ if $P(A) = \frac{1}{4}$ and $P(B) = \frac{1}{2}$, where A and B are overlapping events?

9. A spinner has 8 equal sections numbered 1 to 8. What is the probability of the spinner stopping on a number that is a multiple of 3 or is greater than 5?

13-4

Practice (continued)

Compound Probability

Form G

10. A local aquarium has 6 turtles, 12 penguins, and 8 sharks. You randomly select 1 animal to watch. What is the probability that you select a turtle or a shark?

11. Writing A bag contains red, green, and blue golf balls and golf tees. You reach into a bag to randomly select one golf ball and one golf tee. Describe how to calculate the probability that you select a red golf ball and a red golf tee.

12. In a local town, 55% of the residents drive to work, 23% of the residents own a dog, and 6% of the residents walk to work. Find the probability that a randomly chosen resident owns a dog or walks to work.

13. You donate 8 baseballs to a local baseball team. Your uncle donates 12 baseballs. If a total of 50 baseballs are donated, what is the probability that the first pitch of the season uses one of your baseballs or one of your uncle's baseballs? Write your answer as a percent.

Use the spinner at the right for Exercises 14–17.

14. What is the probability of the arrow stopping on a consonant or one of the first 4 letters of the alphabet?

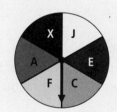

15. What is the probability of the arrow stopping on "X" on the first spin and "F" on the second spin?

16. What is the probability of the arrow stopping on "J" or "A" on one spin?

17. Reasoning What is the probability of the arrow stopping on "J" and "A" on one spin? Explain.

13-4 Standardized Test Prep
Compound Probability

Multiple Choice

For Exercises 1–4, choose the correct letter.

1. What is the probability of rolling a 5 on a number cube and randomly drawing the 2 of Clubs from a deck of cards?

   Ⓐ $\frac{1}{312}$ 　　Ⓑ $\frac{1}{260}$ 　　Ⓒ $\frac{1}{24}$ 　　Ⓓ $\frac{1}{2}$

2. In one class, 19% of the students received an A on the last test and 13% of the students received a C. What is the probability that a randomly chosen student received an A or a C?

   Ⓕ 0.06 　　Ⓖ 0.13 　　Ⓗ 0.16 　　Ⓘ 0.32

3. What is the probability of rolling a 3 or a number less than 4 on a number cube?

   Ⓐ $\frac{5}{19}$ 　　Ⓑ $\frac{1}{2}$ 　　Ⓒ $\frac{2}{3}$ 　　Ⓓ $\frac{3}{4}$

4. You win 6 out of every 10 races you run. Your friend wins 7 out of every 9 dancing competitions she enters. What is the probability of you both winning your next events?

   Ⓕ $\frac{7}{16}$ 　　Ⓖ $\frac{7}{15}$ 　　Ⓗ $\frac{21}{40}$ 　　Ⓘ $\frac{13}{19}$

Short Response

5. The results of a survey revealed that 26% of the students read fiction in their spare time, 21% of the students read non-fiction, and 7% don't read in their spare time. What is the probability that a randomly chosen student reads fiction or doesn't read in her spare time?

13-5

Think About a Plan

Probability Models

Healthcare The table at the right is a relative frequency distribution for healthy people under the age of 65.

a. Copy and complete the table.
b. What is the probability of getting the flu given you are vaccinated?
c. What is the probability of getting the flu given you have not been vaccinated?

	Got the Flu	Did not Get the Flu	Totals
Vaccinated	■	54%	60%
Not Vaccinated	■	■	■
Totals	15%	■	100%

Understanding the Problem

1. Because the events are mutually exclusive, what operation(s) can you use to find missing probabilities in the table?

2. How is the two-way frequency table helpful in finding the probabilities?

Planning the Solution

3. Write the formula for conditional probability.

Getting an Answer

4. Complete the table. Remember that the sum of each pair of values in the row or column should equal the amount in the Total row or column, respectively.

	Got the Flu	Did not Get the Flu	Totals
Vaccinated		54%	60%
Not Vaccinated			
Totals	15%		100%

5. Use the formula from Step 3 to find the probability of getting the flu, given you are vaccinated.

$$P(\text{got the flu} \mid \text{vaccinated}) = \frac{P(\text{got the flu and vaccinated})}{P(\text{vaccinated})} =$$

6. Use the formula from Step 3 to find the probability of getting the flu, given you have not been vaccinated.

$$P(\text{got the flu} \mid \text{not vaccinated}) =$$

13-5 Practice

Probability Models

Form G

For Exercises 1–4, use the two-way frequency table below. It shows the number of one doctor's female patients who caught a cold one winter and whether or not they exercised regularly.

	Caught a cold	Did not catch a cold	Totals
Exercised	8	30	38
Did not exercise	10	2	12
Totals	18	32	50

1. How many patients exercised?

2. What is the probability that a randomly chosen patient caught a cold and did not exercise?

3. What is the probability that a randomly chosen patient exercised and did not catch a cold?

4. What is P(did not exercise | did not catch a cold)?

The table below shows the students in a physical education class. Use this information for Exercises 5–7.

	Has played tennis	Has not played tennis	Totals
Boys	10	6	16
Girls	10	4	14
Totals	20	10	30

5. What is P(girl)?

6. What is P(has not played tennis)?

7. What is the probability that a randomly chosen student has played tennis given he is a boy?

13-5

Practice (continued)

Probability Models

For Exercises 8–10, use the table below. It shows the relative frequencies of students in a science club who have pets, and whether or not they have a yard.

	Pets	No pets	Totals
Yard	0.60	0.05	0.65
No yard	0.25	0.10	0.35
Totals	0.85	0.15	1

8. What is the probability that a randomly selected student has a yard given that they have pets?

9. What is $P(\text{does not have a yard} \mid \text{have no pets})$?

10. Error Analysis Your friend determines that $P(\text{has a yard} \mid \text{has no pets})$ is 0.08. What error did your friend make? What is the correct probability?

A biologist surveyed one type of plant growing on a wooded acre. Use his results, shown in the table below, for Exercises 11 and 12.

	Lobed Leaves	Non-lobed Leaves	Totals
Red Berries	12	48	60
No Red Berries	40	0	40
Totals	52	48	100

11. What is $P(\text{has red berries} \mid \text{has lobed leaves})$?

12. What is $P(\text{has lobed leaves} \mid \text{has red berries})$?

13-5 Standardized Test Prep

Probability Models

Multiple Choice

For Exercises 1–4, choose the correct letter.

The table below shows the number of participants at a charity event who walked or ran, and who wore a red t-shirt or a blue t-shirt. Use the table for Exercises 1–4.

	Blue t-shirt	Red t-shirt	Totals
Walk	80	30	110
Run	20	30	50
Totals	100	60	160

1. What is the probability that a randomly chosen person ran and wore a blue t-shirt?

   Ⓐ 0.125   Ⓑ 0.25   Ⓒ 0.4   Ⓓ 25

2. What is the probability that a randomly chosen person walked and wore a red t-shirt?

   Ⓕ 0.18   Ⓖ 0.1875   Ⓗ 0.3525   Ⓘ 0.5

3. What is $P(\text{ran} \mid \text{wore a blue t-shirt})$?

   Ⓐ 0.2   Ⓑ 0.25   Ⓒ 0.4   Ⓓ 0.8

4. What is the probability that a randomly chosen runner wore a blue t-shirt?

   Ⓕ 0.3   Ⓖ 0.4   Ⓗ 0.5   Ⓘ 0.6

Short Response

5. When calculating $P(B \mid A)$, why is $P(A)$ in the denominator?

13-6 Think About a Plan

Conditional Probability Formulas

Chemistry A scientist discovered that a certain element was present in 35% of the samples she studied. In 15% of those samples, the element was found in a special compound. What is the probability that the compound is in a sample that contains the element?

Understanding the Problem

1. What percent of the samples contain the element?

2. What percent of the samples contain the special compound *and* contain the element?

3. Will you use the percent of the samples that did *not* contain the element?

Planning the Solution

4. Write the formula for conditional probability.

5. What is the value of $P(A$ and $B)$?

6. What is the value of $P(B)$?

Getting an Answer

7. Evaluate the conditional probability formula using the values for A and B.

8. What is the probability that the compound is in a sample that contains the element?

13-6

Practice

Form G

Conditional Probability Formulas

At a recent swim meet, half of the swim club members experienced an improvement in their race times over a previous swim meet. The probability of a swim club member experiencing an improvement in their race time and training the week before the meet was 30%.

1. What is the probability that a swimmer trained the week before the meet given that his or her race time improved?

2. The probability that a swimmer did not experience an improvement in his or her race times and trained the week before the meet was 10%. What is $P(\text{trained} \mid \text{did not improve})$?

3. Half of a class took Form A of a test, and half took Form B. Of the students who took Form B, 39% passed. What is the conditional probability that a randomly chosen student took Form B and passed?

4. Three-fourths of a research team worked in a lab while one-fourth of the team worked near a pond. Of the researchers who worked near the pond, 14% collected insects. What is the probability that a randomly chosen researcher worked near the pond and collected insects?

5. In the senior class, 24% of the students play softball, 32% of the students play field hockey, and 14% play both. What are the probabilities that a softball player also plays field hockey, and a field hockey player also plays softball?

Use the diagram at the right for Exercises 6 and 7.

The tree diagram shows the percentages of plants that received sunlight and whether or not they grew.

6. What is the combined probability that a plant grew?

7. What is the combined probability that a plant did not grow?

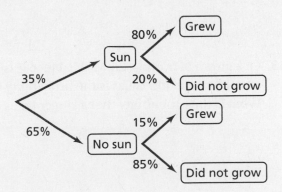

13-6 Practice (continued) Form G
Conditional Probability Formulas

Of the people who went to an amusement park last week, 85% rode a rollercoaster, 45% attended a musical review show, and 18% did both.

8. What is the conditional probability that a person who rode a rollercoaster also attended a musical review show?

9. **Writing** Explain the meaning of P(rode a rollercoaster | attended musical review). Then calculate the probability.

10. **Writing** Half of your 200 classmates went to the zoo. Of the students who went to the zoo, 25% saw the dolphin show. Explain how to calculate the number of students that attended the dolphin show.

The diagram at the right shows the percent of blue-eyed voters and brown-eyed voters that voted for 2 candidates. Use the table for Exercises 11 and 12.

11. What is the combined probability that Candidate A won?

12. **Error Analysis** Your friend says the combined probability of Candidate B winning is 80%. What error did she make? What is the correct combined probability?

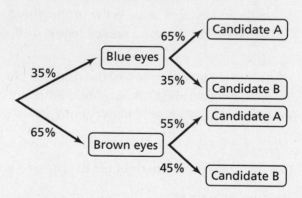

13. Of a group of friends, 28% take dance lessons, 32% take singing lessons, and 8% take both. What is the probability that a dancer takes singing lessons? What is the probability that a singer takes dance lessons?

13-6 Standardized Test Prep
Conditional Probability Formulas

Multiple Choice

For Exercises 1–4, choose the correct letter.

A physician determined that on average, 40% of his patients get the flu each year. Of this group, 10% received the flu vaccine. Of the patients who do not get the flu, 20% received the flu vaccine. Use this information for Exercises 1 and 2.

1. What is the probability that someone who did not receive the vaccine got the flu?

   Ⓐ 0.25   Ⓑ 0.43   Ⓒ 0.75   Ⓓ 0.75

2. What is the probability that someone who received the vaccine got the flu?

   Ⓕ 0.25   Ⓖ 0.33   Ⓗ 0.5   Ⓘ 0.66

3. Of the 85% of the students in a class who studied for a test, 75% passed the test. Of the 15% of the students who did not study, 30% passed. What is the combined probability of passing?

   Ⓐ 0.3   Ⓑ 0.6375   Ⓒ 0.6825   Ⓓ 0.75

4. In a survey, 60% of the people own a laptop computer, 80% own a desktop computer, and 30% own both. What is the conditional probability that a laptop computer owner also owns a desktop computer?

   Ⓕ 0.3   Ⓖ 0.4   Ⓗ 0.5   Ⓘ 0.6

Short Response

5. When calculating $P(B \mid A)$, what does A represent?

13-7 Think About a Plan

Modeling Randomness

Games A bag contains 10 marbles: 4 are red, 5 are yellow, and 1 is blue. You draw one marble from the bag without looking. If you draw a blue marble, you win $10. If you draw a red marble, you win $5, and if you draw a yellow marble, you win $3. What is the expected value you will win or lose? Would you play this game for $5? Explain.

Understanding the Problem

1. How many possibilities are there?

2. What is the combined probability of the events?

Planning the Solution

3. Write a formula for the expected value of these events.

4. What is the probability of drawing a blue marble? How much will you win if you draw a blue marble?

5. What is the probability of drawing a red marble? How much will you win if you draw a red marble?

6. What is the probability of drawing a yellow marble? How much will you win if you draw a yellow marble?

Getting an Answer

7. Use the expected value formula from Step 3 to find the expected value you will win or lose in the game. Show your work.

   The expected value is a _____ of _____ .

8. Would you play this game for $5? Why or why not?

13-7 Practice

Form G

Modeling Randomness

For Exercises 1 and 2, use the lines from a random number table to select numbers to use in each problem.

1. Choose 4 relatives from a group of 24 relatives.

   15287   69109   65187   09154   48712   07934   63825

2. Choose 5 customers from a group of 52 customers.

   73546   87013   67823   68454   76984   57934   90853

3. A manufacturer makes five types of car, represented by the numbers 1 through 5. Using the random number table below, how many randomly chosen cars are picked before all 4 types have been chosen?

   15132   53521   35123   35441   14243

4. At halftime of a basketball game, 8 different types of t-shirts are thrown into the crowd. Using the random number table below, how many randomly chosen t-shirts are thrown before all 8 types have been distributed?

   53636   45227   45424   31115   21428   53737   82763   61732   72181

5. In each hand of a card game, there is a 54% chance of winning 3 points and a 46% chance of losing 4 points. What is the expected gain or loss on each hand?

6. On a certain test, 2 points are awarded for a correct answer and 1 point is deducted for each incorrect answer. The last time the test was given, the students answered correctly 68% of the time. What is the expected value for each question?

7. A certain basketball player has success rates of 39% for her 3-point shots and 51% for her 2-point shots. Find the expected values and compare them using $<$, $>$, or $=$.

   3-point ____ ☐ ____ 2-point

8. In a trivia game, you answer correctly on 26% of the 5-point bonus questions, and you answer correctly on 68% of the 2-point questions. Find the expected values and compare them using $<$, $>$, or $=$.

   5-point ____ ☐ ____ 2-point

13-7 **Practice** (continued)   Form G
Modeling Randomness

9. **Reasoning** Two strategic moves in a board game have expected values of 0.9 and 0.95. Are you guaranteed to perform better by continuously using the move with the greater expected value? Why or why not?

10. The directors of 7 different community choirs are asked to provide 30 vocalists to perform in a special holiday concert. The choirs are represented by the numbers 1 through 7 in the random number table below. How many random choices of vocalists are made until all 7 choirs are represented in the concert by one vocalist each?

    71762   65624   22261   42512   73141   64572

11. In a carnival game, contestants can throw at 2 targets to win prizes. There is a 12% success rate of hitting target A, which yields a $7 prize. There is a 48% success rate of hitting target B, which yields a $3 prize. Compare the expected values using $<$, $>$, or $=$.

    $7 prize ____ ▢ ____ $3 prize

12. **Error Analysis** Your friend uses the random number table below to choose 4 baseball players from a group of 13 baseball players.

    04855   91291   08956   51342   48291   18275   19172

    He picks the numbers 4, 12, 8, and 11. What error did he make?

13. A theater coach is able to send only 5 of his 26 students to a special acting workshop. He wants to be fair and choose them randomly. Using the random number table below, which numbers will he use to help choose the students?

    09364   97140   29376   30287   45008   43875   83926   31248   26075

14. A board game uses a spinner with equal-sized sections numbered 1, 2, 3, 4, 5, 6, and 7. Spinning an even number enables a player to move 2 spaces forward. Spinning an odd number makes a player move 1 space backward. What is the expected value, in fraction form, of each spin?

13-7 Standardized Test Prep

Modeling Randomness

Multiple Choice

For Exercises 1–4, choose the correct letter.

For Exercises 1 and 2, use the lines from a random number table to select numbers to use in each problem.

1. Using the table below, which numbers would you use to choose 3 students from a group of 50 students?

   36674   86790   98265   42947   20763

   Ⓐ 36, 48, 42   Ⓑ 36, 48, 26   Ⓒ 36, 48, 9   Ⓓ 48, 26, 42

2. There are students from 4 different towns at a conference. Using the random number table below, how many students would be randomly chosen until one from each town is chosen?

   13231   23121   42314   13423

   Ⓕ 3   Ⓖ 10   Ⓗ 11   Ⓘ 15

3. In each roll of a game piece, there is a 64% chance of losing 2 points and a 36% chance of winning 7 points. What is the expected value for each roll?

   Ⓐ −1.28   Ⓑ 1.24   Ⓒ 2.52   Ⓓ 3.8

4. In a game at the fair, a player has a 43% chance of making a 3-point shot and a 32% chance of making a 4-point shot. Which shows the greater probability shot and difference between expected values?

   Ⓕ 4-point by 0.01   Ⓖ 4-point by 0.08   Ⓗ 3-point by 0.01   Ⓘ 3-point by 0.08

Extended Response

5. In a game at a fundraiser, Choice A has a 12% of winning 8 prize tickets and Choice B has a 46% chance of winning 2 prize tickets. Describe how you would choose between playing Choice A or Choice B.